CAROLE PATEMAN

Carole Pateman's writings have been innovatory precisely for their qualities of engagement, pursued at the height of intellectual rigour. This book draws from her vast output of articles, chapters, books and speeches to provide a thematic yet integrated account of her innovations in political theory and contributions to the politics of policy-making. The editors have focused on work in three key areas:

Democracy

Pateman's perspective is rooted in practicality, enquiring into and speculating about forms of participation over and above the 'traditional' exclusions through which representative systems have been variously constructed over time. Her work pushes hard on theorists and politicians who make easy assumptions about apathy and public opinion, who bracket off the workplace and the home, and who see politics only in partisan activity, voter behaviour and governmental policy.

Women

Pateman's innovatory and still-cited work on participation antedates the feminist revolution in political theory and many of the practical struggles that developed through the later 1970s. While woman-centred, her concerns were always worked through larger conceptions of social class, economic advantage, power differentials, 'liberal' individualism and contracts including marriage. Her feminism was innovative in political theory, and within feminism itself. As a feminist, Pateman defies categorization, and her concepts of 'the sexual contract' and 'Wollstonecraft's dilemma' are canonical.

Welfare

Pateman's innovation here is an integration of welfare issues – in particular the proposals for a 'basic income' or for a 'capital stake' – into her broad but always rigorous conception of democracy. This is argued through in terms of citizenship, taken as the result of a social contract. In that way, Pateman puts liberalism itself through an imminent critique, drawing in the practicalities and risks of life in late capitalist societies. Her theory as always is political, taking in neo-liberal attacks on 'welfare states' and the stark realities of international inequalities. Pateman's career achievements in democratic and feminist theory are brought productively to bear on debates that would otherwise occur in more limited, and less provocative, academic and political contexts.

Terrell Carver is Professor of Political Theory at the University of Bristol, UK. He has published extensively on theoretical and substantive issues relevant to Marx, Engels and Marxism, and to sex, gender and sexuality.

Samuel A. Chambers is Associate Professor at The Johns Hopkins University, Baltimore, MD, USA. He writes broadly in contemporary thought, including work on language and media, popular culture and the politics of gender and sexuality.

Routledge Innovators in Political Theory

Edited by Terrell Carver, University of Bristol and Samuel A. Chambers, The Johns Hopkins University

Routledge Innovators in Political Theory focuses on leading contemporary thinkers in political theory, highlighting the major innovations in their thought that have reshaped the field. Each volume collects both published and unpublished texts, and combines them with an interview with the thinker. The editorial introduction articulates the innovator's key contributions in relation to political theory, and contextualizes the writer's work. Volumes in the series will be required reading for both students and scholars of 21st century politics.

1. William E. Connolly
Democracy, pluralism & political theory
Edited by Samuel A. Chambers and Terrell Carver

2. Carole Pateman
Democracy, feminism, welfare
Edited by Terrell Carver and Samuel A. Chambers

CAROLE PATEMAN

Democracy, feminism, welfare

Edited by Terrell Carver and
Samuel A. Chambers

Routledge
Taylor & Francis Group

LONDON AND NEW YORK

First published 2011
by Routledge
2 Park Square, Milton Park, Abingdon, Oxon OX14 4RN

Simultaneously published in the USA and Canada
by Routledge
711 Third Avenue, New York, NY 10017

Routledge is an imprint of the Taylor & Francis Group, an informa business

British Library Cataloguing in Publication Data
A catalogue record for this book is available from the British Library

Library of Congress Cataloging-in-Publication Data
Carole Pateman : democracy, feminism, welfare / edited by Terrell Carver and Samuel A. Chambers.
    p. cm. — (Routledge innovators in political theory ; 2)
Includes bibliographical references and index.
ISBN 978-0-415-78111-4 (hardback) — ISBN 978-0-415-78112-1 (pbk.) — ISBN 978-0-203-81060-6 (e-book) 1. Feminist theory. 2. Democracy. 3. Social policy. 4. Pateman, Carole. I. Chambers, Samuel Allen, 1972- II. Carver, Terrell.
HQ1190.C375 2011
305.4201—dc22   2010052898

ISBN 13: 978-0-415-78111-4 (hbk)
ISBN 13: 978-0-415-78112-1 (pbk)
ISBN 13: 978-0-203-81060-6 (ebk)

Typeset in Bembo by RefineCatch Limited, Bungay, Suffolk

MIX
Paper from
responsible sources
FSC® C004839
www.fsc.org

Printed and bound in Great Britain by
TJ International Ltd, Padstow, Cornwall

CONTENTS

ACKNOWLEDGEMENTS

The work in this collection has been published previously in a variety of different forms. We would like to thank the publishers for granting permission to use the following copyright material:

Pateman, Carole, 'Political Culture, Political Structure and Political Change'. *British Journal of Political Science*, 1(3): 291–305, 1971. © Cambridge University Press, reprinted with permission

Pateman, Carole, 'A Contribution to the Political Theory of Organizational Democracy'. *Administration and Society*, 7(1): 5–26, 1975. © Sage, reprinted with permission

Pateman, Carole, 'Political Obligation and the Sword of Leviathan'. Chapter 3 in C. Pateman, *The Problem of Political Obligation: A Critique of Liberal Theory*, pp. 37–60, 1979. © Wiley, reprinted with permission

Pateman, Carole, 'If Voting Could Change Anything, It Would Be Illegal'. *Politics*, XIV(2): 304–7, 1979. © Wiley, reprinted with permission

Pateman, Carole, 'Feminism and Democracy'. Chapter 13 in G. Duncan (ed.), *Democratic Theory and Practice*, pp. 204–17. Cambridge: 1983. © Cambridge University Press, reprinted with permission

Pateman, Carole, 'The Shame of the Marriage Contract'. Chapter 4 in J. Stiehm (ed.), *Women's Views of the Political World of Men*, pp. 67–97. New York: Transnational, 1984. © Brill, reprinted with permission

Pateman, Carole, 'Sex and Power'. *Ethics* 100(2): 398–407, 1990. © University of Chicago Press

Pateman, Carole, 'Equality, Difference, Subordination: The Politics of Motherhood and Women's Citizenship'. Chapter 1 in G. Bock and S. James (eds), *Beyond Equality and Difference: Citizenship: Feminist Politics and Female Subjectivity*, pp. 17–31. London, Routledge, 1992. Reprinted with permission

Pateman, Carole, 'Three Questions about Womanhood Suffrage'. Chapter 17 in C. Daley and M. Nolan (eds), *Suffrage and Beyond: International Feminist Perspectives*, pp. 331–46. New York: New York University Press, 1994. Reprinted with permission

Pateman, Carole, 'The Legacy of T.H. Marshall'. Oslo University publication (public lecture, 1996)

Pateman, Carole, 'Freedom and Democratization: Why Basic Income is to be Preferred to Basic Capital'. Chapter 8 in K. Dowding, J. De Wispelaere and S. White (eds), *The Ethics of Stakeholding*, pp. 130–48. London & New York: Palgrave, 2003.

Pateman, Carole, 'Another Way Forward: Welfare, Social Reproduction, and a Basic Income'. Chapter 2 in L. Mead and C. Beem (eds), *Welfare Reform and Political Theory*, Russell Sage Foundation, 2005.

INTRODUCTION

Doing politics with theory: the writings of Carole Pateman

Terrell Carver and Samuel A. Chambers

Carole Pateman is one of the most cited and reprinted political theorists of our time, chiefly for her work on participation and obligation in democratic theory, her notable feminist conception 'the sexual contract', and more recently her policy-related conceptualisation of welfare in terms of basic income. Whether one judges these engagements as innovation or renovation is a tricky point, but one on which nothing very much turns in the end. This volume puts a larger context around her work on these themes by collecting some of the unreprinted and less-frequently reproduced items, along with some of the 'classics' – grouping them under three broad headings: 'Democracy and political theory', 'Women in political theory', and 'Political theory of welfare'. Significantly all three are areas of 'real world' interests and concerns, as opposed to the more rarefied debates concerning knowledge, truth and certainty that so often engage political theorists, particularly since the post-structuralist and 'linguistic' turns of the 1980s. Pateman's work in political theory is overwhelmingly interventionist, not just into academic literatures and debates, such as in political science and ethics, but into the wider worlds of political judgement and policy-making. Pateman was the first woman President of the International Political Science Association (1991–94) and is a very recent President of the American Political Science Association (2010–11); in both cases there could not have been a better choice.

Pateman has held full-time academic posts at the University of Sydney, Australia, the University of California at Los Angeles (UCLA) in the USA, and Cardiff University, Wales, as well as visiting posts at numerous universities, including Stanford, Princeton, the Australian National University, and the University of British Columbia. She has honorary doctorates from the University of Helsinki, the National University of Ireland, and the Australian National University, and she is in receipt of the Lifetime Achievement Award from the Political Studies Association of the United Kingdom.

While no one is groomed for political theory from an early age, at school or elsewhere, Pateman's career is unusual in its origins, given the hierarchies of sex and class at the time, and her own experiences of family, school and work. Her route into political theory was to enroll for Oxford University's Diploma in Economics and Political Science at Ruskin College, Oxford, in 1963. This was an independent organisation with affiliations to the University, itself a federation of 'traditional' colleges and halls. A 'non-traditional' affiliate, Ruskin was supported by trade unions and other organisations promoting higher education for working class students, who would very likely be 'mature'. This was in a culture where the normal route to university was via academic selection straight from schools, and indeed from the kinds of schools where working-class pupils were a rarity. There were not very many universities at the time, and therefore few university places at all in relation to the general population. Hence the number of university places that were 'won' by middle-class pupils was vastly disproportionate, and by upper-class ones even more so. The class (and sex) divide and hierarchy were obvious for all to see, and indeed hotly defended by some on grounds of tradition as a good in itself or of selection on (allegedly) meritocratic principles.

Pateman 'left' secondary school in 1957, as pupils do in Britain, for employment, and she took up clerical work at the Land Registry offices near her family's home in Sussex. The later enrollment at Ruskin College was highly successful. Obtaining a distinction in the pre-university diploma (and being the only woman to sit the examination), she went on to complete her B.A. in Philosophy, Politics and Economics at Lady Margaret Hall, one of the 'traditional' Oxford women's colleges (as they were in those sex-segregated days – former men's and women's colleges are now all mixed). Graduate study at the time was relatively unusual, though the age and sex ratios were probably somewhat less skewed than for undergraduates. However, the number of Oxford (or indeed any) graduate students in England from working-class backgrounds, and from a route of 'mature' student university entrance (without the usual requisite of 'A-level' study and examinations), must have been very tiny indeed. Pateman published her book *Participation and Democratic Theory* in 1970 with Cambridge University Press, and was awarded her D.Phil. on that subject by Oxford University in 1971.

Pateman's concerns with women, democracy and welfare might look almost sociological. Her work follows on from Max Weber, Joseph Schumpeter, Talcott Parsons and numerous others on down the line to Anthony Giddens, scholars who approach the modern industrial state, its institutions and its citizens, with their eyes on participation, inclusion, reform and progress. What puts Pateman firmly on the political theory side of things is her focus on well known issues that define the discipline: the problem of obligation, the theory of democracy, the conceptualisation of freedom, the limits of liberalism, and the distribution of political rights and citizen responsibilities. Moreover there are few who can compete with Pateman as a reader, interpreter and *user* of the political theory classics, the *locus* where political theorists love to be. Those classic texts include Plato, Aristotle, Hobbes, Locke, Rousseau, Marx and J.S. Mill, amongst many others, which – after her scholarly work, and that of other feminist associates – came to include a sprinkling of women, such as Wollstonecraft. Over and beyond these achievements there are few in the discipline who can compete with Pateman on the detailed historical research required to understand the genealogy of the present, and to grasp the malleability of 'human nature' and institutions over time.

Pateman did not 'learn' academic feminism and then 'take on' political science, political institutions, policy studies and ethics in order 'to gender' them – since academic feminism didn't exist at the time she started out, this trajectory wasn't really possible. She studied political science and political theory and had well developed interests and ambitions there before she began to do any academic feminist work, which dated from the later 1970s. From the feminist perspective then, the thrust of her work was as thorough as it was innovatory. Given that conventional political studies were all founded on the exclusion of women, how then – Pateman asked – are we to *re-understand* them all from a perspective that made such an exclusion *entirely* illegitimate? This would be a perspective that would license women to speak no matter what, and would presume that any reconstruction must be as thorough as is required. This kind of thoroughness, all the way down, is itself an innovation, and the works collected in this volume are testimony not just to the clarity of Pateman's feminism, but to a complementary depth in her grasp of the necessary sciences and relevant subjects to which she has directed her formidable intellect, in particular her prior and primary work on democracy, and her feminist critique and re-theorisation of the welfare state.

Democracy and political theory

Pateman's work is firmly centred in the theory and practice of modern, representative, liberal democracies, though in precisely what sense our theoretical constructs and day-to-practices are really 'liberal' is one of her major preoccupations. In Chapter 1, 'Political Culture, Political Structure and Political Change' (pp. 3–17) Pateman's focus is on change, and the way that 'evaluative assumptions and conceptual confusions' in studies of political culture, particularly the highly influential work of Almond and Verba (1965), presumed that existing political structures in democratic societies were responsive to citizens, and that their job was to assess the role of 'culture' in contributing to, or detracting from, 'stability'. Pateman argues trenchantly that this whole analysis was caught out by the 'participation explosion' of the 60s and 70s in their own societies, rather than in 'the modernizing countries', the venue where Almond and Verba assumed that radical change – and a dynamic of destablization – was 'the problem'. On the conceptual side Pateman unravels Almond and Verba's misuse of Parsons; the Parsonian framework rules out Almond and Verba's starting point – an incongruence between political culture and political structure – at the outset. Beneath the lengthy critique there is, as ever, Pateman's overriding concern not with democratic 'systems' but with the democratic citizens who do – or don't do – democracy.

As Pateman says in Chapter 2, 'A Contribution to the Political Theory of Organizational Democracy' (pp. 18–32), 'theory must be taken into account together with practical problems', when considering 'organizational democracy' as a problem. The logic of the central arguments of liberal democratic theory leads, so Pateman argues, to the democratisation of organisations outside the state, including industries and indeed any organisation where management is a feature. However, separation of social life into two 'autonomous' spheres – 'the political or public and the private' – where 'private' includes 'enterprise', is a structural feature of liberal democratic thought. Pateman's discussion of 'industrial democracy' zeroes in on this tension, not simply to reflect on democratisation outside the state, but rather to note that the *general* concepts of democracy and 'the political' need re-thinking, once the supposed autonomy of the public from the private is breached. Or to put it the other way round, if the public/private spheres are presupposed, then arguments for 'organizational democracy' are disabled, because they represent an 'importation' of 'politics' into an alien sphere. In another twist of the argument, Pateman aligns 'organizational democracy' with a participatory or self-managing set of practices, rather than with the representative structures of 'liberal democracy', where democratic citizenship is largely reduced to periodic voting. Conversely, where democracy as a practical activity broadens the context and experience of citizenship, the tendency – in numerous works of political science – to liken 'voter behaviour' to 'consumer behaviour' will fall by the wayside.

Chapter 3, 'Political Obligation and the Sword of Leviathan' (pp. 33–58), drawn from Pateman's book-length 'critique of liberal theory', *The Problem of Political Obligation*, takes up the case of Hobbes. Despite his obviously illiberal arguments for absolute and undivided sovereignty, Hobbes and his 'uncompromising individualism' represent for Pateman a highly productive point at which to note the problems that liberal theory faces when it bases the right to govern on a 'self-assumed obligation'. Pateman takes considerable care to explicate the argument in *Leviathan* (1991 [1651]), which established 'a pattern of argument followed by subsequent liberal theorists'. Against C.B. Macpherson, Pateman makes the very telling point that contractarianism itself explains why liberal individuals are ready to submit themselves to the market (where theoretical equality results in inequality in practice), and why the then separate sphere of *political* equality insulates the market economy itself from egalitarian criticisms. As liberals back off from the Hobbesian absolutism that follows from his radical individualism, so the problem of political obligation seems to disappear – until, as was the case when Pateman wrote this classic work on liberalism – civil disobedience causes the problem to reappear and to provoke, from some liberals, anyway, a Hobbesian resolution.

Voting is the focal point of Pateman's review article now republished as Chapter 4, 'If Voting Could Change Anything, It would be Illegal' (pp. 59–65), where her analytical interests in democracy and participation come together with feminism and social class. The upshot is a critique of both the way that political science frames its studies of voting behavior, and the way that contemporary representative systems disable democratic modes of decision-making. Pateman argues that modern democracies have confined 'the political' to voting, and have thus sidelined other forms of participation, so voting – which merely circulates elites and changes little – has only a symbolic and legitimating function. Her view is that those who struggled hard for the franchise, such as women and workers, had clear political objectives and a broader notion of 'the political' in terms of actions and activities drawing on citizen participation in many forms. Political science merely takes the system at face value, and so fails to draw the critical conclusions that Pateman derives from her more historically and sociologically astute approach.

Pateman's book chapter, 'Feminism and Democracy' (pp. 66–79) neatly draws these two major threads together, that is, the incompatibility between the continued subjection of women and the democratic requirements that individuals are free and must be treated as equals. As Chapter 5 this work closes the section on 'Democracy and Political Theory'. The treatment of the subject ranges from wry hilarity at liberal contradictions and hypocrisies to a notable *mea culpa* regarding her own pre-vious work. On her title-subject, 'Feminism and Democracy', Pateman comments tartly: 'A feminist might dispose briskly of the subject of this essay. For feminists, democracy has never existed; women have never been and still are not admitted as full and equal members and citizens in any country known as a "democracy"' (p. 66). And including her own book, *Participation and Democratic Theory* (1970) in her critical sights, she comments: 'By failing to take into account the feminist con-ception of "private" life, by ignoring the family, participatory democratic arguments for the democratization of economic life have neglected a crucial dimension of democratic social transformation' (p. 75). She also notes that the edited collection on *Democratic Theory and Practice* (Duncan, 1983), to which she is contributing, has 'a token paper by a woman writer', namely herself (p. 66). Her overall argument is the very broad one that democratic citizenship and 'equal opportunity' cannot continue to presuppose the public/private divide through which liberalism has secured the patriarchal relations of marriage and the household, nor can it continue to obscure the concomitant inequalities in economic relations and elsewhere in the public sphere that disadvantage women in relation to men. Ultimately this is because women are defined in a contradictory way with respect to consent, the quintessential moment of rationality for the 'individual':

> Women have exemplified the beings whom political theorists have regarded as lacking the capacities to attain the status of individual and citizen or to participate in the practice of consent, but women have, simultaneously, been perceived as beings who, in their personal lives, always consent, and whose explicit refusal of consent can be disregarded and reinterpreted as agreement (p. 74).

Thus the 'creation of a free and egalitarian sexual and personal life' is fundamental to the whole project of liberal democracy, which is yet to be delivered (pp. 76–77).

Women in political theory

Pateman's (1988) landmark book *The Sexual Contract* has a pre-history in hard thinking about social institutions as scrutinised by feminists, in particular feminist historians, such as traditional marriage. Noting the taken-for-granted quality of marriage as an institution and wife as a status within the philosophy, history and sociology of the time (written by men) – Pateman zeroed in on the exceptions. Her chapter, 'The Shame of the Marriage Contract' (pp. 83–102), references Hegel (who thought the contractual approach to marriage shameful) but skillfully focuses the discussion on the wider issue of contract itself as an increasingly popular model for social relations among 'individuals'. In Chapter 6 she examines the 'social contract' and the classic theories of rule by consent, and then the problematic status of the marriage contract itself within this matrix: '...almost everything about the marriage contract', Pateman says, 'is questionable – even its existence' (p. 84).

Pateman's argument is this: while liberal political theory can give polite regard to the social contract as a fiction, liberalism ignores the fictional, rather than properly contractual, quality of marriage. The 'signing' ceremony, she says, merely confirms the patriarchal superiority of husbands to wives, and with that, the political mystification entailed when a woman 'consents' to this institution of subjection (an indignity spared to the slave). Pateman links 'wife' to 'woman', arguing that the latter in liberal theories to date is naturalised as man's inferior (because destined for wifehood and 'the home') and thus not truly an individual equal to any other in consenting (or not) to a contract of mutual advantage, such as would occur between men. The theoretical links in Pateman's argument are precise and ingenious; the methodology neatly distinguishes between fiction and mystification. The marriage contract is fictional, because it isn't a 'real' contract, but rather a confirmation of superior/inferior status that is independent of the contracting parties. An individual woman's consent is a mystification, because she is not in fact a consenting individual (i.e. a man), legalistic appearances of 'equal contractors' to the contrary.

Continuing this devastating critique – devastating in that it ruthlessly exposes the contradictions through which (male) liberals accommodate their revolutionary 'individualism' to patriarchalist naturalism – Pateman finds the same fault in Hegel's attack on Kant's 'shameful' contractarian conception of marriage (Hegel finds it degrading to the individuals involved and untrue to the ethical status of family life). Hegel, no less than liberal theorists, invests his theory with female inferiority – and male superiority, finessed as 'individuality' – and so, Pateman concludes, 'The contractarian conception of marriage and Hegel's unique marriage contract are both covered in shame' (p. 93).

What follows is a remarkable essay in political philosophy, evaluating the strengths and weaknesses of contractarianism in social relations within a historical and sociological account of a long-term movement from status to contract. In particular Pateman exposes the economic and other social changes that would have to occur in order for women to be individuals, not merely as 'equals' to men (who are already assumed to be 'individuals'), but as persons within a feminist conception of egalitarian individuality. This would entail females having 'bodily integrity and autonomy' in ways that would necessarily differ from men's, without – Pateman notes – an unnecessary ascription of childrearing to women as their essential responsibility. Rejecting the status/contract binary for human relationships, and thus any reductionism of all relationships involving freedom and equality to those that can be captured in a voluntary contractualism, Pateman then offers a view of 'personal association' arising through promise. In this way bonds of 'mutuality' could allow autonomy, individuality and love to flourish.

The flip side of this is Pateman's exposure of contractualism as an ideological construction within liberalism, or if separate, very much allied to it. In her view contractualism obscures the structures of patriarchal domination, particularly when men and women contract into marriage as 'equals' (much as Marx criticised the wage contract for obscuring the domination of capital over labour when workers contract as 'equals' with capitalists). And in the same mode, for Pateman, the dissolution of such ideological coherence comes not with mere intellectual critique, but rather takes place when widespread questioning erupts into political action, as indeed it would in the 'revival of the organized feminist movement' (p. 94). It is clear from her writing that for Pateman, the unity of theory and practice was itself a practice, not just an idea in theory.

Pateman's engagement with Catherine A. MacKinnon's (1987) book *Feminism Unmodified: Discourses on Life and Law* comes in a notable essay on 'Sex and Power' (pp. 103–113), which is Chapter 7 in this volume. Her assessment is more than calm and thoughtful, in that she carefully notes the points where her feminism, and that of the controversial anti-pornography campaigner, overlap, as well as analysing precisely where she thinks MacKinnon's reductionism doesn't work. At a crucial point, Pateman writes that 'Mackinnon's argument lacks historical depth and an appreciation of the paradoxes and contradictions of women's position' (p. 106).

The focus on men's power over women is where the two overlap, and Pateman says that MacKinnon's insistence on this is welcome. Pateman notes that political theorists, particularly contract theorists and utopian socialists, did at one time discuss this topic – but that in more recent times the subject has disappeared, until feminists made it a focus. Contract theorists of the 17th and 18th centuries had raised the revolutionary potential for sexual relations inherent in their doctrines of natural freedom and equality among apparently de-gendered 'men'. But they had dealt with this politically by presuming a 'sexual contract' through which women were already subjugated and in men's power when civil society was created through contract and consent. Ironically, Pateman notes, this exclusion became accepted by later liberals as 'a valid limitation on the scope of political inquiry' (p. 104).

The paradoxes and contradictions of women's position in specifically liberal societies arise, Pateman argues, because the 'standard for equality between the sexes is made in the male image' (p. 105). Moreover supposedly gender-neutral laws and policies measure women against a masculine ideal and a male body. On the latter point, Pateman criticises MacKinnon's attempts to derive sex difference itself from power alone, and in particular power exerted in (hetero)sexual relations, iconically so in pornography. Humankind has 'two bodies', Pateman insists, while noting that neither meanings nor power follow straightforwardly and unambiguously from anatomical facts (specifically, the possibility and reality of pregnancy) (p. 107). Solutions to the oppression of women cannot come from arguments and strategies that reduce the politics and economics involved to a question of power as such, any more than to a question about the body as such. Thus Pateman's review ends by framing feminism in political theory terms as a practical problem of 'freedom, justice, equality, and democracy', rather than in philosophical terms – however provocative or even persuasive the polemic, however logically deductive the argument (p. 113).

'Wollstonecraft's dilemma' is undoubtedly one of Pateman's most powerfully analytical contributions to political theory, arising out of her head-on engagement with the equality/difference debate in feminism. Chapter 8, 'Equality, Difference, Subordination: the politics of motherhood and women's citizenship' (pp. 114–127) uses this concept to pose a major paradox to which women are subject politically. One is that they have been both excluded from, and included within, the polity on the basis of 'the very same capacities and attributes': their sexual difference from men was said to make them unfit for citizenship as 'women', but their reproductive difference from men was said to make them essential citizens as 'mothers'. Pateman finds this reflected theoretically in the then current feminist debate between 'maternal' thinkers of 'difference' and their 'political' critics arguing for equality, as well as historically in a multitude of examples, most particularly the distribution of rights, benefits, contributions and privileges of industrialised welfare states. Wollstonecraft's dilemma arises because:

> within the existing patriarchal conception of citizenship, the choice always has to be made between equality and difference, or between equality and womanhood. On the one hand, to demand 'equality' is to strive for equality with men...On the other hand, to insist...that women's distinctive attributes, capacities and activities be revalued and treated as a contribution to citizenship is to demand the impossible; such 'difference' is precisely what patriarchal citizenship excludes (p. 117).

Pateman's highly productive analytical strategy is to found any discussion on the realities of subordination and exclusion, and then to relate any framing of the issues to that, thus exposing the extent to which conventional conceptualisations – too often adopted uncritically – both disguise and reproduce the guilty secrets that liberalism exposed, and then tried to cover up.

Chapter 9, 'Three Questions about Womanhood Suffrage' (pp. 128–143) rounds off this central section on 'Women and Political Theory'. This is a cracking piece in which Pateman turns conventional wisdom inside out. The extension of the franchise was not a smooth trajectory of inclusiveness, eventually 'getting down to' women. Rather the landmark acts extending the franchise beyond a very privileged and favoured few were the first acts that specifically excluded women. Most men demanding further extensions were for universal *manhood* suffrage and against votes for women. Women suffragists were thus stuck with the tactical difficulty of supporting such extensions on principle, even though they promised nothing for women, or opposing such extensions, and so appearing undemocratic. Enthusiasm among men for the enfranchisement of even *some* women was notably absent. Pateman interprets this near universality of male exclusionary views as a straightforward defence of sex (and sexual) privilege. Control over women at home in traditional ways might be threatened if they attained a public and political voice: who knows what would happen then? The private/public division of spaces, and with that of power, was thus becoming a very public issue.

Pateman's three questions are startling and provocative: Why did womanhood suffrage take so long? Why did women organise against their own enfranchisement? And why did women win the vote? Her questions alone are enough to shatter the view that women's suffrage is a boring topic that generates no significant puzzles. On the contrary, her answers raise important questions about victors' histories, ideological erasures, the normalisation of subordination, the continuing relevance of women's history, and the analytical and political power of fearless feminism.

Political theory of welfare

Feminist democratisation is thus the final theme of this collection, in that Pateman takes up the practicalities of the capitalist economy and the 'Political Theory of the Welfare State' with those considerations in mind. In Chapter 10 she broadens her already published critical reflections on the welfare state with 'The Legacy of T.H. Marshall' (pp. 147–163), an address given at the University of Oslo and published here with slight changes. Besides detailing his complicity with patriarchalism, which is anti-democratic in its very principles, Pateman also criticises Marshall for his Anglocentrism with respect to other nations of the British Isles, and indeed of the Empire and Commonwealth. A discussion of citizenship informed by more careful fact-finding would reveal the skewed and inaccurate character of the very views and proposals for which he is best known. Pateman then turns to his concept of 'social rights', through which the tensions between the capitalist labour market and full and equal citizenship could be resolved, or at least substantially ameliorated. In a strong formulation social rights would amount to a universal right to an income not proportionate to an individual's market value, and in a weaker version, to an entitlement to welfare conditional on an obligation to work – and in an even weaker version, an entitlement dependent on social or economic disability and the state of public finances. In the end Pateman argues for a strong version of social rights as an essential element in the way that citizens are made ready to be full and equal participants in social and political life.

Characteristically Pateman gives her theorisation of democratic citizenship in relation to the welfare state specific form through an engagement with policy-related work on the 'stakeholder' society. This takes place in Chapter 11, 'Freedom and Democratization: why basic income is to be preferred to basic capital' (pp. 164–179) – a contribution to a multi-author volume *The Ethics of Stakeholding*

(Dowding *et al.*, 2003). In considering the alternative proposals for a right to a basic income or a right to a 'stake' (i.e. a one-off capital grant), Pateman finds the conflation of freedom *tout court* with economic opportunity an inadequate way to conceptualise the issues. She suggests that these issues must be grasped under the rubric of autonomy, thereby raising questions concerning the full standing as citizens for all individuals, her touchstone for realizing democracy. However, economic opportunity and security is certainly essential for this, in Pateman's conception, and – relating her discussion again to Marshall's classic work on class and citizenship – Pateman comes down on the side of the democratic right to a basic income (as opposed to a right to a capital grant, as proposed by some radical libertarians). Also characteristically Pateman raises structural interrelationships that the economistic and masculinising libertarians omit or unreflectively presume – marriage, household and caring work, voluntary welfare activities, for instance – and thus she considers women's lives in relation to the particular kind of freedoms that a basic income would afford. Basic income would thus be a step forward in the democratisation of society, but only if women's freedom were explicitly catered for. To be politically significant basic income would entail a strong critique of an 'abstractly individualistic theoretical framework' that has been imported into political theory from neo-classical economics. The structure of institutions, most particularly 'private' or 'traditional' ones such as marriage and the concomitant status of women, has a clear bearing for Pateman on any defensible conceptions of freedom, democracy and citizenship.

At the close of this section on 'The Political Theory of Welfare' Chapter 12, 'Another Way Forward: welfare, social reproduction, and a basic income' (pp. 180–206) tackles the subject the other way round, as it were, via current 'reforms' of welfare into 'workfare' (in particular the 1996 legislative changes in the USA). The latter concept marked an attempt to 'reform' the principles and practicalities of modern welfare states in fundamental ways in the USA. Noting the peculiarly limited character of social welfare provision in the broad sense (limited national insurance benefits, no comprehensive national health insurance scheme, even for children, etc.), Pateman addresses general issues of social reproduction, including, but not limited to, the raising of the next generation of citizens and the characteristic way that women's unpaid labour is allocated to this social good. This of course raises crucial issues of full and equal citizenship, as well as raising concerns over the time-balance between the paid and unpaid labouring activities required to secure the reproduction of society in ways that are consistent with the fulfillment of democratic norms as a universal.

On the specific proposals 'reforming' welfare into 'workfare' Pateman draws on Marshall's contrast between a logic of social rights and a logic associated with the former Poor Law regime, under which the recipients of minimal benefits received them only through coerced labour. Because of that they entered a realm of reduced civil rights and second-class citizen status. In a novel twist the focus of Poor Law-style workfare shifted in current proposals and policies from men as heads of households to women as single mothers, where Pateman's critique gives careful attention to the consequences for child care, on the one hand, and the supposed 'virtue' of marital households, on the other. Overall Pateman works to loosen the linkage in norms and practice between employment and the full benefits and status to which all democratic citizens are equally entitled. A basic income for all citizens, she says, 'would open up time and resources to citizens and help put social reproduction at the forefront of debate', contrary to the Poor Law logic of 'workfare', through which paid employment is overrated, and unpaid labour devalued or worse (p. 193). A basic income is thus a necessary but not sufficient step in order to realise democratic citizenship as a universal. Public provision of goods and services is also required for 'good quality education in well-equipped schools, affordable housing, access to health care, violence free neighborhoods, access to cultural amenities, or the cultivation of individual capacities within the democratized institutions of a robust democracy' (p. 200).

Pateman as an innovator: democracy, feminism, welfare

The heading above perhaps sums up the innovative way that Pateman has worked as a political theorist. Her thought refuses the usual academic distinctions between theoretical and applied, historical and analytical, mainstream and feminist. Even more important, perhaps, is the way that the highest standards of historical scholarship, analytical argumentation and empirical work are consistent features of her overt concerns with 'real-world' issues. There is steely determination here to use political theory to make a difference in the political sphere itself, something she shares with a number of classic theorists, but perhaps rather fewer of the moderns. Her method could perhaps be characterised as factual deconstruction (rather than deconstruction of 'facts'), in that she is characteristically dissatisfied with generalities – to do with say, women, democracy, or welfare – and instead pursues specificities. No stranger to detailed factuality as a matter of history, law, economic figures, or civil status, Pateman's work persuades through registers of knowledge and credibility that are widely accessible. The method thus suits the project, and the project has an immediacy and a depth that make her work distinctive. Renovation can be innovation.

This volume closes with Chapter 13 (pp. 207–218), an interview given specially to the editors in which Pateman reflects on how far political theory has come in her career of over forty years in the subject...and how far it has yet to go. Her engagement with liberalism and feminism in theory and practice has been remarkable, and the interview draws out her current views on participatory or 'organizational' democracy, contractualism, gender politics, the welfare state, and the warfare state post-9/11.

References

Almond, G.A. and S. Verba. 1965. *The Civic Culture and Political Development*. Princeton, NJ: Princeton University Press.

Dowding, K., J. de Wispelaere and S. White (eds). 2003. *The Ethics of Stakeholding.* Basingstoke: Palgrave Macmillan.

Duncan, G. (ed.). 1983. *Democratic Theory and Practice.* Cambridge: Cambridge University Press.

Hobbes, T. 1991 [1651]. In R. Tuck (ed.) *Leviathan.* Cambridge: Cambridge University Press.

MacKinnon, C.A. 1987. *Feminism Unmodified: Discourses on Life and Law.* Cambridge, MA and London: Harvard University Press.

Pateman, C. 1970. *Participation and Democratic Theory.* Cambridge: Cambridge University Press.

— 1988. *The Sexual Contract.* Cambridge: Polity.

PART I

Democracy and political theory

1

POLITICAL CULTURE, POLITICAL STRUCTURE AND POLITICAL CHANGE (1971)

In *The Civic Culture,* perhaps the best known study of political culture, Almond and Verba say that 'the relationship between political culture and political structure [is] one of the most significant researchable aspects of the problem of political stability and change' (1965: 33). I want to look at the way this relationship has been treated in one particular area, an area very relevant to questions of political stability and change in our own society; that is, in studies of political participation and apathy, especially research into the sense of political efficacy or competence. This is the area with which *The Civic Culture* itself is largely concerned, and it is now well established that individuals low in a sense of political efficacy tend to be apathetic about politics; indeed, Almond and Verba consider the sense of efficacy or competence to be a 'key political attitude' (1965: 207).

The major claim made for the usefulness of the concept of political culture is, in the words of *The Civic Culture,* that it provides 'the connecting link between micro and macropolitics' (1965: 32). Similarly, Pye states that 'it is the problem of aggregation — which involves the adding up of the discoveries of individual psychology in such a manner as to make community-wide behaviour understandable in the light of individual actions —...for which the concept of political culture holds such great promise' (1965: 9). In discussions of political participation, the use of the concept of political culture has not fulfilled this promise. Attention has remained almost entirely focused at the level of individual psychology. Furthermore, that political participation does pose a problem of 'community-wide behaviour' has hardly been recognized.

The problem is that of the social pattern of political participation, and the social distribution of a low, and high sense, of political efficacy. Empirical studies show that aspects of our own political culture, such as a low sense of political efficacy, that are related to low rates of political participation, tend to be concentrated (like apathy itself) among individuals from a low SES background.[1] A relatively random distribution of different levels of the sense of efficacy would be unremarkable but the existing pattern, on the face of it, does call for some attempt to be made at an explanation. Yet in most recent work on democracy and participation no such attempt is made; in fact it is argued that the existing pattern of political participation and apathy must be taken as the starting point for discussions of democracy. It is claimed that if we are to talk *realistically* about democracy then we must accept that the ordinary citizen is unlikely to become more interested or active in political affairs than he is at present.[2]

To argue that we must take the existing social pattern of political participation as unchangeable or given is to say that we must take the existing political culture, or at least part of it, as given, and this leads to a one-sided view of the relationship between political culture and political structure. In his article on 'Political Culture' in the *International Encyclopedia of the Social Sciences* (1968), Pye states that 'if the concept of political culture is to be effectively utilized, it needs to be supplemented with structural analysis, but the difficulty is that political structures can be seen on the one hand as products reflecting the political culture, while on the other hand they are also "givens" which shape the political culture'. It is this second aspect of the relationship that has been neglected in recent discussions. Attention has been focused on the way in which the political structure reflects the existing political culture as, for instance, in the various, and now familiar, discussions of the contribution to the maintenance of a stable democratic structure made by those aspects of our own political culture related to political apathy and disinterest. If it is assumed that the social pattern of political participation, and the culture that underlies this pattern, cannot be significantly changed, then there is no point in looking at the neglected side of the political culture/structure relationship; the features of the culture in question have already been assumed to be incapable of being 'shaped' in a more participatory direction.

Several factors have contributed to this conclusion about the pattern of Anglo-American political participation and political culture, including the tendency for researchers into political socialization to concentrate on childhood socialization and an implicit evaluative assumption, in many discussions, about the way in which the existing system does work. Both these aspects will be discussed later. Also important is a lack of clarity in the use of the concept of political culture itself. The multi-dimensional nature of the concept is often obscured because attention is focused on one of its components, the psychological, at the expense of another element that would raise the question of the significance of the neglected side of the political culture/structure relationship.

The concept of political culture is used to cover an extremely wide range of political phenomena.[3] However, it is typically summed up along the lines suggested by Dawson and Prewitt (1969): 'Political culture, conceptualized roughly, is the pattern of distribution of orientations members of a political community have towards politics' (1969: 27). These writers do not define 'orientations' but it is clear that they are using it to cover all the ways in which the individual can regard politics, that is to refer to 'all the perceptions (cognitions, knowledge), affects (feelings and attitudes), and evaluations (values and norms) through which a person relates himself to social objects' (Easton and Dennis 1969: 5). An investigation of a political culture, therefore, will include the three sides of the individual citizen's relationship to politics: his value perspective; any relevant personality or psychological factors; and cognitive aspects, i.e. his knowledge and beliefs about his own political structure and the way it operates. Thus if all three aspects of a political culture were considered the neglected side of the relationship between political culture and political structure could not be avoided. The cognitive element contains a built-in reference to the impact of political structure on political culture.

One reason that this connection is often overlooked is that the term 'orientations' is also used more narrowly to refer to the psychological aspect of the political culture. This is how, following Parsons, it is used in *The Civic Culture* (although, notwithstanding their definitions, Almond and Verba attempt to stretch the term to cover all three aspects). It is worth looking more closely at the definitions in *The Civic Culture* and, briefly, at what Parsons has to say about culture because the Parsonian framework remains focused at the micro level and has nothing to say about the problem of the relationship between culture and structure; indeed, it eliminates any such problem.

Gabriel Almond is usually credited with introducing the notion of political culture to the study of politics in his essay on *Comparative Political Systems,* published in 1956, and most recent discussions refer one back to that source. In that essay Almond says that Parsons has provided the basis for his approach and he defines political culture as 'patterns of orientation to political action', and orientations as 'attitudes towards politics' (Almond 1956: 396). In *The Civic Culture* Almond and Verba state that they are using the concept of culture in the sense of '*psychological* orientation toward social objects' (my emphasis) and that orientation 'refers to the internalized aspects of objects and relationships'; political culture then refers to 'the political system as internalized in the cognitions, feelings, and evaluations of its population' (Almond and Verba 1965: 13–14).[4] However, they do not make clear why orientations should be defined as 'psychological' and 'internalized' when part of what is covered by the notion is cognitive factors, i.e. beliefs and knowledge about the political system. What does 'internalized' mean in such a context? It becomes clear a few pages later, during Almond and Verba's discussion of their typology of political cultures, the parochial, the subject, and the participant, that essentially all that is meant by 'internalized' is that the individual 'understands' or is 'aware' that he is a member of a political system with a central political authority, and that he has some knowledge of, and feelings about, that authority. It is this that is lacking in the parochial political culture (Almond and Verba 1965: 16ff).

These muddles in the Almond and Verba definition of political culture illustrate some of the difficulties of attempting to use Parsons' conceptual framework to talk about political culture; difficulties that do not generally seem to be appreciated by the writers who so frequently refer to him and so, presumably, regard his work as helpful. Parsons has a good deal to say about culture and socialization but it is odd that his work is rarely discussed in writings about political culture.[5]

Orientation is an extremely important concept in Parsons' theory and he says that it is 'a structural concept and designates a relatively stable aspect of a system' (Parsons 1961: 337). Action has an orientation 'when it is guided by the meaning which the actor attaches to it' (Parsons and Shills 1951: 4). The orientation of the actor 'concerns the "how" of his relation to the object world, the patterns or ways in which his relations to it are organized' (Parsons 1951: 7). How does the actor obtain, or come to have, the orientation that he has? The answer that Parsons gives to this question is that it is a result of socialization, of the internalization of culture; more specifically, of normative culture because it is, says Parsons, 'inherent in an action system that action is… "normatively oriented" ' (1951: 36).

Culture, or the cultural system, of which political culture is a sub-system, plays a crucial role in the Parsonian framework; it is from culture that the 'order' in the system derives. The cultural system is concerned with 'patterns of meaning' (Parsons, Shills, Naegele and Pitts 1961: 34) and it is not precisely analogous to the social or personality systems in that it has, as it were, a dual status. Parsons says that cultural patterns can be both 'an object of orientation' and an 'element in the orientation of action' and can be 'transferred' from being an object to become an element in orientation (Parsons and Shills 1951: 6–7, 67). This transference can be illustrated by the dyadic model. If a stable pattern of interaction is to be maintained between ego and alter then they must have mutual (normative) expectations about each other's behaviour and their situation must have a common normative meaning or definition for them both. That is to say, the expectations, the culture or patterns of meaning, must not be merely 'an object of orientation' for ego and alter but they must both have *internalized* it to become 'an element in the orientation of action', part of their motivation, their psychologies. 'What was once an object becomes a constitutive part of the actor…it is part of his personality' (Parsons and Shills 1951: 8). Thus the concept of orientation in Parsons' theory is essentially psychological, and Black, in his well-known critique of Parsons, paraphrases orientations as 'acquired predispositions to respond in certain ways to given stimuli' (Black 1961: 272).

Parsons stresses that although the social and cultural systems are analytically distinct they are also, and this is a central feature of systems of action, 'interpenetrating' (Parsons *et al.* 1961: 990). This interpenetration has just been described: it is the internalization (in the personality system) of normative culture that gives rise to and 'controls', or institutionalizes, stable patterns of interaction – or social structures. Parsons places great emphasis on the fact that 'a fundamental proposition about the structure of action systems [is]…that their structure as treated within the frame of reference of action *consists* in institutionalized patterns of normative culture' (Parsons *et al.* 1961: 36; Parsons' emphasis). Thus if the notions of orientation and internalization are used in their Parsonian sense, there is no question of a problematical relationship between culture and structure; culture, in one of its aspects, *is* structure.

If the Parsonian framework is to be used to discuss political culture and structure, the political structure has therefore to be seen as a structure of shared political values (or shared, internalized, normative culture) that defines their political situation, and underwrites the collective (political) goals, for the members of the polity.

Political power can then be seen in consensual terms as a 'generalized capacity' for achieving these collective goals through the exercise of decision making by the occupants of leadership (authority) positions (Parsons 1967). Since Almond and Verba wish to 'avoid the assumption of congruence between political culture and political structure' (Almond and Verba 1965: 32–33) their references to Parsons and their definitions of 'orientations' and 'political culture' are particularly misleading; their approach presupposes that a viewpoint other than the Parsonian one is taken. That is, that the individual's political behaviour is seen as deriving from more than the internalization of (shared) values and norms, from more than psychological factors. One aspect which must be considered is the influence of the impact upon the individual of the political structure itself, a political structure seen in terms of a structure of power and authority that is, at least sometimes, exercised non-consensually and which places an *external* constraint on the individual and influences his behaviour and attitudes, i.e. which helps 'shape' the political culture.

Almond and Verba also differ from Parsons over the relative importance for political behaviour of childhood and adult socialization. Although Parsons states that learning continues throughout life much of his attention has been focused on childhood socialization within the family, and he argues that the major value orientation patterns, including presumably the political orientations, are laid down in childhood. These form the core of the basic structure of personality and 'are not on a large scale subject to drastic alteration during adult life' (Parsons 1951: 203, 208). Adult ego and alter have, so to speak, the process of internalization largely behind them.

This aspect of the Parsonian framework has important consequences for questions of political change. For Parsons all questions about political structure boil down to questions about individual psychology, or at least to questions about the childhood socialization process through which internalization occurs. The only problematical element is internalization; a change in political structure is a change in the socialization process, a change in individual psychology. Parsons states that 'institutionalization is embedded in the non-rational layers of motivational organization. It is not accessible to change simply through the presentation to an actor of rational advantages in the external definition of the situation' (Parsons *et al.* 1961: 74–75). In the political sphere any citizens with 'non-consensual' attitudes are regarded as cases of faulty or incomplete internalization. Parsons says that 'the primary function of superior authority is clearly to define the situation for the lower echelons of the collectivity. The problem of overcoming opposition in the form of *dispositions* to noncompliance then arises from the incomplete institutionalization of the power of the higher authority holder' (my emphasis) (Parsons 1967: 318). Again, as Giddens has pointed out, when Parsons talks of 'power deflation', i.e. a progressive loss of confidence in political leaders, he 'conceives the process as basically a psychological one' (Giddens 1968: 266).

Most recent writers on political socialization, like Parsons, state that socialization is a process continuing throughout life, but the tendency has been for the emphasis to be placed on the earlier years. Dawson and Prewitt, for example, state that 'new orientations are acquired, but in most instances they occur within bounds established by the deep and persistent orientations acquired during childhood' and they suggest that the adult is unlikely to alter the more 'basic' orientations such as 'his conception of the legitimate means of selecting political rulers, or broad ideological goals' (Dawson and Prewitt 1969: 56). The important point is that an interpretation of adult political behaviour basically in terms of childhood socialization (irrespective of definitions of orientation or political culture) will be a largely psychological interpretation. Moreover, since patterns of childhood socialization are not easy to influence, this approach tends to support the claim that it is not feasible to change the existing pattern of political participation. Nor does this approach offer much help towards an explanation of the existing pattern of participation. Even if individuals having a low or high sense of political efficacy have been socialized differently as children this does not explain why parents from different SES backgrounds should typically adopt such divergent methods of socialization. I shall return to this point, but next I shall discuss an example of the 'psychological' approach specifically concerned with the sense of political efficacy.

A paper by Easton and Dennis provides an interesting example of the way in which concentration on childhood socialization obscures a possible explanation for the political apathy and disinterest of the majority of ordinary citizens, an explanation in terms of the impact of the political structure on the individual. Easton and Dennis are concerned with the *norm* of political efficacy, a norm which involves that in a democracy citizens should be politically active and leaders should be responsive to citizens' demands. They argue that the early 'internalization' of this norm of political efficacy is crucial for adult political behaviour, because it provides a reservoir of 'diffuse support' for the political system. That is, it may offset adult experiences that 'undermine the political importance of the ordinary member' of the polity; childhood socialization helps 'contain' the 'frustration' that adult citizens might feel both 'in normal times, when members may feel that their capacity to manipulate the political environment is not living up to their expectations, and in special periods of stress, when popular participation may appear to be pure illusion or when political outputs fail to measure up to insistent demands' (Easton and Dennis 1967: 38). But Easton and Dennis offer no convincing arguments to show that this is what does happen. Given the postulated motivation, it seems far more plausible that if the adult citizen finds his political expectations are continually frustrated and that 'insistent demands' fail to meet with any worthwhile result, then either of two things is likely to happen. Either he will demand that the political environment is changed so that participation ceases to be 'pure illusion', or he will give up trying to influence the political process and lapse into apathy.[6]

If the second alternative is adopted then there is a simple and straightforward explanation for the low rates of political participation of ordinary citizens. Given their experiences of, and perception of the operation of the political structure, apathy is a realistic response, it does not seem worthwhile to participate. This explanation, it should be noted, is in terms of adult, not childhood experiences, and in terms of cognitive, not psychological factors. Additional support for this suggestion can be derived from an examination of the pattern of replies of respondents from different SES backgrounds to the statements that make up the political efficacy scale. So far, the concept of political efficacy has been taken as fairly unproblematical, but, as with the concept of political culture itself, recent discussions have overlooked that political efficacy is a multidimensional concept and attention has been concentrated on its psychological component.

A scale to measure the individual's sense of political efficacy was first devised by Campbell, Gurin and Miller in the early 1950s. They described the sense of efficacy as 'the feeling that individual political action does have, or can have, an impact on the political process, i.e. that it is worthwhile to perform one's civic duties. It is the feeling that political and social change is possible, and that the individual citizen can play a part in bringing about this change' (Campbell *et al.* 1954: 187). Almond and Verba's definition of 'subjective competence' in *The Civic Culture* is similar. They say that the political influence of a group or individual is 'the degree to which government officials act to benefit that group or individual because the officials believe that they will risk some deprivation…if they do not so act'. If an individual 'believes he can exert such influence, we shall view him as subjectively competent' (Almond and Verba 1965: 136–37). Campbell *et al.* have also suggested that a more general personality or psychological trait lies behind the sense of political efficacy or competence, namely 'ego strength', a 'sense of personal effectiveness', or a 'sense of control or mastery over the environment' (Campbell *et al.* 1960: 516–18). The sense of personal effectiveness and the sense of political efficacy have been found to be correlated. In *Political Life,* Lane's definition of political efficacy combines both these aspects; 'it has…two components – the image of the self and the image of democratic government. – and contains the tacit implication that an image of the self as effective is intimately related to the image of democratic government as responsive to the people' (Lane 1959: 149). However, we have already seen that Easton and Dennis also distinguish a third aspect of political efficacy, namely a norm of efficacy. So, like political culture, the concept of a sense of political efficacy involves three dimensions: the evaluative or normative, the psychological (the feeling of personal effectiveness, or ego strength), and the cognitive (knowledge and belief about the operation of the democratic political structure).

The original political efficacy scale, which more recent investigations follow closely, contained these statements:

1. I don't think public officials care much what people like me think.
2. The way people vote is the main thing that decides how things are run in this country.
3. Voting is the only way people like me can have any say about how the government runs things.
4. People like me don't have any say about what the government does.
5. Sometimes politics and government seems so complicated that people like me can't really understand what's going on (Campbell *et al.* 1954: 187–88).[7]

On the face of it a reasonable interpretation of the replies to these statements is that they indicate how the individual citizen perceives his political environment. The differential scores obtained by respondents from low and high SES backgrounds (those from higher SES backgrounds tending to obtain the highest scores) would indicate that they differ in the extent to which they regard the government as responsive to their demands and needs. Thus, if the ordinary citizen from a lower SES background regards the political structure as unresponsive, one arrives at the explanation for his apathy suggested earlier: apathy is a realistic response, participation is seen as pointless. There is other evidence to show that individuals from different SES backgrounds do differ in this way in their perceptions of the political structure.[8] Why then has this fairly obvious interpretation of the social pattern of political participation been overlooked?

Among the features that, I claimed earlier, contributed to the one-sided view of the political culture/structure relationship was an evaluative assumption about the way in which the existing democratic political structure does in fact operate. This assumption is precisely that the system *is* responsive to the demands and needs of all citizens. That this is an evaluative assumption can be seen, for example, from Prewitt's examination of the claim of many recent theorists of democracy that elected leaders are in fact accountable to the ordinary citizen (the concept of accountability embodying much the same notions about the operations of the system as responsiveness). Prewitt argues that the notion that elections legitimize leaders has been 'converted into a statement about the process which holds them accountable'. He shows that the assumption of accountability is often unjustified in city government, and to a lesser extent at higher levels in the USA because of the prevalence of volunteerism, i.e. a situation where 'both the choosers and the chosen come to think of movement into and out of political office as being regulated by self-selection and self-eliminating patterns rather than electoral challenge'. He comments that volunteerism might be connected to 'political disillusionment' among the electorate (Prewitt 1970).[9]

The assumption enters into arguments about the sense of political efficacy and participation in two ways. It is assumed that it is, in principle, worthwhile for all citizens to participate, and it is also assumed that for the majority of ordinary citizens such activity is only rarely required, that it is realistic and rational for them to be apathetic and disinterested most of the time. To look at this first assumption slightly differently: that the results of investigations showing the social distribution of a low and high sense of efficacy have been used to support the arguments of recent writers on participation and apathy, depends upon the assumption that the replies of individuals from higher SES backgrounds to the political efficacy scale *accurately* reflect the realities of the political structure. Conflicting replies can thus only be implicitly interpreted as telling us something about the respondents' psychology.

An illustration of how such an implicit evaluative assumption can influence arguments about political efficacy is provided in the recent study by Langton on *Political Socialisation*. Langton suggests that a developed sense of political efficacy arises from the individual's participation in a politicized group or social environment. 'In the family, for example, this may come about through the child's internalization of the politicized parental role, or by a more indirect means. In the latter case the politicized group environment may inspire a process which translates ego strength into political efficacy, i.e. it makes ego politically relevant' (Langton 1969: 143). What Langton does not explain is how the 'translation' is made from ego strength, a psychological feeling of effectiveness, to political efficacy, a belief that one can make an impact on political affairs. Interaction in a 'politicized' environment might lead one to believe that the existing political structure gives little or no scope for the ordinary citizen to influence political affairs; one may come to believe that ego is politically *irrelevant,* even though one may feel (psychologically) effective in everyday affairs. That is, the argument is only convincing on the implicit assumption that the political structure is such that participation is worthwhile. But once the assumption is made then apathy can appear to derive solely from a feature of the individual's psychological make-up.

A similar argument can be found in *The Civic Culture,* together with another explanation for apathy which provides an example of the second of the two uses of the evaluative assumption. The first of Almond and Verba's arguments arises from their investigation of the political socialization process that produces a developed sense of political efficacy. They found that it is opportunities to participate within the authority structures of different social spheres, the home, the school, the workplace, that is of crucial importance. They also found that socialization in the workplace is the most important of all, i.e. that it is adult socialization that is vital for the development of a high sense of political efficacy. They argue that the individual will generalize from his experiences within the authority structures of areas like the workplace to the political sphere. If the individual has the chance to participate, to exercise influence over decisions, at work then he will see the political sphere as offering similar opportunities (Almond and Verba 1965: 271–73, 294–99, Tables XI. 6–8).[10] However, in the discussion in the final chapter of *The Civic Culture* the assumption is that the existing democratic political structure is responsive to citizens' demands, that citizens can influence political decisions. An implicit explanation for apathy, therefore, is that apathetic citizens are making an erroneous generalization from their experiences in the workplace onto the political sphere.

Almond and Verba's alternative explanation of the apathy of the ordinary citizen is that it is a realistic response to his political environment. They argue that given the complexity of political affairs and the difficulties of obtaining information, then it is irrational for the average citizen to use his time and energy taking a keen and active interest in politics (Almond and Verba 1965: 340).[11] The assumption is that even *without* active participation the individual's interests will be secured; the fact that the individual could participate is assumed to be enough to keep democratic leaders responsive. But respondents' replies to Almond and Verba's subjective competence scale follow the same pattern as replies to other efficacy scales, so it is reasonable to conclude that many of their respondents do not agree with their assumption about the responsiveness of the existing political structure.[12]

The conclusion of studies of the aspects of the Anglo-American political culture relevant to the sense of political efficacy, and so to political participation, is that change is neither required nor feasible. Or, rather more accurately, because it is assumed that the existing political structure is responsive to citizen's needs and demands and that the only real task is to see how the existing political culture contributes to or detracts from the stability of that structure, we are confronted with a premise rather than a conclusion. It is assumed that questions about radical changes in political culture are relevant to the modernizing or developing countries, not to our own; consider the question posed by Almond and Verba of what kind of political culture it is that 'fits' a democratic political structure (Almond and Verba 1965: 337, 360). Given that they assume that we do have a stable, successful, democratic structure, their answer is hardly surprising, that it is our own 'civic culture' that provides the best 'fit'. What is problematical is whether the modernizing countries, where Almond and Verba see a 'participation explosion' occurring, will also develop this culture (Almond and Verba 1965: 2).

The ironical aspect of all this is that the writers on political efficacy and participation, due to their own assumptions and approach, have been taken completely unawares by the demands for a 'participation explosion' within their own polities. Not only have their arguments failed to recognize or explain the problem of the existing social pattern of participation, but nor do they give any hint that there would be demands for an increase in participation in various social spheres. The other side of this failure is that the concepts of political culture and the sense of political efficacy have not been properly recognized as multidimensional. The gap between the largely psychological arguments used at the micro level and the 'community-wide' or macro level political behaviour and attitudes can only be bridged if the three aspects of the sense of political efficacy are treated not as separate, or separable, but as three components of a complex whole.

From this perspective the evidence of *The Civic Culture* can be reinterpreted. The replies to Almond and Verba's subjective competence scale are tapping the cognitive element of the sense of political efficacy. What the evidence on the socialization process in the family, school and workplace reveals is, I suggest, the psychological element, ego strength or the sense of personal effectiveness. As already stated these two aspects have been found to be correlated; both must enter into any explanation of the social pattern of participation. An outline for such an explanation could run as follows.

The result of the socialization process for the individual from a lower SES background, especially socialization through the authority structure of the workplace, is such that, typically, he feels ineffective in his dealings with the world; thus he tends not to participate in political affairs. This feeling of ineffectiveness no doubt contributes to a view of the political structure as unresponsive, but the ordinary citizen's experiences and observations of that structure lead him to conclude that participation would be pointless. This, in turn, reinforces the feeling of ineffectiveness and so on. In other words, political culture and political structure are mutually interdependent and reinforcing. This is not, of course, a particularly original observation, but it is something, despite Pye's remark quoted earlier, that tends to be forgotten in discussions of participation and apathy.

The relationship between political culture and political structure is doubly complicated. The implicit reference when talking of 'political structure' is to the national political structure; certainly this is what Almond and Verba mean. However, it is being argued here that it is not just the impact of the national political structure that helps 'shape' the political culture, but authority structures, that is, political structures on a wide definition of the term 'political', in various social spheres; the impact of the authority structure of the workplace being particularly important. Other writers on political socialization have agreed with Almond and Verba about the importance of the authority structure of the family and school, but few have considered the possible implications of the impact of the authority structures within which the individual interacts in adult life. Hence the unsatisfactory position that I noted above. The differences in levels of political efficacy found in children (which follow the same social pattern as in adults) can be explained in terms of the different views on child-rearing and so the different family authority structures typically provided by parents of different SES backgrounds, those of higher SES backgrounds being more participatory (Greenstein 1965: 91–92; Kohn 1968).[13] But this does not explain why the parents (adults) should differ in this respect, nor the pattern of levels of sense of political efficacy in adults. Interesting evidence on this point has been almost completely neglected in discussions of political socialization, evidence supporting Almond and Verba's argument that it is socialization in the workplace, i.e. adult socialization that is crucial for (some aspects at least) of political socialization. This evidence suggests that it is the non-participatory role of the ordinary man in the workplace that is a major influence on his whole view of the world, including his views on child-rearing, and especially on his feeling of ineffectiveness (Kohn and Schooler 1969; Lipsitz 1964).[14] Those who tend to be politically apathetic, individuals from lower SES backgrounds, have typically had few or no opportunities to participate in different social spheres from childhood through to adult life. Thus this evidence provides the missing link between the studies of childhood socialization and the psychological aspect of adult political behaviour.

If this argument is at all convincing, it throws considerable doubt on the claim that existing patterns of political participation must be taken as given. If an explanation can be found for the tendency for low rates of political participation to be concentrated among citizens from low SES backgrounds, then, at the very least, the question of whether these rates could be increased is still an open one, awaiting further empirical investigation. My argument suggests that the changes required would be radical ones. It would not be enough to modify the national political structure to make participation more worthwhile if the citizens required to participate do not feel (psychologically) confident to do so; to influence the latter aspect a change in the socialization process, a change in the 'intermediate' authority structures, especially that of the workplace, is also required.

It might be objected that this conclusion has been reached by ignoring one element in the concept of the sense of political efficacy, the evaluative or normative;

the different elements have not been treated as it has been claimed that they should. The normative aspect is, perhaps, the most confused part of the discussions of political culture and participation and requires more analysis than is possible in this context. However, a few brief points can be made. Following Parsons it would seem that if the individual has 'internalized' the norm of political efficacy at an early age (that citizens should be active and leaders responsive in a democracy), then there should be few problems about his adult political 'orientation' or behaviour, he should have few 'dispositions to non-compliance'. But how, on this kind of argument, do we make sense of the recent phenomenon of a demand for a 'participation explosion'; do the demands and political activities of some young people, young people being those most prominently involved, indicate that their socialization was 'faulty'?

First, if the psychological and cognitive components of the sense of political efficacy are considered in this context, it is not surprising that these young people are politically active. Their social background is typically such that they will feel highly (psychologically) effective, yet this goes together with a view of the political structure like that attributed above to the typically apathetic citizen, namely that it is unresponsive to the needs and demands of citizens. Second, that they are demanding a change in the political structure in the specific form of a move toward greater popular participation in various social spheres can be explained by the very fact that they *have* 'internalized' the norm of political efficacy. 'Internalization' itself is a notion that is used in several different ways in the literature, but even on a 'strong' Parsonian interpretation, to the effect that through internalization the norm somehow becomes part of the personality and 'controls' what the individual wants, the demands are intelligible. Indeed, if one took a much looser interpretation of 'internalization', perhaps 'accept' or 'believe in', then probably the majority of the population in the Anglo-American democracies have internalized the norm. In either case, the crucial point that is overlooked in discussions in general terms of the internalization of norms is that there is more than one way to *interpret* the norm of political efficacy and the other norms and values traditionally associated with democracy; there is more than one view on what 'really' constitutes responsiveness of leaders and so on, and these differences in interpretation also encompass divergent notions of what form of democratic institutions actually embody, or give practical expression to those norms and values.

Thus so far as the third component of the sense of political efficacy is concerned, the difference between the typical young 'protester' and the typical apathetic citizen (who both share the same view of the political structure) lies in the interpretation of the norm. The latter, while believing that the existing structure does not live up to expectations based on the norm, cannot clearly envisage an alternative democratic structure.[15] This forms another element in the 'circle' of apathy. On the other hand, the advocate of a move toward a more participatory structure does see an alternative, based on adherence to (on 'internalization' of), but a different interpretation of, the norm of political efficacy. Whether or not the alternative advocated is empirically feasible is a question, central though it is to the issue of political change in our own society, that has been dismissed without examination, lost behind the evaluative assumptions and the conceptual confusions in studies of political culture and participation. Investigations of political culture and political socialization may have formed one of the growth points in the study of politics in the last decade but they have made only a minimal contribution to 'the problem of political stability and change'.

Notes

1 See, for example, the first study of political efficacy (Campbell, Gurin and Miller, 1954: 192 and Table A3). A summary of findings on political efficacy can be found in Milbrath (1965: 56ff). 'SES' is 'socio-economic status'.

2 This is the major argument of those recent theorists of democracy, the majority, who claim that the 'classical' theory of democracy is unrealistic and needs drastic revision. The final chapter of *The Civic Culture* (Almond and Verba, 1965) provides one example of this argument; other examples are briefly discussed in Pateman (1970: 3–14).

3 For example, this characterization: political culture 'includes political traditions and folk heroes, the spirit of public institutions, political passions of the citizenry, goals articulated by the political ideology, and both formal and informal rules of the political game… political stereotypes, political style, political moods, the tone of political exchanges… some sense of what is appropriately political and what is not' (Dawson and Prewitt, 1969: 26).

4 Compare these two definitions from other writers who follow Parsons. Orientations are 'stable, internalized, dispositional traits, underlying and guiding individual behaviour' (Nordlinger, 1967: 46). Political culture is 'the "internalized" expectations in terms of which the political roles of individuals are defined and through which political institutions (in the sense of regularized behaviour patterns) come into being' (Eckstein, 1963: 26).

5 There is a brief discussion in Kim (1964). Mitchell (1967) devotes a short section to political culture suggesting that Parsons provides a fruitful approach in this area as in others.

6 Apathy may be an example of the 'containment' of frustration but, even so, the point is that it is far from clear that this results from the 'internalization' of a norm in childhood.

7 Agreement with statements 1, 3, 4, 5 indicates inefficaciousness, and disagreement with 2.

8 The typical working-class view of a gulf between 'us' and 'them', in contrast to the middleclass view of society as an ordered hierarchy, has often been remarked upon. One investigator found that manual workers interviewed had a general picture of government as 'a group of men who arrange to keep themselves in power and don't care about the interests of the common people' (Lipsitz 1964: 958). Evidence of the divergent views of the political structure of different income groups in the USA can be found in Form and Rytina (1969). In a very interesting article Mann (1970) has collected together evidence of different perspectives of middle- and working-class individuals over a variety of areas.

9 See also evidence on the belief in the efficacy of elections in Dennis (1970).

10 'The structure of authority at the workplace is probably the most significant – and salient–…with which the average man finds himself in daily contact' (Almond and Verba 1965: 294).

11 Almond and Verba also argue that because, like any other government, a democratic government must govern, i.e. 'have power and leadership and make decisions', citizens cannot be very active politically; that would upset the 'balance' between 'power and responsiveness' of leaders necessary for democratic government (1965: 340–44). This argument that a stable democratic system *requires* apathy is common to many recent writers on democratic theory, who stress the dangers to stability of a significant increase in popular activity. One of the more emphatic statements on these lines can be found

in Sartori (1965). Sartori also argues that apathy 'is nobody's fault in particular, and it is time we stopped seeking scapegoats' (1965: 88).

12 See Almond and Verba (1965) figures VI.1 and 2 showing that the higher the educational attainment of the respondents the higher their level of competence.

13 For descriptions of English family structures, see e.g. Klein (1965).

14 See also the discussion of other studies supporting the argument that the authority structure of the workplace is a major influence on the sense of effectiveness in Pateman (1970); and see the comments on the factory in Inkeles (1969).

15 See the discussion in Mann (1970).

References

Almond, Gabriel A. 1956. 'Comparative Political Systems'. *Journal of Politics* 18: 391–409.

Almond, Gabriel A. and Sidney Verba. 1965. *The Civic Culture: Political Attitudes and Democracy in Five Nations*. Boston: Little, Brown.

Black, Max (ed.) 1961. *The Social Theories of Talcott Parsons*. Englewood Cliffs, N.J.: Prentice-Hall.

Campbell, Angus and Phillip Converse, Warren Miller and Donald Stokes. 1960. *The American Voter*. New York: Wiley.

Campbell, Angus, Gerald Gurin and Warren Miller. 1954. *The Voter Decides*. Illinois: Row, Peterson.

Dawson, Richard E. and Kenneth Prewitt. 1969. *Political Socialisation*. Boston: Little, Brown.

Dennis, Jack. 1970. 'Support for the Institution of Election by the Mass Public'. *American Political Science Review* 64: 819–35.

Easton, David and Jack Dennis. 1967. 'The Child's Acquisition of Regime Norms: Political Efficacy'. *The American Political Science Review* 61: 25–38.

—— 1969. *Children in the Political System: Origins of Political Legitimacy*. New York: McGraw Hill.

Eckstein, Harry. 1963. 'Introduction'. In Harry Eckstein and David E. Apter (eds) *Comparative Politics*. New York: Free Press.

Form, William H. and Joan Rytina. 1969. 'Ideological Beliefs on the Distribution of Power in the United States'. *American Sociological Review* 34: 19–31.

Giddens, Anthony. 1968. '"Power" in the Recent Writings of Talcott Parsons'. *Sociology* 11: 257–72.

Greenstein, Fred I. 1965. *Children and Politics*. New Haven: Yale University Press.

Inkeles, Alex. 1969. 'Making Men Modern'. *American Journal of Sociology* 75: 208–25.

Kim, Y.C. 1964. 'The Concept of Political Culture in Comparative Politics'. *Journal of Politics* 26: 313–36.

Klein, Josephine. 1965. *Samples from English Cultures*. London: Routledge & Kegan Paul.

Kohn, Melvin L. 1968. 'Social Class and Parent–Child Relationships: an Interpretation'. *American Journal of Sociology* 68: 471–80.

Kohn, Melvin L. and Carmi Schooler. 1969. 'Class, Occupation and Orientation'. *American Sociological Review* 34: 659–78.

Lane, Robert E. 1959. *Political Life: Why and How People Get Involved in Politics*. New York: Free Press.

Langton, Kenneth P. 1969. *Political Socialisation*. London: Oxford University Press.

Lipsitz, Lewis. 1964. 'Work Life and Political Attitudes'. *The American Political Science Review* 58: 951–62.

Mann, Michael. 1970. 'The Social Cohesion of Liberal Democracy'. *American Sociological Review* 35: 423–37.

Milbrath, Lester W. 1965. *Political Participation*. Chicago: Rand McNally.

Mitchell, W.C. 1967. *Sociological Analysis and Politics: The Theories of Talcott Parsons*. Englewood Cliffs, N.J.: Prentice Hall.

Nordlinger, Eric A. 1967. *The Working-Class Tories*. London: MacGibbon & Kee.

Parsons, Talcott. 1951. *The Social System*. New York: Free Press.

— 1961. 'The Point of View of the Author'. In *The Social Theories of Talcott Parsons*, ed. Max Black. Englewood Cliffs, N.J.: Prentice-Hall.

— 1967. 'On the Concept of Political Power'. In Talcott Parsons, *Sociological Theory and Modern Society*. New York: Free Press.

Parsons, Talcott, Edward A. Shills, Kaspar D. Naegele and Jesse R. Pitts (eds). 1961. *Theories of Society: Foundations of Modern Sociological Theory*. New York: Free Press.

Parsons, Talcott and Edward A. Shills (eds). 1951. *Towards a General Theory of Action*. Cambridge, MA: Harvard University Press.

Pateman, Carole. 1970. *Participation and Democratic Theory*. Cambridge: Cambridge University Press.

Prewitt, Kenneth. 1970. 'Political Ambitions, Volunteerism, and Electoral Accountability'. *American Political Science Review* 64: 5–17.

Pye, Lucian W. 1965. 'Introduction'. In *Political Culture and Political Development*. Princeton: Princeton University Press.

Sartori, Giovanni. 1965. *Democratic Theory*. New York: Praeger.

2

A CONTRIBUTION TO THE POLITICAL THEORY OF ORGANIZATIONAL DEMOCRACY (1975)

At the heart of liberal democratic theory lies the assumption that because 'democracy' is a political concept it properly refers only to the government (national and local) of the state. To use the term to refer to organizations that fall within the jurisdiction of the state – as in 'industrial democracy' – is seen as either illegitimate or involving some special sense of the term; that is, a nonpolitical sense.

Thus to take a recent example, a political scientist argues that economic enterprises are not political: 'to condition or influence political power is not the same as to wield it' (Sartori 1973: 21). Management and organization theorists writing on 'industrial democracy' usually implicitly or explicitly reject democracy in the political sense. Rhenman, for instance, states that 'a management cannot be elected in the same way as, for example, the parliament and government of a democracy' (Rhenman 1968: 3, 42).[1] Such arguments presuppose the separation of social life into two 'autonomous' spheres, the political or public and the private. This reflects a fundamental structural feature of liberal democratic theory and the tradition of thought about political life to which it belongs.[2]

However, not all writers on democracy agree that the term has no application to the organizations of the private sphere. In his recent book, *After the Revolution?* Dahl, for example, introduces industrial democracy, or self-management, as a legitimate part of polyarchical democracy. Indeed, he remarks that as a solution to certain contemporary problems it is 'too obvious to be ignored' (Dahl 1970: 134). Dahl does not explicitly argue that industrial democracy entails that the economic enterprise is therefore political. However, the problem with which he is concerned is that of the 'appropriation of public authority by private rulers' in the huge corporations (Dahl 1970: 115), and 'public' authority has usually been seen as political authority (see Wolin 1961; Arendt 1959).[3] Moreover, that Dahl has no 'special' sense of democracy in mind is clear, because he is arguing for self-management of the enterprise, for the election by the employees of a representative council ('government'). That is to say, the enterprise is being seen as a miniature political polyarchy.

The introduction of self-management into *After the Revolution?* (Dahl 1970) marks a considerable departure from Dahl's earlier writings on democratic theory – although he does not seem to regard it that way himself. His introduction of self-management suggests that organizational democracy poses no problems for liberal democratic theory. In this paper I shall argue that this view is mistaken.

My argument will be that the logic of some of the central arguments of liberal democratic theory itself leads to organizational democracy. However, to admit this as a legitimate element in democratic theory is to undermine a central, structural feature of liberal democratic theory: namely, the separation or autonomy of the political and private spheres. The theoretical changes required to encompass organizational democracy cannot be contained within liberal democratic theory itself. Thus the logic of some of the central arguments of the theory leads to its transformation into a theory of participatory or self-managing democracy.

The theoretical arguments here may appear somewhat remote from the practical problems involved in the implementation of organizational democracy. But to treat organizational democracy in isolation from democratic theory as a whole means that, implicitly, it is being seen in terms of the theory of the existing politic-economic system, i.e., liberal democratic theory. Problems will neither be dealt with adequately nor, in some cases, even be recognized as problems if refracted through the perspective of an inappropriate theory – a mystifying theory. The decisive impact of organizational democracy on democratic theory, and the very conception of democracy itself, is obscured all the time that it is assumed that organizations can be treated apart from 'political' democracy as a whole. This encourages suspicion and hostility to organizational self-management because it is not seen as a legitimate part of democracy. That is to say, conceptions of democracy and the political sphere are a crucial part of the *problem* of achieving organizational democracy; theory must be taken into account together with practical problems.

In this paper I shall approach the problem of organizational democracy through an initial discussion of some of the central claims of liberal democratic theory: those concerned with democratic voting.

I

The distinguishing feature of a democratic political system is widely held to be the existence of periodic, free elections for competing candidates, with a universal (sane, adult) franchise.[4] It needs to be emphasized that the *only* democratic element in this conception of democracy is universal suffrage. Historically, this has been combined with an otherwise liberal theory of representative government to form contemporary liberal democracy.

The liberal theory of representative democracy developed as the theory of, indeed as part and parcel of, the development of capitalist society in the modern Western world.[5] One of the most striking features of contemporary liberal democratic theory is the frequency with which the analogy is drawn between the electoral mechanism and the free market economy. As Schumpeter put it, in democratic voting, 'the social function is fulfilled, as it were, incidentally – in the same sense as production is incidental to the making of profits (Schumpeter 1943: 282; see also Macpherson 1973). The basis for the analogy is that the same conception of the social actor is common to both liberal economic and liberal political theory. This conception of the free individual *qua* individual, is abstracted from specific social relationships; see the starting point in Dahl's (1970) argument in *After the Revolution?* the free individual, acting rationally in an instrumentally functional way, conscientiously deciding for himself, pursuing his chosen interests, freely entering into contracts – or voting.[6] The private, self-interests of these individuals are systematically brought together through the market, the division of labor, and the electoral mechanism.

As Wolin has pointed out, the liberal theory of representative government was subsumed under the division of labor (Wolin 1961: 304). This is of the greatest importance for the structure of liberal democratic theory. Most liberal writers regard the 'inconveniences' arising from the individual pursuit of private interests as great enough to warrant a special, impartial body (Locke's 'umpire') to enforce the rules required for orderly interaction. But despite this extension of the division of labor, the analogy with the market is misleading in a crucial respect. Theoretically, in economic life, notwithstanding the division of labor, all individuals freely decide for themselves and are responsible for their actions. However, once government is subsumed under the division of labor, political decisions theoretically become, uniquely, the responsibility of a few individuals only, the representatives. This is why Pranger sees representative government as a variant of a certain kind of politics; politics as power: 'in every form of representative politics the most typical feature is *plena potestas,* the arming of select individuals…with plenary power to act in place of and with full authorization of the constituents, the ordinary citizens' (Pranger 1968: 13–14). In liberal representative theory, except on special occasions, ordinary individuals have no need to concern themselves with the political sphere; *homo civicus* is not naturally a political animal. Under the division of political labor it is the job of the representatives to 'get on with governing', and political decisions are their responsibility.

Thus, a central, structural feature of liberal democratic theory is the separation, or autonomy, of the political sphere from the rest of social life. When Dahl remarks that it is 'absurd' to see the contemporary economic corporation as 'private', this is – implicitly – to step outside the framework of liberal democratic theory. Within that theory, far from being absurd, it is required. The two spheres, the private and the political, are brought together, in theory, through voting (democratic voting with the introduction of universal suffrage); individuals vote as citizens; that is, they vote as political not private actors. The formal, equal status of citizenship gives to everyone, under universal suffrage, an equal political resource, no matter what their private status.

The relatively tenuous connection between liberal representative government and universal suffrage or democratic voting is shown by Schumpeter's willingness to exclude persons from the suffrage on grounds of sex, race, and religion in his democracy (Schumpeter 1943: 244–45). But the liberal argument for democratic voting is that it ensures that representatives do not ignore any interests in their decision-making. Elections provide the sanction – the threat of loss of office – that ensures that everyone's interests are looked after. The corollary of this is that voting, like other (rational) actions in liberal theory, is instrumentally functional. The point of voting is to receive a benefit: the protection and furtherance of individual, private, interests, using the currency, as in the economic market, as frugally as possible.

Contemporary liberal democratic theory follows this conception of voting; it abounds with references to the electoral 'responsiveness' and 'accountability' of representatives that are required for instrumentally functional voting. As one of the most recent empirical studies states, an instrumentally effective vote will increase 'the likelihood that the government will perform as (the citizen) desires', and 'the participant must be able to tell whether he has had any success' (Verba and Nie 1972: 103).

The logic of liberal democratic theory is that democratic voting ensures that representatives are responsive to all citizens, that all interests are protected and looked after. It is assumed, that is, that the nondemocratic nature of the organizations in the private sphere is unrelated to the realization of the theoretical claims made for democratic voting. This assumption is one that many writers on democratic theory are all too eager to embrace.

II

The structural division of social life, within liberal democratic theory, into separate spheres of the private and the political provides a barrier against consideration of the question of organizational democracy. But this is not the only reason, even for those working within the liberal democratic theoretical framework, why the possibility of an extension of citizenship and democratic voting to the organizations of everyday life is so seldom raised. It is also widely assumed that democratic voting works as it is held to in democratic theory. Indeed, that is precisely why liberal democratic theory is so often presented by its proponents as a purely descriptive theory.

It is assumed that an account of the liberal democratic system in terms of an electoral mechanism, where democratic voting is instrumentally effective and representatives are responsive to all citizens and accountable to the electorate, is an accurate description. Given this assumption, it has been possible for writers on democracy to spend a great deal of time scrutinizing the characteristics of individual voters (are they rational?) – thus conveniently avoiding the question whether voting itself appears rational to individual citizens, i.e., whether it does actually work as claimed and whether it is worthwhile.

General observation of the operation of liberal democracies might cause one to pause when confronted with the theoretical claims made for democratic voting. Given that poverty, discrimination, homelessness, and a large class of claimants existed even during the period that the most uncritical democratic theory was written, a cynic might see those changes that have occurred in the writings of theorists of liberal democracy as a variant on the theme of Dr. Johnson's about-to-be-hanged man; lootings, burnings, squatting, work-ins appearing on the television screen and in the headlines all concentrate the mind wonderfully – but not enough where claims for democratic voting are concerned.

The difficulties facing a citizen trying to assess how 'successful' a vote has been through the proliferation of 'images', and the marketing of parties and candidates by advertising and public relations techniques, and perhaps even systematic deceit by representatives, are too obvious to need more comment. Many citizens, particularly those from lower SES [socio-economic status] groups, seem dubious that their votes are instrumentally effective.[7] About half the electorate find that 'whoever you vote for, things go on pretty much the same' (McClosky 1970: 396), and about the same proportion are doubtful whether 'the way people vote is the main thing that decides how things are run in this country' (Dennis 1970: 829), or whether elections mean that governments pay 'a good deal' of attention to what the people think (Butler and Stokes 1969: 32). There seems to have been a decline in the extent to which people value elections for their 'participatory effects' (Dennis 1970: 829) – and the poor tend to feel cheated (Lipsitz 1970: 165; see also Form and Rytina 1969: 19–31, and Hindess 1971: esp. ch. 7).

Fascination with the economic analogy has led democratic theorists to make the same mistake as the economists, a mistake that has been nicely characterized by Parry:

> It is not a necessary truth in a competitive political situation all interests will be considered, let alone accommodated. A comparison can be made with a competitive market in economics…It does not attend to the *needs* of everyone in the community since not all needs may be backed by purchasing power, and such needs do not go forward as demands.
>
> (Parry 1969: 124–25; emphasis in original)

Which is to argue, as Bachrach and Baratz have done, that the other 'face' of politics as power is that some interests may be systematically neglected through non-decision-making (Bachrach and Baratz 1970; see also Crenson 1971). The common assumption, that because competing packages of 'issues' are put forward at elections all interests are protected and catered for, and can, therefore, rationally be voted for, cannot be accepted until it is also known what the issues do *not* include.

The evidence which perhaps best highlights the disparity between the liberal democratic theory of voting and the reality is Verba and Nie's conclusion in *Participation in America* that political participation, including voting, *'helps those who are already better off'* (Verba and Nie 1972: 338; emphasis added). They find that representatives are not equally responsive to all citizens; what Verba and Nie call 'concurrence' goes disproportionately to the most politically active, i.e., upper-SES citizens (Verba and Nie 1972: 337). Significantly, they also argue that instrumental voting is impeded by 'the nature of the electoral mechanism itself'; voters having no say in when, for what, or for whom they vote (Verba and Nie 1972: 114, 106).[8]

It might be suggested that the apparent instrumental ineffectiveness of the ordinary citizen's vote supports the emphasis of many liberal democratic theorists on interelectoral political activity, pressure groups, and so on. The first problem with this argument is that insofar as elections become unimportant, so the distinction between liberal democratic and other political systems becomes obscured. Second, voting is the only political activity engaged in by many, especially lower-SES citizens, and the vote is the only political resource that is equally distributed. To emphasize interelectoral organizational activity, when it is commonplace that some interests are a great deal better organized than others, can only reinforce a situation where political participation helps the already advantaged.

Such an emphasis is, however, not surprising given the vast changes that have occurred since the early development of liberal democratic theory – changes that have undermined in practice whatever validity the theoretical separation of the political or public sphere and the private sphere may once have had. The relationship with government of many organizations active interelectorally is such that the liberal democratic political 'umpire' now has begun to look more like part of an interlocked web of corporate oligarchies. Some 'pressure groups' are a good deal more successful than others just because they have become an integral part of the governmental apparatus. Economic organizations are the obvious example woven into the public sphere through governmental committees, regulatory boards, and so forth and in liberal democracies private industry is hugely subsidized by the government by a variety of means – which is to echo Dahl's argument that it is absurd to see these 'corporate leviathans' as private.

Dahl puts forward the democratization of these economic organizations as a way to end such an appropriation of public authority by private rulers. But he presents this as a particular solution to a particular problem, when self-management is required as a general solution in response to a much more general problem: that of the realization of the central claims of liberal democratic theory. It seems clear that if democratic voting is to be instrumentally effective then it has to be extended into organizations which vitally affect the interests of every citizen, yet which, being seen as private, are responsible only to themselves.

The extension of citizenship and democratic voting into the corporate leviathans, i.e., recognition of the organizations of everyday life as part of the political sphere, strikes at the heart of the central structural feature of liberal democratic theory. The political and the private can no longer be seen as separate, but must be seen as interrelated. This is one reason why organizational democracy cannot be slotted, as it were, into the existing liberal democratic theoretical framework. The difficulties, however, do not stop there.

The empirical evidence suggests that although substantive results for all citizens are held to follow from use of the electoral mechanism, this is often far from the case. Democratic voting, rather than being instrumentally effective, is often merely a periodic, formal exercise of a formal political status for most citizens. My argument is that, within liberal democracy, voting and representation are doomed to remain largely formal matters. Modification of the electoral mechanism and the introduction of organizational democracy necessary to change this situation would lead away from liberal democracy in both theory and practice. Democratic theory, according to Dahl, is 'potentially a revolutionary doctrine' (Dahl 1970: 4). If this is so for liberal democratic theory, it is only because the logic of the theory leads to its own transformation.

III

It is important that organizational democracy is seen in terms of a participatory theory of democracy, or the tendency will be that it will *appear* that an extension of democracy must be confined to the formalities of liberal democractic representation.

The distinguishing features of a democratic system according to liberal democratic theory are formal or procedural ones; for example, the electoral mechanism, the formal equality of the status of citizenship, the procedural guarantees of civil liberties, the formal separation of private and political power. Similarly, the liberal democratic conception of representation is a formal one. Pitkin has distinguished two views of 'formalistic' representation: authorization and accountability. The first view (see Pranger's comment on *plena potestas* cited earlier) 'equates elections with a grant of authority'; the second 'equates elections with a holding-to-account' (Pitkin 1967: 56). As Pitkin states, these formal views say nothing about the actual activity of representing, 'about what goes on *during* representation, how a representative ought to act or what he is expected to do, how to tell whether he has represented well or badly. Such questions do not even make sense in terms of formalistic definitions' (Pitkin 1967: 58). Liberal democratic theory, of course, does say something about the substantive activity of representatives; they are expected to protect individual interests and can be judged, held to account, on that basis. But whereas elections certainly formally authorize, or legitimize, representatives, it is not clear in exactly what sense accountability takes place, other than the formal standing for re-election.

Citizenship is a formal political status. But in the liberal democratic conception the citizen is, in one crucial respect, like the liberal democratic individual, a private animal. When the citizen actually votes, the vote is cast on the basis of, and in defense of, private interests; it is precisely for that reason that the vote can act as a sanction against representatives who have failed to protect those interests. Although, theoretically, the two spheres of social life are brought together in an election, in practice the citizen does not leave, so to speak, the private sphere. The autonomy of the political sphere remains inviolate, and the sole responsibility of representatives for political decisions remains unimpaired.

Thus, the effect of the judgment of citizens at elections is always uncertain. From the citizens' viewpoint each election renews the permanent alienation of political action, decision making, and responsibility to a select few. It is obscure how these citizens could hold representatives politically to account except in the purely formal sense that they are required to stand for re-election. If a new set of representatives is authorized to take office, the sense – exceedingly weak – in which this could be held to be a holding to account of their predecessors depends on the actual performance that ensues; they may continue along virtually the same lines until they too are accountable at the next election.

If the democratization of organizations is seen as a matter of replicating liberal democracy, i.e., electing a representative government in each organization, it is being seen as an extension of citizenship and democratic voting in a largely formal sense. Of course, it would mark a great change from the present authority structure in organizations if it actually took place, but, nevertheless, democratic voting within organizations operating as miniature liberal democracies is likely to resemble democratic voting in the wider liberal democracy at present. The same problems of the purely formal nature of accountability and the question of ensuring responsiveness of representatives would remain. What must be stressed at this point is that not only is there an alternative conception of democracy and organizational democracy available, but that once the legitimacy of organizational democracy is conceded, then liberal democratic theory is no longer appropriate.

The question 'How can the instrumental effectiveness of democratic voting best be ensured?' has not yet been directly confronted. But the answer is clear: only if the votes of citizens actually serve to make decisions. That is to say, the logic of democratic voting leads to direct democracy.

From the perspective of liberal democratic theory, representative and direct democracy appear as two separate and formally distinct authority structures. Dahl, in *After the Revolution?* treats 'primary' and representative democracy in this way (Dahl 1970: 67–77).[9] Direct democracy runs counter to a liberal theory's assumption that political decision-making and responsibility must always be given up to representatives. And, apart from this theoretical difficulty, once direct democracy is seen in isolation as a unique form of authority structure, then, in contemporary industrialized society and in contemporary organizations, it appears as unrealistic and unreasonable.

Appearances are often deceptive. The introduction of organizational democracy opens the way for a reconsideration of other aspects of democratic liberal theory. Democratic voting is not unique to liberal democratic theory; indeed, as I have suggested, its connection with that theory is relatively tenuous. Democratic voting can also form part, an integral and central part, of a participatory or self-managing theory of democracy. This theory is based on a democratic and not a liberal conception of the citizen, and it begins with direct democracy.

In a directly democratic situation citizens are responsible for political decision-making (as well as having responsibility for their own, private lives); citizens are judged, as it were, by themselves as individuals, and they are responsible to themselves for the subsequent results of their collective decision-making. This conception of citizenship need not be abandoned with recognition of the empirical necessity of representation within contemporary organizations – representation, that is, in a democratic not a liberal sense. Here the focus is on representation as a 'substantive

activity' rather than a formal status; and to ensure that representatives act appropriately, that the content of their decisions does not run against the interests of the
citizens of the organization, accountability and responsiveness are essential.
These can be brought about – in a substantive sense – by devices such as recall
of representatives for information and explanation, and also, more importantly,
because citizens have not alienated their responsibility for political decision-
making. Through democratic voting when meeting as a collective body, citizens,
when necessary, can change decisions and not merely replace their representatives.

In a participatory or self-managing democracy, direct and representative democracy are no longer seen as two separate forms of the authority structure. Instead
both take their place as two aspects, dialectically interrelated aspects, of one democratic authority structure. Thus representation does not necessarily involve *plena potestas;* once the move is made to the other form of politics distinguished by Pranger,
politics as participation, areas of political authority may be temporarily delegated
to accountable representatives, but never alienated by citizens. Within participatory
democratic practice the citizens no longer emerge periodically from private life
(or, at least, theoretically do so) to put on their 'political lion skins' (Marx 1967:
226).[10] They have no need to do so because they are participating in the political sphere everyday as actual political citizens; political participation – democratic
citizenship – is as much a part of everyday life as the individual's private activities.

IV

It is now possible to turn from this rather abstract discussion to some of the problems of organizational democracy itself. The aim of organizational democracy is
democracy. It is not primarily increased productivity, efficiency, or better industrial
relations (even though these things may even result from organizational democracy);
rather it is to further justice, equality, freedom, the rights of citizens, and the
protection of the interests of citizens, all familiar democratic aims. The participatory
or self-managing democracy required if democratic voting is to be instrumentally
effective is not only a 'political method' (though it is that too, of course), but
also a means of developing the capacities and perspective on sociopolitical life demanded by democratic – in contrast to liberal – citizenship: that development
being itself another major aim of organizational democracy. This last consideration
leads to a further reason why organizational democracy should not be seen in
isolation from democratic theory in general, or seen merely as an extension and
replication of liberal democracy in new social spheres; namely, that given such an
approach, organizational democracy is unlikely to operate successfully.

Dahl argues that one difficulty in the introduction of self-management in industry is that many employees will probably not be interested in participating (Dahl
1970: 135–36). This will no doubt be the case – if organizational democracy is
seen in terms of setting up a miniature liberal democracy, i.e., the election of a
central managing council with all else within the enterprise remaining as before.
In that situation there will be little reason why the newly enfranchized citizens of

the enterprise should expect their organizational representatives to be any more responsive or accountable than those they are already familiar with, or why their feeling of powerlessness should disappear.[11] Democratic voting and participation will seem hardly more worthwhile than in the wider context of the present liberal democratic state. Moreover, citizens will all have been thoroughly socialized into the ways and outlooks of nondemocratic organizations (and liberal democratic citizenship) and thus will not be equipped with the capacities, confidence, and perspective required to participate in the full. That 'management should manage' is an outlook perhaps even more deeply entrenched than the idea that representatives, not citizens, should govern.

'One can sense the degree to which people are "programmed" with behaviour that is congruent with the pyramidal structure…[when] individuals uninitiated to T groups still tend to begin them with attempts to create little pyramidal systems within their group' (Argyris 1973: 43). To overcome such legacies from liberal democracy and nondemocratic organizational structures, a central representative council must be combined with areas of direct democracy at the everyday, shop-floor level – there may also be representative councils at this level – and with decision-making meetings of the whole collective body of the enterprise. This will achieve two things: responsiveness and accountability of representatives and an immediately relevant and practical illustration that democratic voting and representation do not always and necessarily mean the permanent alienation by citizens of political decision-making, i.e., it will provide experience of participatory citizenship. Experience of self-management at the familiar everyday level is essential if the democratization of the organization as a whole is to be meaningful and accessible to citizens (Pateman 1970: chs 4 and 5). The organization thus ceases to be two separate spheres of management and workers, government and governed, but becomes a complex of interlocking and interrelated democratically structured units. Under the latest constitutional measures in Yugoslavia, the self-managed enterprise is seen along these lines as a 'federation' of its basic 'organizations of united work'.

It is within such a self-managing organizational democracy that contemporary theories of 'participative management' and the many current experiments with job enlargement, job enrichment, project management, and the rest can take their place. Such measures are often treated with suspicion by radicals and unions, and they do often, but not always, amount to little more than pseudo-participation (Pateman 1970: chs 4 and 5); on the other hand, seen in the right way, they might provide a basis for 'encroaching control' in present nondemocratic organizations, and they also provide valuable experience and information for the democratized organization itself. Participation in the running of the day-to-day work process is just as important as participation in wider management decisions for the development of the skills and capacities required in a self-managing democracy. Measures such as rotation of persons in supervisory positions, which operates successfully in Israeli kibbutz industry (see Rosner 1972–73: 103–22; Fine 1973), are especially important in helping members to play a full role within the organization. This is especially so of those who, like women, have been systematically socialized to regard themselves as 'naturally' incapable of exercising their citizenship or participating in the control of their work-life.

It is only a radical, participatory approach to organizational democracy that is likely to foster the expertise, skills, and confidence, both in the daily work process and in the exercise of democratic citizenship with the enterprise, that are vital if members of the organization as a whole are to be equipped to meet the challenge for control that will come from the technostructure. In his discussion of guild socialism, Cole remarked that the choice of experts did not 'raise the democratic issue' (Cole 1920: 52–59); if their choice does not, their role once chosen certainly does if organizational democracy is to be more than a formal structure.

The evidence from Yugoslavia illustrates the importance, and difficulty of this problem,[12] but this must be seen in the light of the evidence that shows that it is the experience of participation within an organizational democracy that increases the interest in and demand for more participation and control (see Pateman 1970; Garson 1974). It is also important to note that it is only from within the perspective of self-managing democracy that the role of the technostructure, like that of representatives, becomes a *problem;* where the authority structure is based on the permanent alienation of decision-making and political responsibility by citizens the problem never arises.

Other problems also look very different once the liberal democratic theoretical perspective is left behind. A comment that is often made about the system of self-management in Yugoslavia is that the central councils in the enterprises are not really autonomous (see Dahl 1970: 131). Sometimes, of course, the reference is to the role of the Communist League; but it also seems to be a demand that the elected representative councils should be completely formally free from 'interference' so that they (like their liberal democratic state counterparts) can 'get on with governing'. Given this, it is not surprising that an objection that is often made to organizational democracy is that it would lead to 'parochialism' and 'selfishness' on the part of each organization; important 'stakeholders' or 'affected interests' or the wider community would be neglected (Kramer 1972: esp. ch. 8).[13]

It is arguable if the neglect would be greater than that of the present 'private rulers' of nondemocratic organizations, and there is a good reason for suggesting that it could be less. From the perspective of self-managing democracy the problem is incorrectly stated, since organizational democracy does not involve a demand for autonomy in the liberal democratic sense of formal separation and absence of interference. It is precisely the conception of two separated spheres of social life that acts as a barrier against perception by citizens of interrelationships between political and private that actually exist.

Within the context of a self-managing democracy such interrelationships would become explicit. Organizational democracy does not preclude, for example, representation of a community council on an enterprise council (or vice versa) both are part of one participatory democratic society, just as representative and direct democracy are parts of one democratic authority structure. Moreover, the multi-dimensional nature of participatory citizenship would make explicit what liberal democratic formal separation of roles obscures – that individuals do belong to more than one stakeholder or interest group. Thus, parochialism and selfishness may be less likely (though no authority structure, of course, could guarantee their absence) because decisions can be taken within one organization with the wider social context of self-managing citizenship consciously in mind (see Garson 1972–73).

Dahl calls Rousseau 'the best advocate of participatory democracy we have' (Dahl 1970: 82), and my arguments in this paper owe a good deal to *The Social Contract*. However, Dahl argues that to take Rousseau's insights and direct democracy seriously would mean that a nation would have to 'dissolve itself into tiny states simply and in order to create a multiplicity of primary democracies' (Dahl 1970: 86). This is to see Rousseau through liberal democratic spectacles. Just as organizations will not 'dissolve' into many tiny, separate organizations, neither need a territorial political unit break up into separate units if it is transformed into a participatory democracy. That self-managing democracy is not a multiplicity of separate little liberal democracies is a central point of my argument. Rather, the self-managing units – or 'Chinese boxes' to use Dahl's term – are interwoven into a complex whole by the dialectical interrelationships of the direct decision-making spheres and the multidimensional nature of citizenship.

Finally, I should like to return to my starting point. Historically, liberal democracy is linked to the market economy. If organizational democracy leads to the transcendence of liberal democracy the question poses itself of what might replace the favorite analogy between democratic voting and the consumer in the market economy. The example of Yugoslavia since the economic reforms of 1965 shows the difficulties in trying to combine a system of self-management and a market economy, but whatever might be the role of the market, the analogy is misplaced and superfluous within a participatory democracy. Democratic voting is not like spending money for the satisfaction of purely individual interests and desires; the importance of voting for the individual is that, exercised within a context of organizational and self-managing democracy, it allows the collective, democratic control by citizens of their own lives and environment.

Notes

1 Rhenman's argument is based on (an essentially liberal democratic) 'stakeholder' view of the organization. An alternative way of seeing the members of the organization and their relation to 'outside' bodies and individuals is presented below.

2 I use the term 'liberal democratic' theory in this paper (and not the 'contemporary' theory of my *Participation and Democratic Theory*) in order to emphasize to which tradition of political thought it belongs (Pateman 1970). The theory is discussed under various other headings: the 'elitist' theory, the 'new' theory, 'polyarchy', and so forth.

3 On Dahl's own definition of a political system – 'any persistent pattern of human relationships that involves to a significant extent, power, rule, or authority' – an economic enterprise is political (Dahl 1963: 6).

4 This section of the paper and the next draw on some of the arguments in Pateman (1973).

5 'Democracy in the sense of our theory of competitive leadership presided over the process of political and institutional change by which the bourgeoisie reshaped, and

from its own point of view rationalized, the social and political structure that preceded its ascendency; the democratic political method was the political tool of that ascendency' (Schumpeter 1943: 297).

6 The individual was almost always, explicitly or implicitly, a male; for a contemporary statement see the description of *homo civicus* in Dahl (1961: 223–25).

7 An explanation of why many people, nevertheless, do go on voting, in terms of the role of liberal democratic theory itself in the political socialization process, and the idea of citizen duty, can be found in Pateman (1973).

8 The finding on concurrence is perhaps not surprising given that another study finds that political office often seems to be a 'by-product' of 'previously achieved status...previously acquired prestige, wealth, leisure, security'; i.e., those that give and receive concurrence tend to come from upper-SES groups (see Prewitt 1970: 16).

9 'The democratic idea is too grand to be trivialized by restricting itself to only one form of authority' (Dahl 1970: 67–77).

10 To avoid misunderstanding I should add at this point that rejection of the liberal conception of citizenship does not necessarily involve rejection of the important (liberal) civil rights and freedoms. On the difference between the liberal and participatory democratic conceptions of individuals and their social relationships, see also Lukes (1973) and Wood (1972).

11 Structural change is required 'to reduce the powerlessness of the ordinary American employee' (Dahl 1970: 139). But a miniature polyarchy is unlikely to be structural change enough. The West German system of codetermination illustrates this point (although it is not a system of industrial democracy). One study found that only half the workers interviewed had any concrete ideas what codetermination meant. The codetermination system 'does not give the individual worker the feeling of personally participating in those decision-making processes affecting his own situation' (Furstenber, 1969: 94–147; see also Schauer 1973).

12 One survey of the empirical evidence states that 'The hierarchical organization has survived within the new institutional shefl of democratic organization' (Zupanov 1972–73: 39; see also Goricar 1972–73; Bucar 1972–73).

13 The terms 'stakeholders' and 'affected interests' are Rhenman's and Dahl's respectively.

References

Arendt, H. 1959. *The Human Condition*. New York: Anchor.

Argyris, C. 1973. 'On Organizations of the Future'. Beverly Hills: Sage Professional Papers in Administrative and Policy Studies 1.

Bachrach, P. and M.S. Baratz. 1970. *Power and Poverty*. New York: Oxford University Press.

Bucar, F. 1972–73. 'The Participation of the State and Political Organizations in the Decisions of the Working Organization'. Participation and Self-Management (Proceedings of the First International Sociological Conference on Participation and Self-Management, Institute for Social Research, Zagreb; hereinafter referenced as 'Self-Management Conference') 1.

Butler, D. and D. Stokes. 1969. *Political Change in Britain*. London: Macmillan.

Cole, G.D.H. 1920. *Guild Socialism Restated*. London: L. Parsons.

Crenson, M.A. 1971. *The Un-Politics of Air Pollution*. Baltimore: Johns Hopkins University Press.

Dahl, R.A. 1961. *Who Governs?* New Haven: Yale University Press.

— 1963. *Modern Political Analysis*. Englewood Cliffs, NJ: Prentice-Hall.

— 1970. *After the Revolution?* New Haven: Yale University Press.

Dennis, J. 1970. 'Support for the Institution of Elections by the Mass Public'. *American Political Science Review* 64.

Easton, L.D. and K.H. Guddat (eds). 1967. *Writings of the Young Marx on Philosophy and Society*. New York: Anchor.

Fine, K. 1973. 'Worker Participation in Israel'. In G. Hunnius, G.D. Garson and J. Case (eds), *Workers' Control*. New York: Random House, 226–67.

Form, W.H. and J. Rytina. 1969. 'Ideological Beliefs on the Distribution of Power in the United States'. *American Sociological Review* 34: 19–31.

Furstenberg, F. 1969. 'Workers' Participation in the Federal Republic of Germany'. *Bulletin of the International Institute for Labor Studies* 6: 94–147.

Garson, G.D. 1974. 'On Democratic Administration and Socialist Self-management: A Comparative Survey Emphasizing Yugoslavia'. Beverly Hills: Sage Professional Papers in Administrative and Policy Studies 3.

Garson, G.D. 1972–73. 'On the Political Theory of Decentralized Socialism'. Self-Management Conference 2.

Goricar, J. 1972–73. 'Workers' Self-management: Ideal Type-Social Reality'. Self-Management Conference 1.

Green, P. and S. Levinson (eds). 1970. *Power and Community: Dissenting Essays in Political Science*. New York: Vintage.

Hindess, B. 1971. *The Decline of Working Class Politics*. London: MacGibbon & Kee.

Hunnius, G., G.D. Garson and J. Case (eds). 1973. *Workers' Control*. New York: Random House.

Kramer, D.C. 1972. *Participatory Democracy*. Cambridge, MA: Schenkman.

Lipsitz, L. 1970. 'On Political Belief: The Grievances of the Poor'. In P. Green and S. Levinson (eds), *Power and Community*. New York: Vintage, 142–72.

Lukes, S. 1973. *Individualism*. Oxford: Blackwell.

McClosky, H. 1970. 'Consensus and Ideology in American Politics'. In R.E. Wolfinger (ed.) *Readings in American Political Behavior*. Englewood Cliffs, NJ: Prentice-Hall.

Macpherson, C.B. 1973. 'Market Concepts in Political Theory'. In C.B. Macpherson (ed.) *Democratic Theory: Essays in Retrieval*. New York: Oxford University Press.

Marx, K. 1967. 'On the Jewish Question'. In L.D. Easton and K.H. Guddat (eds) *Writings of the Young Marx on Philosophy and Society*. New York: Anchor, 216–48; originally published in 1844.

Parry, G. 1969. *Political Elites*. London: Allen & Unwin.

Pateman, C. 1970. *Participation and Democratic Theory*. New York: Cambridge University Press.

— 1973. 'Vote, Vote, Vote for…? Some Theoretical Reflections on Democratic Voting' (unpublished paper).

Pitkin, H. 1967. *The Concept of Representation*. Berkeley: University of California Press.

Pranger, R.J. 1968. *The Eclipse of Citizenship*. New York: Holt, Rinehart & Winston.

Prewitt, K. 1970. 'Political Ambitions, Volunteerism, and Electoral Accountability'. *American Political Science Review* 64.

Rhenman, E. 1968. *Industrial Democracy and Industrial Management*. London: Tavistock.

Rosner, M. 1972–73. 'Self-management in Kibbutz Industry: Organizational Patterns and Psychological Effects'. Self-Management Conference 4: 103–22.

Sartori, G. 1973. 'What is "Politics"?' *Political Theory* 1.

Schauer, H. 1973. 'Critique of Codetermination'. In G. Hunnius, G.D. Garson and J. Case (eds), *Workers' Control*. New York: Random House, 210–25.

Schumpeter, J.A. 1943. *Capitalism, Socialism and Democracy*. London: Allen & Unwin.

Verba, S. and N.H. Nie. 1972. *Participation in America: Political Democracy and Social Equality*. New York: Harper & Row.

Wolin, S. 1961. *Politics and Vision*. London: Allen & Unwin.

Wood, E.M. 1972. *Mind and Politics*. Berkeley: University of California Press.

Zupanov, J. 1972–73. 'Employees' Participation and Social Power in Industry'. Self-Management Conference 1.

3

POLITICAL OBLIGATION AND THE SWORD OF LEVIATHAN (1979)

'A society as conceived by individualism has never existed anywhere'.

L. Dumont, *Homo Hierarchicus*.

The problems of political authority and political obligation to which the emergence of liberal individualism gives rise are nowhere better laid bare than in Hobbes' (1968) *Leviathan*. It might be thought that Hobbes' theory is hardly the place to begin an examination of the historical roots of liberal voluntarism; Leviathan is not a liberal ruler. Nevertheless, Hobbes 'had in him more of the philosophy of liberalism than most of its professed defenders' (Oakeshott 1975: 63). His theory is based on central liberal assumptions and values, and his radically abstract individualism presents a particularly clear statement of the problems surrounding self-assumed obligation. Hobbes' uncompromising individualism leads him to the extreme solution of absolute rule and unconditional political obedience, but, because he takes his arguments to their logical conclusion, they are all the more instructive for contemporary discussions of political obligation in the liberal democratic state. In particular, his arguments throw some interesting light onto the costs of assuming that political obligation is unproblematic.

The interpretation of Hobbes' theory, and especially his theory of obligation, is a matter of some controversy, However, much argument, especially over the status of the laws of nature, is due to a failure by many of his commentators to distinguish 'ought' from 'obligation'. Nor is the radically voluntarist character of Hobbes' theory always appreciated. It is true that his conception of 'consent' stands at the limits of hypothetical voluntarism, and that he ends by claiming that all rulers who preserve order, no matter what the ostensible basis of their power, rule by virtue of their subjects' 'consent'. But the peculiarities of Hobbes' conception of 'consent' do not mean, as some writers have argued, that he is not a consent theorist at all. Voluntarism – self-assumed obligation, consent, and the social contract – is at the heart of *Leviathan*. In this chapter I shall comment further on the general significance of liberal social contract theory. Hobbes' version of the contract story, notwithstanding its singular features, establishes a pattern of argument followed by subsequent liberal theorists.

Hobbes aimed to place his argument about political obligation on such a certain footing that his conclusions could no more be doubted than the conclusion of a geometric theorem. It is possible to arrive at demonstrable conclusions about commonwealths because, as in geometry, we are arguing about something which is the artificial creation of humans themselves. In *Leviathan* Hobbes does not work through the whole process of his method of 'resolution' and 'composition', but begins from the result of an imaginative 'resolution' of a commonwealth into a collection of individuals, which are themselves 'resolved' into machines in perpetual motion; he then takes his readers through the process of 'composition' (Macpherson 1962: 30). It should be emphasized that Hobbes' methodology leads him to base his argument on a radically abstract and atomistic individualism. Machines in perpetual motion, or mere physiological entities, have no natural connections with each other. Hobbes not only removes the bonds of civil law from his individuals but all bonds and relationships whatsoever. His conception of the 'condition of meer nature', as he calls the state of nature, is thus a logical abstraction in the most complete sense. But any logical abstraction is an abstraction from an actual form of social life. The entities have to be reconstituted as individuals before they can be seen in their 'natural' state or as subjects in a commonwealth, but the allegedly 'natural' characteristics with which Hobbes equips the entities during the process of 'composition' are socially familiar ones. How else could he claim that his readers had only to look into themselves and examine their own passions and fears to find his argument irresistible? Hobbes' individuals' 'natural' qualities are admirably suited to people living at a time when the traditional social order, bolstered by claims about the divine right of kings and patriarchal arguments, was beginning to pass away and the first stages of the market economy and a liberal society and state were making their appearance.

The state of nature

The 'problem' of promising discussed by Pateman (1979: ch. 2) is a particular case of the general problem of moving from the perspective of a single, isolated individual to a coherent conception of social life and its multiplicity of social practices. The general problem is a consequence of radical, abstract individualism, and it is exemplified in Hobbes' account of the state of nature. His account makes sense only because he (and his readers) implicitly presupposes the social attributes, relationships, and practices that he attempts to strip away. Hobbes' state of nature shows us a world as it would be if inhabited by individuals who are each confined within a purely subjective viewpoint. Since each one is considered singularly, individuals can have no other outlook than an entirely private and self-interested one. They are possessive individuals who judge the world, and others, solely in terms of subjective evaluations of self-interest, in terms of the protection and enlargement of what they own, including, most importantly for Hobbes, the protection of the property they have in their own bodies and lives. The well-known features of Hobbes' state of nature are a direct consequence of this radically individualist perspective.

Hobbes' natural individuals are able to reason and they can speak to each other. Without speech, Hobbes says, 'there had been amongst men, neither Commonwealth, nor Society, nor Contract, nor Peace, no more than amongst Lyons, Bears, and Wolves' (1968: ch. IV; 100). For the nominalist Hobbes words, 'names', depend on the will and the judgement of the individuals who are speaking. Meaning is a matter for private judgement. In the natural condition *everything* is a matter of individual private judgement. Hobbes argues that 'True and False are attributes of Speech, not of Things' (1968: ch. IV; 105). The same things affect individuals differently, and affect the same individual differently at different times, so their names will be of 'inconstant signification' and it will therefore be an arbitrary matter how individuals evaluate others and their environment. What one person calls cruelty another will call justice, and similarly with 'good' and 'bad'; everyone calls 'good' whatever it is they happen to desire, and things that they are trying to avoid are called 'bad'. There is nothing that 'naturally' leads to any consistency in naming, and in 'the condition of meer Nature…private Appetite is the measure of Good, and Evill' (1968: ch. XV; 216).

Hobbes' examples of the subjective attribution of meaning are of moral words. However, there is no good reason why 'private appetite' is not the measure of *all* words. Unconnected, atomistic individuals have to decide for themselves what their words mean, and this makes it extremely difficult to see how language would ever arise at all. If, as Hobbes argues, society requires speech, the development of speech also requires a set of social relationships. Speech is learnt, it is not generated anew each day by isolated individuals.[1] This is just one example of Hobbes implicitly presupposing what he has ostensibly abstracted from his argument. He is implicitly falling back on a conception of social individuals and social relationships in order to get his imaginative reconstruction off the ground at all. In reading these passages of *Leviathan* we, and Hobbes, implicitly assume a social background of agreed meanings, or a language, in which only the meanings of moral words remain to be arbitrarily assigned. Without this assumption the state of nature would not be inhabited by speaking individuals, but his machines or, rather, as Rousseau saw, dumb animals who are potentially human.

Hobbes also assumes that although there is no agreement about the meaning of moral words in the state of nature, his individuals, nevertheless, do possess a capacity for understanding what these words would mean in a condition of social peace.[2] Indeed, he must make this assumption; if his individuals did not have this capacity they could not enter into civil society. It is not individuals or their 'natures' that change during the transition from the state of nature to civil society, but their socio-political situation. Therefore, if individuals did not *already* understand what kinds of relationships were indicated by words such as 'justice', 'obligation', 'peace', 'promise' and 'contract', there could be no social contract and no political obligation in civil society.

Hobbes argues that individuals will try to obtain as much as possible of whatever they desire and call 'good'. He calls the means to fulfil these desires 'power', and this can be all kinds of things, from riches, or strength, to a reputation of power (1968: ch. X; 150–51). Insofar as individuals are able to satisfy their desires through use of their power they obtain 'felicity' or a 'continual prospering'. Hobbes sees the striving for felicity as a continual struggle, the fulfilment of one desire being merely a step on the way to another. To keep felicity and power at a constant level demands more power, and so Hobbes arrives at his famous statement of the 'generall inclination of all mankind, a perpetuall and restlesse desire of Power after power, that ceaseth onely in Death' (1968: ch. XI; 161).

These characteristics of individuals have been established before Hobbes deals with the 'natural condition' of mankind in Chapter 13 of *Leviathan* (Macpherson 1968: 40; 1962: 34–35). He then considers what will happen when they come together with no social rules or civil laws to regulate their interaction. It is at this point that Hobbes introduces the postulate of a fundamental equality between individuals. In fact, this postulate necessarily follows from the assumptions of abstract individualism. Seen singularly, each with the same 'natural' attributes, individuals must be regarded as equals; there is no reason why 'naturally' they should be otherwise. It should be noted that Hobbes regards the sex of the individual as irrelevant; individuals are equal whether they are male or female (1968: ch. XX; 253). Hobbes is extremely unusual in the consistency of his individualism on this point and in his willingness to challenge the patriarchal claim that women are 'naturally' weaker than, and thus subordinate to, men (although Hobbes' challenge does not extend to his argument about civil society). Each individual, whether male or female, is strong enough to kill another, and with experience, all are equally capable of the reasoning and cunning required to use their strength to kill. If two individuals both desire the same thing, and only one of them can enjoy it, 'they become enemies; and… endeavour to destroy, or subdue one an other' (1968: ch. XIII; 184).

Each individual in the state of nature has a natural right to everything that is required for self-preservation. Since individuals judge their needs entirely subjectively, it follows that there can be no general limitation upon their natural right. Hobbes' individuals have a natural right to all things – even to each others' bodies; 'there is nothing he can make use of, that may not be a help unto him, in preserving his life against his enemyes' (1968: ch. XIV; 189–90). No one, except the individual concerned, can judge whether the natural right has been properly exercised in a given case.

The paradox of a situation where individual private judgement is paramount is that the absolute freedom of the right to everything involves no real liberty or rights at all. Instead it leads to complete insecurity and a condition of pure arbitrariness. Individuals will attack each other at random at any time in their competition to attain felicity. It will always be advantageous for an individual to act first, to make what would today be called a pre-emptive strike, in anticipation of another's actions: as Hobbes states, 'there is no way for any man to secure himselfe, so reasonable, as Anticipation; that is, by force, or wiles, to master the persons of all men he can' (1968: ch. XIII; 184). In the state of nature there can be no ideas of 'justice', no notions of 'mine' and 'thine', and no matrimonial laws; all will take what they can get and keep it for as long as they can. The natural condition is therefore a state of mutual war between individuals; war will break out every time any individual judges it advantageous to attack another. It is, as Hobbes describes it in one of the most famous passages in the whole literature of political theory, a nasty, brutish condition. Life is short where there is 'no place for Industry…no Culture of the Earth…no Navigation…no commodious Building…no account of Time; no Arts; no Letters; no Society' (1968: ch. XIII; 186).

'No Society' – but it is usually assumed that the absence of a 'common power' in Hobbes' state of nature implies only that a political sovereign, a government, or state, and a set of civil laws, is lacking, but Hobbes' individualist state of nature lacks much more than this. It has no social or moral rules or relationships; that is to say, it is not a social state. The task of Leviathan is correspondingly enormous; his sword has to bring into being not only a civil government but social life itself. This tends to be overlooked because it is usually erroneously assumed that a 'common power' would not exist in a society where people voluntarily and willingly complied with rules and laws, and no specialized, external rule-enforcement agency was required. Yet, if offences did occur, these people would be prepared to take action against the offenders, although it need not be violently coercive action: 'In order that a society should be describable as having no "common power" it would have to be positively committed to abstaining from *any* sort of action which could bring any substantial evil on the heads of offenders' (McNeilly 1968: 188). In other words, all 'societies' will have a common power. Indeed, outside of a society the conception of an 'offender' makes no sense, for an 'offender' presupposes that there is something, namely a framework of ordered social relationships, to be 'offended' against. Without such relationships, all that remains is a collection of atomized individuals in Hobbes' asocial natural condition. They have no social constraints on their wills, judgements, and actions, and therefore no conception of an 'offence'.

The sociological and anthropological oddity of Hobbes' picture of the state of nature, and the radical task that Leviathan is called upon to perform, is usually underestimated precisely because the social and moral relationships that Hobbes has attempted to strip away are implicitly read back in. One of the questions that has greatly exercised Hobbes' commentators is whether moral obligations exist in his state of nature. As we have seen, Hobbes' individuals have the capacity to understand what an 'obligation' is, but, nevertheless, his state of nature is extremely unlikely to contain obligations.

Obligation in the state of nature

Hobbes' individuals are unrelated to each other in their natural condition and they therefore have to create *all* their social relationships for themselves, including relations of obligation. Hobbes states there is 'no Obligation on any man, which ariseth not from some Act of his own; for all men equally, are by Nature Free' (1968: ch.

XXI; 268). Paradigm cases of such acts are a contract, a promise, a covenant, consent. An individual takes on an obligation by giving up the right to all things, either by general renunciation, or by transferring it to some specific person or persons. Once this is done, 'he is said to be OBLIGED, or BOUND, not to hinder those, to whom such Right is granted, or abandoned, from the benefit of it' (1968: ch. XIV; 191).

Hobbes goes on to argue that, once the individual is bound, it is self-contradictory not to perform the obligation. It would be 'absurd' if it were not carried out. This is just one example of how Hobbes hopes to make his argument as watertight as a geometric theorem. It is 'absurd' to question the conclusion of a theorem and, similarly, because all voluntary acts, according to Hobbes, are performed only because individuals expect that they will result in some good to themselves, it is 'absurd' to try to hinder their consequences. One aspect of the right to everything cannot be renounced or transferred to form part of an obligation. No individual can give up the right of self-preservation or self-protection. Hobbes goes so far as to say that anyone who appears not to want to preserve their life, 'is not to be understood as if he meant it, or that it was his will; but that he was ignorant of how such words and actions were to be interpreted' (1968: ch. XIV; 192).

Hobbes distinguishes two basic forms of self-assumed obligation: a contract, where there is a mutual transfer of rights; and a covenant, where one party is trusted by the other to perform their part of the agreement at some later date.[3] The 'bonds' of an obligation are constituted by the appropriate words and actions that indicate that a contract or covenant has been made. However, these bonds have no strength 'from their own Nature'; words alone are not sufficient to hold individuals to their obligations. Bonds constituted by words 'are too weak to bridle mens ambition, avarice, anger and other Passions', all of which lead men to break faith (1968: ch. XIV; 192). If obligations are to be fulfilled, individuals must be sufficiently fearful of the consequences of breaking them, and the only completely effective fear is that brought about by the sword of an absolute sovereign. It should be emphasized, however, that Hobbes is *not* saying that words cannot create an obligation – to say 'I contract…' or 'I promise…' *is* to put oneself under an obligation. Rather, words alone are not enough to bring about the *keeping* of obligations.

In the state of nature words are so ineffective that it is very unlikely that any agreements will be kept. In discussing the example of a covenant, Hobbes says that 'upon any reasonable suspicion, it is Voyd'. Individuals have only their own subjective judgements of the possible actions of others to guide them. It is always advantageous to anticipate the actions of others, so that the slightest hint that one individual will not keep an agreement, or that it would be disadvantageous for an individual to perform his or her side of the covenant, will mean that the words have become void.[4] Fear of what the other person will do (or fail to do) means that covenants are unlikely ever to be fulfilled: 'He which performeth first, does but betray himselfe to his enemy' (1968: ch. XIV; 196).

Hobbes says that the reason for the fear must be something that arises after the making of the covenant, but there seems no good reason, given Hobbes' characterization of the state of nature, why any covenants should be entered into. It is difficult to see why the words 'I covenant…' should ever be spoken and why obligations arising from covenants should ever exist in the state of nature. If the words are to be spoken meaningfully, individuals must understand that covenants involve trust on the part of one party at least, and their experience would have shown them that it is never beneficial to oneself to trust anybody. That is the first lesson of prudence that comes with experience; to trust someone, to perform your part of the covenant first, is to betray yourself to an enemy. The prudential thing to do would be *to enter no covenants at all*. If an individual could always be sure that he or she would never perform first, then it would be beneficial to enter a covenant – because he or she would always break the trust. However, other individuals would also learn that this is advantageous, and so would demand to perform second or be trusted…Thus it is extremely unlikely that there would be obligations arising from covenants in Hobbes' state of nature because there is little reason for covenants to take place.

This conclusion might be contested in the light of Hobbes' own affirmative answer to the problem: 'where one of the parties has performed already…there is the question whether it be against reason, that is, against the benefit of the other to performe, or not' (1968: ch. XV; 204).[5] The important point here is the exact force of Hobbes' reference to 'against reason'. If the 'benefit' is to be assessed subjectively by an individual alone, then it is 'against reason' for the second party to fulfill the agreement. Seen solely in terms of the 'individual reason' of an abstract individual, it is always beneficial for the individual *not* to keep an agreement. He who performs first has betrayed himself to his enemy, to the second (non)performer. However, this particular example is concerned with someone in the state of nature who, in order to protect himself more securely, has entered into a defensive agreement with others. Now, I have argued that the existence of social relationships of any kind is problematic in the state of nature. Let us suppose, however, that an individual has entered into an agreement with some confederates for mutual defence. If, Hobbes argues, this individual now declares that it is reasonable for him not to keep his part of the bargain, he 'cannot be received into any Society, that unite themselves for Peace and Defence, but by the errour of them that receive him'. This is, indeed, now the appropriate conclusion. The hypothesis of the defensive confederation has, in one small area, transformed the anomie and war of the state of nature into social life, and it has, therefore, transformed the problem of performing second.

The keeping of covenants must now be considered from the perspective of individuals in a mutual relationship (the confederation or small society), *not* from the subjective perspective of an isolated individual. The communal or social perspective gives a different answer to the question of what is 'against reason' than the subjective judgement of the single, isolated individual.[6] If there is to be any social life, as I shall show shortly in discussing the laws of nature, individuals must understand that, generally, agreements should be kept, and that it is 'against reason' to insist to the contrary. In the state of nature there is no peace, and cannot be, because each individual reasons purely subjectively; hence there can be no limitations on what is, or is not, 'against reason'. Individuals have the right to all things and so, strictly speaking, the idea of something being 'against reason' makes no sense. This is why Hobbes' hypothesis of a confederation is an improbable one. In the state of nature confederations are unlikely to form because each individual will judge it beneficial to break agreements when they have (foolishly) been trusted by others – and all will learn from experience.

There is, however, another way in which the confederation can come into being: through what I shall call an enforced covenant. Our understanding of the 'acts of our own' that give rise to obligations is that they must be free and voluntary. Usually, if I have been forced under threats to say 'I promise', my promise will not be regarded as valid; it is not a 'real' promise. However, Hobbes treats as 'voluntary' even those acts performed under threat of violence or death. Fear and liberty are compatible, and thus Hobbes argues that covenants 'entered into by fear in the condition of meer Nature, are obligatory' (1968: ch. XIV; 198). If, therefore, a confederation is formed because one individual is able to terrorize others into joining with him, their 'obligation' to perform their part of the agreement is, according to Hobbes, just as valid as if they had all willingly banded together. He also argues that if you have agreed to pay an armed robber a ransom in return for your life, then you must pay when the time comes. The reasonableness of 'performing second' in this case, if one may safely refuse to do so, can well be questioned. More importantly, Hobbes' notion of an enforced covenant is central to his conception of obligation and 'consent'.

In Pateman (1979: ch. 1) I drew a distinction between the two forms of self-assumed obligation: self-assumed obligation as the free creation of obligations, and self-assumed obligation as consent. Initially, Hobbes' discussion of obligation appears to focus on the first form; obligations are created when individuals freely say certain words. Hobbes' radical individualism means that he must begin with this form of self-assumed obligation. Nevertheless, his argument is actually based on self-assumed obligation as consent – and the 'consent' in question is that involved in an enforced covenant. Hobbes' theory provides a particularly clear example of the way in which voluntarism can be transformed into the most empty form of hypothetical voluntarism. If a robber makes a demand backed by the threat of death then, Hobbes argues, the individual will always 'consent' to the demand to save his or her life. The individual's submission can *always* be interpreted as 'consent'; 'obligation' can always be inferred from forced submission. Hobbes uses 'consent' in the same sense when he refers to the relation between parent and child, between conqueror and subject, and, as I shall show later, between Leviathan and the individuals who authorize his rule. Hobbes states that 'the Rights and Consequences of both Paternall and Despoticall Dominion, are the very same with those of a Soveraign by institution; and for the same reasons' (1968: ch. XX; 256). The reason is that they are all based on 'consent'. An individual, whether a victim facing a robber's gun, a prisoner facing a conqueror's sword, or a child facing a parent who can expose it, will always 'consent' to be ruled rather than forfeit his or her life. It is not the power or force that is exercised that is relevant to the subsequent right to rule, but the 'consent' that can always be inferred from the individual's submission. Hobbes is a completely consistent – and completely hypothetical – conventionalist. All authority, he argues, whether that of a parent over a child, or the conqueror over defeated subjects, is based on 'consent': 'command alone has no more significance in Hobbes than power alone' (Riley 1973: 504).

The only 'obligations', arising from covenants, likely to be found in the state of nature are those implied by the 'consent' to enforced covenants. But, based on threats and force, these covenants cannot be accepted as constituting valid obligations. What then of contracts? There are no special problems about contracts in the Hobbesian state of nature, providing that the mutual transfer of right takes place simultaneously between individuals. If the contract takes the form where both parties agree to perform together at a future date, all the problems about trust and keeping faith, already discussed, arise once more. The major difficulty about contracts is whether they constitute anything that can properly be called 'obligation'. As Hobbes is well aware, a relationship of 'obligation' is one based on keeping faith; to have assumed an obligation *is* to have committed oneself in a relationship of trust. In introducing the notion of a contract Hobbes refers to economic exchanges and transactions (1968: ch. XIV; 193). Hobbesian contracts are nothing more than simultaneous exchanges by possessive individuals, in which each individual independently judges that the exchange will be advantageous. Contracts do not provide an example of obligation in the state of nature. Their significance lies in what they reveal about the form and character of (uncoerced) social relationships that can be derived from a radically abstract individualism; 'social life' can be seen only as a series of discrete exchanges between individuals.[7] Not all theorists draw Hobbes' absolutist conclusions from this reductionist view of social relationships. In Pateman (1979: ch. 7) I consider Godwin's philosophical anarchist alternative to the rule of Leviathan.

One further comment needs to be made about Hobbes' treatment of these topics. Individuals can threaten others, but they can also give them things; Hobbes says that where an individual makes an offer unilaterally to gain friends, or enhance reputation, this is not a contract or covenant but a 'GIFT, FREE-GIFT, GRACE which words signifie one and the same thing' (1968: ch. XIV; 193). It is worth digressing slightly at this point because many present-day theorists insist that obligations including political obligations, can arise from the receipt of benefits, or 'grace' (an argument that I criticize in Pateman 1979: ch. 6). Hobbes says that 'benefits oblige' and that gratitude, or cheerful acceptance, is due to a superior who bestows a benefit (1968: ch. XI 162–63). However, this cannot, as he implies, be the case in the state of nature; the benefit would merely be seized with no question of 'gratitude' arising. Later, Hobbes discusses gratitude in the context of the laws of nature, and he says that individual must 'Endeavour that he which giveth [a benefit] have no reasonable cause to repen him of his good will' (1968: ch. XV; 209). But this, as I shall show in the next section, does not involve an obligation but, rather, that individuals who desire peace ought to act in this way.

The laws of nature

I have so far said nothing about the place of the laws of nature in Hobbes' discussion of covenants, contracts and the natural condition. The status and role of the laws of nature has given rise to a major controversy in recent studies of Hobbes' political theory. A great variety of interpretations is to be found, ranging from Watkins characterization of the laws of nature as 'assertoric hypothetical imperatives', the McNeilly view that they are a purely formal statement of the necessary means the peace, and Warrender's much discussed argument that Hobbes' laws of nature and laws of nature in the traditional, pre-modern, sense of God's law in the world, and that they are binding on individuals for that reason (Watkins 1973: ch. 5; McNeilly 1968: ch. 8; Warrender 1957).

I have argued that we can make sense of Hobbes' state of nature only because certain social qualities and relationships are implicitly presupposed; these include the relationships summed up in the laws of nature. Once the abstractly individual-ised character of the natural condition has been established, it can be seen that the laws of nature provide an essential social background, necessary if the transition to civil society is to be possible. The laws of nature provide the necessary conceptual and empirical minimal conditions for a moral and social order, for a 'society', to exist. On to make the point in a different way, in terms of the distinction I drew in Pateman 1979: ch. 2, Hobbes' laws of nature provide a background of 'oughts' against which 'obligations' can be freely assumed. In the state of nature the keep-ing of agreements is always a 'problem'; indeed, to say that they *ought* to be kept is meaningless, because there is a right to all things, and nothing that generally ought to be done or not done. On the other hand, as I noted earlier, individuals in the natural condition have a capacity for understanding what moral words would mean in a situation of social peace. If it is possible for an individual in Hobbes' state of nature meaningfully to say 'I covenant' or 'I promise', then it is being taken for granted that the individual understands the nature of the relationships involved in a covenant, and understands that commitments *ought* to be carried out. In short, it presupposes an understanding of the social practice of covenanting, or presup-poses Hobbes' third law of nature, 'that men performe their Covenants made'. And this, according to Hobbes, means that we are presupposing some notion of justice. In the third law of nature 'consisteth the Fountain and Originall of JUSTICE… the definition of INJUSTICE, is no other than the not Performance of Covenant' (1968: ch. XV; 202).

Hobbes tells us that his individuals are not doomed to remain in the natural con-dition. Both their passions and their reason enable them to create a peaceful civil society, the overriding passion being, of course, the fear of premature death. The passions are aided by reason which 'suggesteth convenient Articles of Peace, upon which men may be drawn to agreement. These Articles, are they, which otherwise are called the Lawes of Nature' (1968: ch. XIII; 188). A few sentences later, Hobbes states that a law of nature 'is a Precept, or generall Rule, found out by Reason, by which a man is forbidden to do, that, which is destructive of his life'. But which sense of 'reason' is this? As the preceding discussion suggests, it is not the 'indi-vidual reason' of the inhabitants of the state of nature. The 'reason' that is capable of discovering and understanding the laws of nature and their social purpose is the reason of individuals who live socially with others. Because we, Hobbes' readers, are able to imagine ourselves independent of all social relationships we can also imagine a purely private, subjective, judgement or reason. But 'individual reason', in this sense, can play its part in Hobbes' state of nature only because it is an imaginative abstraction from a conception of reason and rational action that is inherently social.

The first three laws of nature cited by Hobbes are the crucially important ones. The first law states that individuals must 'endeavour' peace where there is hope that it is possible. The second prescribes that each individual should be willing, when others are too, to give up the right to all things in exchange for limited, but mutually equal, rights and freedoms (1968: ch. XIV; 189–90). The third, as stated, underwrites the social practice of covenanting. The laws thus prescribe what individuals *ought* to do if they desire to live socially and at peace with one another. Social life and peace require mutual, equal forbearance, and some general rules to regulate individual judgement and action. The laws of nature provide a statement of the fundamental conceptual requirements for a coherent notion of 'social life'; in that sense they are formally or logically necessary. However, they are not only conceptual necessities. The laws of nature are also empirically necessary. If there actually is no mutual trust (justice), mutual aid, and forbearance, then, as Hobbes' account of the state of nature shows so graphically, social life falls apart into a war between arbitrarily acting individuals.

These basic relationships are moral as well as social. Hobbes states that the science of the laws of nature 'is the true and onely Moral Philosophy' (1968: ch. XV; 215–16), but it is a major source of disagreement among his students whether there is a proper moral philosophy to be found in *Leviathan*. The presentation of the characteristics of possessive individuals as 'natural' human features tends to mislead Hobbes' commentators here (the more so since these individuals are abstracted from a form of social life that has been greatly consolidated and enlarged since Hobbes wrote). Hobbes contends that all voluntary actions are self-interested, and it seems to many theorists that a theory resting entirely on the claims of self-interest cannot contain a properly moral philosophy. However, Hobbes' contention follows logically from the theoretical perspective of abstract individualism, and should not be confused with his general argument about the laws of nature. The laws provide the necessary basis for moral relationships to exist. Without an understanding by individuals of the 'meaning' of the laws of nature no morality would be possible at all. Individuals understand that the laws of nature are in their 'interest' because without them they would have no security and small hope of achieving their desires and needs and wants. This general moral 'interest' of individuals seen socially, not severally, must not be confused with the specific, self-interested 'natural morality' with which Hobbes equips his individuals.

It is often assumed that if Hobbes' laws of nature are moral laws, then they must be 'laws of nature' in the traditional sense, and so impose obligations on the inhabitants of the state of nature. By calling his rules 'laws of nature' Hobbes has contributed to the confusion. His conception of the rules is a modern one; it has nothing in common, except the name, with the long tradition of political argument that called upon God's natural law of the universe. The traditional conception of natural law was of a Divine Law that stood above civil laws, which could be used to evaluate them, placing a limitation upon the scope of the powers of temporal rulers. This idea of a higher law was anathema to Hobbes; nevertheless, he writes of the 'laws of nature' because he

> has not fully emancipated himself from the medieval conception of natural law. He is not fully aware of his own originality...Hobbes's label, law of nature, misleads in containing 'law'. But only we, who are the beneficiaries of the revolution in moral and political concepts which Hobbes, among others, initiated, are in a position to draw clearly the conceptual lines with which Hobbes struggled.
>
> (Gauthier 1969: 70–71)

As I shall show in more detail later, it is a cornerstone of Hobbes' political theory that the sovereign must be the sole lawful interpreter of God's word. God Himself appears in Hobbes' political theory only as mediated through the commands of the sovereign. It is only when God's commands are also the commands of the sovereign that they are, properly, laws. The Word of God, supreme commander of humanity, is traditionally called 'law'. But, Hobbes states, law 'properly is the word of him, that by right hath command over others' (1968: ch. XV; 216). Only an absolute sovereign has both the right to command and can exercise *effective* command. God's commands have to be carried out by people, and, in their natural condition, they are unable to act as God would have them act. God's commands are *called* laws, but they are not properly laws because in the state of nature they will not, and cannot, be acted upon or enforced:

> For the Lawes of Nature...in the condition of meer Nature...are not properly Lawes, but qualities that dispose men to peace, and to obedience. When a Common-wealth is once settled, then are they actually Lawes, and not before...For it is the Soveraign Power that obliges men to obey them.
>
> (1968: ch. XXVI; 314: also 322–23)

The laws of nature are, then, principles of reason that enable men to live peacefully or socially. They are a statement of what individuals necessarily ought to do to this end. Hobbes does, however, sometimes imply that they are more than this, but on these occasions he is, like many present-day theorists, using 'obligation' or 'oblige' as shorthand for all those actions which we ought to perform. I drew attention, earlier, to one instance of this when Hobbes is discussing gratitude. Another example occurs in Hobbes' statement that 'The Lawes of Nature oblige *in foro interno* but *in foro externo;* that is, to the putting them in act, not alwayes'. The laws ought to be followed, but, in the state of nature, they will invariably be ignored. If the individual tries to follow them 'where no man els should do so, he should but make himselfe a prey to others, and procure his own certain ruine' (1968: ch. XV; 215). There has been no covenant or contract to follow the laws, and could not be with God because he cannot be covenanted with, so they cannot, according to Hobbes' own definition, constitute 'obligations' (1968: ch. XIV; 197).

This has been denied by some commentators who argue, to use Warrender's words, that 'Hobbes's theory of obligation is based upon natural law and not upon promise-keeping as such' (Warrender 1957: 237). There are two important points to make about this argument. The first is that Warrender discusses Hobbes' theory in terms of the 'validating conditions' for obligations which render them 'operative' or 'inoperative'. This, however, is begging the question about the existence of obligations in Hobbes' state of nature, for the formulation assumes that they do exist and that what matters is whether they are 'operative'. Secondly, to assume that obligations exist means that individuals can only consent to the obligations; they cannot freely create them for themselves. Warrender ignores the radically voluntarist character of Hobbes' theory. He claims that God's commands are proper laws and obligatory because of God's omnipotence, and so assimilates 'obligation' to enforced covenants. It is fear of God's irresistible power that 'validates' the obligation, just as fear of the robber's threats gives rise to an enforced covenant through 'consent' to his demands (Warrender 1957: 281).[8]

To fill Hobbes' state of nature with Divinely sanctioned relationships of obligation is to rob it of its originality, and also to fail to see why it is a condition so dreadful that Leviathan's absolute rule is the only alternative. Hobbes' political argument depends upon the fact that, no matter how strongly it is held that the laws of nature *ought* to be obeyed, when all individuals' actions are based on individual subjective judgement, it will always be 'unreasonable' actually to obey them. Warrender interprets Hobbes to mean not that there is no obligation to obey the laws of nature, but that the reference to *'in foro interno'* implies that the laws *oblige* in conscience; *'all* the obligations of men in the State of Nature could be described as obligations in conscience' (Warrender 1957: 70). To talk of 'obligations in conscience' begs the vital question whether, in the state of nature, 'conscience' can refer to anything other than the absolute right of individual judgement or the right to all things. The last thing that Hobbes would want is that 'conscience' in the conventional sense should be enshrined at the heart of his political argument; he makes it very clear that conscience has no politically relevant place in civil society.

To allow that individuals have conscientious obligations placed upon them by God would enable them to question the rightness and justice of Leviathan's rule in the name of God. This is precisely what Hobbes wishes to avoid in civil society. Any such questioning is, in his eyes, a return to the state of nature and the ideological conflict that he saw as the cause of the English Civil War. When Leviathan's word and sword replace the traditional Word of God—and who exactly could rightfully wield His sword?—it is impossible for any limitation to be placed on Leviathan's rule if peace is to be secured.

The social contract and the authorization of the sovereign

Before turning to Hobbes' account of the social contract and the institution of Leviathan, I want to say something about the general significance of liberal social contract theory. The idea of the social contract supplies a voluntarist explanation of how 'in the beginning' free and equal individuals could legitimately be governed. The transition from the state of nature to civil society is accomplished through the medium of the liberal social contract. The contract brings a new political association into being and it also establishes a new political status for individuals. During the social contract, individuals exchange their 'natural' freedom and equality for the status of civil subject with civil freedom and equality; they 'put to the act' Hobbes' second law of nature. By entering the social contract, individuals, through their own actions, institute a new political status and the rules which govern it. They become formally equal subjects whose freedom is equally protected through the impartially administered rule of civil law. It should be emphasized that the new political status exists independently of any differences between individuals; all individuals are formally equal as political subjects no matter what social inequalities may divide them. All this is, however, only part of the liberal social contract. The contract, conceptually, is a two-stage process; in Hobbes' version the two stages are simultaneous, but in Locke's theory, which is discussed in the next chapter, the two parts are more easily discerned. In the second part of the liberal contract individuals agree to alienate to a government of representatives the right to make political decisions. It is thus the second stage that is crucial for liberal voluntarist arguments about political obligation; individuals take upon themselves the obligation to let representatives decide upon the content of their political obligation.

Contemporary writers on political obligation implicitly assume that the second stage of the contract is indispensable. The question they are concerned with is how individuals can be said to consent to this arrangement, or voluntarily oblige themselves. I am arguing that, taken seriously as a political ideal, self-assumed obligation undermines this assumption and requires that very different questions are asked. In *The Political Theory of Possessive Individualism,* Macpherson reaches an apparently similar conclusion; he states that it is 'impossible' today 'to derive a valid theory of obligation from the assumptions [of possessive individualism]' (1962: 271). However, Macpherson's interpretation of Hobbes and Locke takes no account of the social contract or of liberal voluntarist arguments about political obligation. He argues that, if individuals are to acknowledge a morally binding political obligation that is not based on God's will, or the purposes of nature, they must be capable 'of seeing themselves as equal in some respect more important than all the respects in which they are unequal' (Macpherson 1962: 83; see also 272). In the seventeenth century the relevant equality was derived from the equal subordination of each individual to the laws of the market. This subordination was regarded as inevitable, and it thus provided individuals with a reason for recognizing an obligation to the political authority that maintained social order in a market society. In the twentieth century, Macpherson argues, this reason no longer holds good. With the development of workers' political consciousness and organizations the laws of the market are no longer seen as an inevitable or natural feature of the world. It is, therefore, no longer accepted that the requisite equality exists, and political obligation has lost its seventeenth-century justification.

One problem with this argument is that, notwithstanding the achievement of the labour movement in the liberal democracies, it is questionable how far it has brought the legitimacy of the liberal democratic state into question. Indeed, it could be argued that it has helped consolidate that legitimacy. It is true that the capitalist market and its inequalities are often criticized by workers' organizations, but by concentrating on the market at the expense of the specifically political aspects of the development of liberal democracy, Macpherson has failed to take into account the extent to which criticism of the market is insulated from criticism of the political institutions that developed with it.

I have emphasized that the development of liberal individualism was an integral part of the development of liberal society, of the capitalist market economy and the constitutional state. 'Free and equal individuals' are necessary for a market economy to operate and, conversely, without the emergence of the market these creatures would not have inhabited the state of nature. However, this is not to say that there is no need to look further than the market for a justification of political obligation. Macpherson gives no explanation of why the social contract and consent are central to Hobbes' and Locke's theories. His argument shows why 'naturally' equal individuals should recognize the need for regulation of the competitive interaction of possessive individuals in the market. But it fails to take into account that 'naturally' free individuals also have voluntarily to agree to institute a political authority to govern them. To ignore the social contract is to ignore that the agreement sets up, in civil society, an equality of exactly the kind that Macpherson argues is needed for justifying political obligation; a formal equality that exists over and above the inequalities of the market or the private sphere.

To ignore the social contract is also to overlook that it stands at the beginning of the long process through which the political sphere has come to be seen as separate from the rest of social life. This helps explain why criticism of the market and the economy can be insulated from criticism of liberal democratic political institutions. The conception of a separate political sphere is also important if the actual development of liberal democracies, rather than the logic of the social contract, is considered. By the mid-twentieth century, with the introduction of universal suffrage and the institutionalization of civil liberties, the formal political status of individuals had been consolidated and extended as the formal political equality of citizenship. Macpherson argues that universal suffrage has undermined another aspect of the seventeenth-century justification of political obligation: the cohesion of self-interest among those, the propertied classes, who chose the representatives (Macpherson 1962: 273). However, universal suffrage and the formal political equality of citizenship have given all individuals a political 'interest' in common. Contemporary liberal voluntarist arguments about voting and consent cannot be fully understood unless the continuity between the liberal social contract story and arguments about universal suffrage is appreciated. It is assumed that all individuals have a reason to enter the contract because it ensures protection of their interests. Similarly, contemporary liberal theory, as I shall show in Pateman (1979: ch. 5), argues that universal suffrage ensures the protection of all citizens' interests irrespective of their substantive social position – hence it is reasonable to infer that consent is given through voting.

Furthermore, without an examination of the political implications of the idea of self-assumed obligation and the role of the second stage of the social contract, the liberal democratic form of political authority remains unquestioned. Macpherson argues that this form can no longer be justified in traditional liberal terms, but he says nothing about the form itself. He argues that in the late twentieth century a justification for obligation can be derived from the equality of insecurity brought about by the development of nuclear weaponry. Although he states that this will look beyond 'a single national state alone', he appears to assume that the liberal democratic form of authority will remain (Macpherson 1962: 276). But by appealing to global insecurity all links to liberalism and self-assumed obligation have been cut. There is little reason, as Hobbes' theory shows, to suppose that an appeal to survival alone will lead to democratic conclusions.

Hobbes concludes from his appeal to self-preservation that an absolute ruler is required, but Leviathan obtains his authority from the consent of his subjects, *not* directly from considerations of security. The principal desire of Hobbes' individuals is protection, but, as 'naturally' free and equal individuals, they must voluntarily enter a contract together to obtain the security of Leviathan's sword. Hobbes' version of the social contract, in one sense, gives expression to the ideal of self-assumed obligation, but its effect is completely to sweep away and transform political 'obligation' into an unconditional political obedience.

> Every man should say to every man, I Authorise and give up my Right of Governing my selfe, to this Man, or to this Assembly of men, on this condition, that thou give up thy Right to him, and Authorise all his Actions in like manner.
>
> (1968: ch. XVII; 227)

It is by saying these words to each other that Hobbes' individuals leave the state of nature and enter civil society. The words create a society and institute a ruler to enforce order. It should be noted that the social contract is a contract, and not a covenant, and so possible in Hobbes' state of nature. Individuals simultaneously exchange certain words and, in so doing, mutually give up their right to all things to the sovereign. The contract is, however, a somewhat magical event. In the short time that it takes for the words to be spoken, a collection of warring individuals is transformed into a peaceful community with Leviathan at their head; a unified body politic is brought into being and individuals become political subjects.

Hobbes' notion of the unity of the new political community is a peculiar one. In the state of nature individuals have no sustained relations with each other; in civil society they are unified through the figure of Leviathan himself who becomes the 'bearer' of their persons and the 'author' of their acts. For political purposes Leviathan and his subjects are one; 'it is a reall Unitie of them all, in one and the same Person' (1968: ch. XVII; 227). Once instituted as sovereign, or representative,

Leviathan makes 'A Multitude of men into One Person…For it is the Unity of the Representer, not the Unity of the Represented, that maketh the Person One' (1968: ch. XVI; 220). The actions and decisions of the sovereign are henceforth to be seen as if they were those of the subjects themselves; they are 'author' of what he does. Leviathan personifies his subjects and, quite literally, according to Hobbes, acts for them.

The two stages of the liberal contract take place simultaneously in Hobbes' version of the contract story. The same words bring individuals into a political association and place Leviathan in authority over them. Given Hobbes' conception of the state of nature, the contract must take place in this way, and the sovereign himself can take no part in it; before the words are spoken there is neither an 'all' to contract together, nor a 'sovereign'.[9] The fact that individuals contract between themselves and not with Leviathan is a crucial element in Hobbes' argument. It can never be claimed that Leviathan has broken his part of the agreement, 'consequently none of his Subjects, by any pretence of forfeiture, can be freed from his Subjection' (1968: ch. XVIII; 230).

Through the contract Hobbes' individuals bring an absolute political obedience into being. They give the sovereign the right to do everything necessary to secure their protection, and, having willed this end, it is 'absurd' for them to hinder the sovereign. I argued above that Hobbes' conception of a contract does not give rise to an 'obligation', but is a simultaneous exchange. During the social contract individuals exchange one status for another; but do they also exchange a condition where obligations would not exist for a condition of political obligation? In one sense the contract gives expression to the principle of self-assumed obligation, for individuals freely say the words. On the other hand, a meaningful sense of 'obligation' disappears as soon as the words have been spoken. At that instant the individuals become subjects, and their relationship to Leviathan and his sword becomes analogous to that between a victim and a robber demanding a ransom in return for life. As the contracting individuals turn themselves into political subjects they also 'consent' to Leviathan's rule, or make an enforced covenant to obey him. Hobbes' equation of 'consent' with enforced covenants is perhaps most clearly revealed in the majority version of the social contract. He states that those that dissent 'must now consent with the rest; that is, be contented to avow all the actions he [the sovereign] shall do, or else justly be destroyed by the rest'. Merely by taking part in the contract, Hobbes declares, the individual has tacitly agreed to accept the majority verdict, so would be acting unjustly not to consent. The minority now stand in relation to the majority like the individual to the conqueror; they must 'consent' or be killed. Hobbes goes even further and argues that anyone who comes within the ambit of the new political society, whether their consent has been asked or not, must submit to the sovereign or otherwise remain in a state of war, and can 'without injustice be destroyed by any man whatsoever' (1968: ch. XVIII; 232).

In Hobbes' theory 'consent' is as much a political fiction as the social contract. In civil society all authority relationships, even between parent and child, are alleged to be based on 'consent', yet the question of how consent might actually be given never arises at any point. Hobbes argues that 'consent' and obedience must last as long as a ruler provides protection. If protection fails then subjects must submit or 'consent' to a new sovereign or face the state of nature. Hobbes' voluntarism is completely hypothetical – and meaningless. His theory contains nothing that can properly be called political 'obligation'. This is not, as is frequently suggested, because of his appeals to self-interest, but because 'obligation' implies free individual judgement, choice and decision that Hobbes ruthlessly eliminates from civil society. The price of leaving the state of nature is absolute and unquestioning political obedience.

Hobbes' absolutist political conclusions follow from the extreme individualism of his state of nature. His theoretical perspective leads to a conception of civil society as a completely artificial condition. Social and moral relationships spring into being all of a piece together with Leviathan and his sword, and their stability and continuity depend upon the strength of that sword alone. Humans do not change in the dramatic passage to civil society. It is because of their fear of Leviathan's sword that they are able to make use of their (implicit) capacities and understanding of what social life would be like, and enter into stable relationships with each other in civil society. But the bonds of civil life rest on the sword, not on individuals' social capacities. The unity of this curious community is appropriately symbolized in the 'person' who sits at its head. Leviathan's presence is so fundamental and far-reaching that it is he who turns words into a meaningful moral language, it is he who legislates a stable understanding of 'good' and 'wrong' into existence: 'Hobbes's ethical scepticism and ethical authoritarianism went hand in hand… there must be one Humpty-Dumpty who really is Master and who determines what moral words shall denote' (Watkins 1973: 110).

Hobbes' Humpty-Dumpty is also a political authoritarian because the artificial civil union is inherently extraordinarily fragile. Social life and an unconditional and unquestioning obedience stand and fall together. Any individual who attempts to question Leviathan's commands is allowing the chaos of the clash of subjective, private judgements to enter civil society. However small the intrusion, it constitutes a shattering of part of the artificial bonds that individuals have created. Hobbes' theoretical perspective has no room for any intermediate state between a peaceful unconditional political obedience and a war between a collection of arbitrarily acting individuals.

Hobbes' discussion of civil society is similar to his picture of the state of nature. The state of nature can be peopled with abstract, isolated individuals only because we already know that individuals live together in society, and because we implicitly invest the 'natural' individuals with some social capacities and characteristics. Similarly, we can imagine a form of civil life held together by the power of Leviathan's sword, because we implicitly envisage its force at work against a background of everyday social life and relationships that do not depend on that sword for their continuity and cohesion. Hobbes is theoretically consistent enough to argue that the family in civil society provides an example of an artificial community in miniature, held together by the consent of its individual members to the jurisdiction of its 'representative person'. On the other hand, he also, unavoidably, writes of the family as if its bonds developed from, and rested upon, the continuing mutual relationships and sympathies of individuals who form a 'natural' community.

When discussing the natural rather than the artificial family Hobbes drops his attack on the patriarchalists and, inconsistently with his radical individualism and conventionalism, allows that the father, as the 'naturally' stronger and more active, will exercise authority within the family.[10] The natural, rather than the artificial, family is seen by Hobbes as an important additional source of political stability and order. Parents can teach their children appropriate political ideas and teach them the necessity of political obedience. Hobbes writes that the necessity of the absolute powers of the sovereign must be 'diligently, and truly taught; because they cannot be maintained by...terrour of legal punishment' (1968: ch. XXX; 377). Hobbes' grasp of the importance of what today would be called political socialization in the maintenance of political obedience and political authority runs counter to his 'demonstration' of the mutual exclusiveness of social order and limited government. If political socialization can supplement, or even, to an extent, provide an alternative to the sword, then such an awesome embodiment of political authority as the sovereign Leviathan may no longer be required. In other words, a less extreme individualism than Hobbes' opens the way to less stark alternatives than posed in his theory. Nevertheless, less extreme, or more conventionally liberal, theorists still have to find a solution to the problems of self-assumed obligation if they are to preserve intact the authority of the liberal state.

The absolute rule of Leviathan is a long way removed from the liberal, constitutional state but, nevertheless, Hobbes' arguments do share some important features with liberal theory. Leviathan is not an arbitrary ruler. The civil status of subject implies certain liberties (and I shall comment on these in the next section) and also equality before the law. Individuals in civil society share an equal subjection and owe an equal obedience like servants before a master (1968: ch. XVIII; 238). In return for giving up the unlimited natural right to all things, they gain equal protection and security within a framework of publicly known and impartially enforced laws. If there is to be security there can be no distinction between rich and poor under the law; the rich 'may have no greater hope of impunity' from legal sanctions than the poorest subject (1968: ch. XXX; 385).

Secondly, Hobbes' theory shares a basic structural feature with liberal theory, namely the separation of the political sphere from the rest of social life. Hobbes' theory illustrates this, as so much else, in a singular and graphic fashion. In entering the social contract Hobbes' individuals take their first, and last, political action. The result of the contract is the total alienation to the ruler of their political rights. In Hobbes' civil society there is only one political actor – Leviathan himself. His actions are those of his subjects; they act vicariously through their 'person'. The political status of subject is thus purely formal and completely subsumed in political obedience. Hobbes' theory establishes an unbridgeable gulf between the everyday life and political obedience of the 'consenting' subjects, and the political sphere, symbolized in the figure of Leviathan and his sword.

Ironically, Hobbes has reintroduced individual judgement in all its arbitrariness at another level. It is true that he allows for the possibility of a sovereign assembly but, for good reason, he prefers an absolute monarch. In an assembly clashes of opinion could endanger peace. To avoid conflict Hobbes also argues that the sovereign should name his successor. Interestingly, he argues, too, that although parents are equal, only one can be the 'representative person' in the (artificial) family because children cannot 'obey two Masters' (1968: ch. XX; 253). The logic of Hobbes' theory requires a single-person Leviathan; security in civil society still depends on the judgement of a sovereign individual.

Political obedience and the right of refusal

In Chapter 29 of *Leviathan* Hobbes discusses 'internall diseases', or seditious doctrines, that may strike a commonwealth, threatening political authority and raising the spectre of the war of the state of nature. The character of these diseases is overlooked by the commentators who wish to treat Hobbes as a traditional natural law theorist and to enshrine the claims of individual conscience at the heart of his political theory. Hobbes explicitly states that, in civil society, to proclaim that it is sinful for a man to act against his conscience is to spread a seditious doctrine. In a civil society the command of the sovereign, 'is the publique Conscience', and individuals cease to have the right to judge whether or not actions demanded of them are good or bad (1968: ch. XXIX; 365–66).

Hobbes rules out all possibility of disobedience by individuals acting on the basis of their own conscientious judgement, whether that judgement is secular or supernaturally inspired. If an individual claims that God has spoken in a personal revelation, although authoritative for the individual concerned, it cannot be taken as God's divine law and thus binding on others. There is no way in which such individual inspiration can be clearly distinguished from dreams, madness, other fancies, or from false testimony made from ambition. If God's Word rests only on individual revelation then 'it were impossible that any Divine Law should be acknowledged' (1968: ch. XXXIII; 426).

Faith is an entirely private, inward matter for the individual, and public religious declarations must be guided by what the sovereign commands: 'Profession with the tongue is but an externall thing, and no more than any other gesture whereby we signifie our obedience' (1968: ch. XLII; 527–28). Political obedience must always come first because the requirements of social order take precedence in this world. Every individual, including the sovereign, must answer to God in the next world; in civil society it is professions that count, even if these constitute a denial of conscientious convictions. Hobbes is ruthlessly consistent in his argument that faith or conscience must never encroach into political life. It is the sovereign, not religious authorities, who must have the final say in matters of religious doctrine. This is central to Hobbes' argument against another 'disease' of the commonwealth, the claim that sovereign power can be divided. There must be no competing voices raised against the sovereign or subjects will be no better off than in the state of nature, with its lack of authoritative interpretation of 'right' and 'just'.

The purpose of Hobbes' very long discussion of religious matters in *Leviathan* is to subordinate the traditional claims of the church to the commands of the sovereign. Hobbes reduces the status of churches to that of any other association or organization, or 'private system', in civil society, and their priests and vicars are required to submit to the decision of the sovereign in doctrinal matters. If peace is to be maintained there can be no religious power on a par with the sovereign, able to sit in judgement on what he commands. A divided sovereign power of this kind serves only to confuse subjects and opens the way to disobedience. 'Temporall and Spirituall Government, are but two words brought into the world, to make men see double, and mistake their Lawfull Soveraign' (1968: ch. XXXIX; 498); there must be no 'Ghostly Authority' to challenge the civil power. If the sovereign 'give away the government of Doctrines', Hobbes caustically remarks, 'men will be frighted into rebellion with the feare of Spirits' (1968: ch. XVIII; 236).

The threat of divided sovereignty is also raised by the seditious doctrine that the sovereign is subject to civil laws. Unless the sovereign stands outside the law his commands can be questioned in the name of the law itself, which is tantamount to setting up another sovereign…and there would be no end to the chaos that would ensue. Similarly, although a major function of the civil law is to protect each individual's property, Hobbes regards it as seditious to argue that the individual's right to his property 'excludeth the Right of the Soveraign' (1968: ch. XXXIX; 367). Individuals, in entering the social contract, gave the sovereign the right to do everything necessary to maintain peace and security, so they cannot exclude the possibility that Leviathan may judge it necessary that they give up some of their property.

Hobbes closes all avenues through which challenges can be made to the authority of the sovereign. He excludes traditional religiously-based questioning, and subjects cannot challenge Leviathan on the grounds that he has broken the social contract or acted unlawfully. Subjects are the authors of their sovereign's commands so they cannot claim to have been injured by them; 'to do injury to ones selfe, is impossible' (1968: ch. XVIII; 232). Moreover, in civil society it is the sovereign who brings a definitive interpretation of 'unjust' and 'wrong' into existence through his commands; 'Hobbes' system excludes the very *possibility* of a wrong or unjust law' (Watkins 1973: 114).

Yet is this the end of the matter? Hobbes devotes a chapter of *Leviathan* to the topic of the liberty of subjects and, more importantly, he has argued that one right, the right of self-preservation, is inalienable. If Hobbes' theory really calls for unquestioning and unconditional political obedience, how could there be 'surprising parallels between Hobbes's arguments and the arguments of recent proponents of civil disobedience'? (Flathman 1972: 239).

The surprising point about these parallels, insofar as they exist, is what they reveal about citizenship in the liberal democratic state rather than about Hobbes' theory. Hobbes never admits that individuals have the right of *political* action, or the *political* right to question the commands of the sovereign; the rights and liberties he allows Leviathan's subjects lie outside political life. In a Hobbesian order, civil disobedience could be seen only as sedition; as a virulent, and probably fatal, disease of the commonwealth. Civil disobedients make precisely the kind of political claims that Hobbes wishes to eliminate. For Hobbes they are engaging in an act of war; they are subjects who 'deliberately deny the Authority of the Common-wealth established', and to whom 'vengeance is lawfully extended, not onely to the Fathers, but also to the third and fourth generation not yet in being...because the nature of this offence, consisteth in the renouncing of subjection' (1968: ch. XXVIII; 360). Hobbes' account of the liberty of subjects is concerned only with the liberty they have in their *private* lives. It is in private, everyday life that free individual judgement and choice, and the principle of self-assumed obligation find their place. Where the law is silent, or where the law allows individuals to act, then they can order their lives as they see fit. In civil society individuals have the:

> Liberty to buy, and sell, and otherwise contract with one another; to choose their own aboad, their own diet, their own trade of life, and institute their children as they themselves think fit; & the like.
>
> (1968: ch. XXI; 264)

Providing that individuals' liberty remains a private matter then, like conscientious religious faith, it can pose no threat to peace and good order.

The sovereign retains the right to regulate any of these matters if security requires it, as Hobbes' comments on the right to private property illustrate, but individuals have an inalienable right to act as they see fit if their self-preservation is at stake. Hobbes introduces this right in the following way: he asks, 'what are the things, which though commanded by the soveraign, [the subjects] may neverthelesse, without injustice, refuse to do' (1968: ch. XXI; 268)? It is not 'unjust' to do something if the right to do it has not been contracted away. Therefore, because the right of self-preservation is inalienable, subjects can legitimately refuse to do things which will endanger their lives. A subject may refuse a command to become a soldier if an adequate substitute can be found, and can 'without injustice' refuse to confess to crimes, or refuse to let himself be assaulted.

Nevertheless, the sovereign has commanded the subject to perform the actions, and his commands are binding and must be enforced. There is no requirement upon the sovereign to allow subjects successfully to exercise a refusal to obey if he has judged that it will put security in danger. A murderer may 'justly' refuse to confess, but he can rightfully be executed, and if the survival of the commonwealth demands that all able-bodied men must fight then they must be compelled to do so. 'The end of Obedience is Protection' (1968: ch. XXI; 272); no one has the right to help another refuse a command of the sovereign even though all have the right of self-defence. If disobedience threatens protection and order, then the 'right' of refusal must be defeated by Leviathan's sword, aided by obedient subjects who must each do what is required to 'protect his Protection' by ensuring the punishment even of 'just' refusers (1968: ch. XXIX; 375).

It is on the question of punishment that Hobbes appears to anticipate recent discussions of civil disobedience (Flathman 1972: 239–40). It is typically argued that, if political disobedience is to be 'civil' disobedience, participants must willingly accept the legal penalties for their breach of the law. In accepting punishment they are distinguishing themselves from revolutionaries and criminals, and affirming that they are acting in good political faith out of a sincerely held conviction that serious injustice exists. At the same time, they are demonstrating that, although they have broken the law for a political reason, they are still allegiant citizens who wish to uphold, not undermine, the rule of law. It is thus tempting for theorists who wish to establish a case for conditional political obligation to look to Hobbes' argument about just refusal and the right of Leviathan to exact a penalty. Hobbes would regard a disobedient as subversive, no matter how willingly he or she embraced punishment or how 'civil' the action was, but the comparison between Hobbes' argument and discussions of civil disobedience is interesting. It raises the question why contemporary writers are so insistent that punishment 'is the natural and proper culmination of [the] disobedient act' (Cohen 1971: 87),[11] when civil disobedients are not seen as subversive but as allegiant citizens.

The orthodox account of civil disobedience, as it has been developed in the academic literature over the past decade or so, has been drawn exceedingly narrowly.[12] For most writers, the idea of civil disobedience is acceptable only to the extent that it can be reduced to an essentially symbolic activity that, in itself, makes no impact on the law or policy at issue. It is seen as a way of showing intensity of feeling, or drawing attention to injustice, rather than as a potentially effective form of political action. This is illustrated in Rawls' discussion, in which civil disobedience is compared to public speech with the aim of appealing to the sense of justice of fellow citizens. This view of civil disobedience reduces it to little more than the 'all-purpose threat' of the little girl in the English children's stories: 'if you don't do it I'll scream and scream until I make myself sick' (Barry 1972: 153; Rawls 1971: sect. 55, 57, 59). The argument that civil disobedients should willingly accept punishment for engaging in what is little more than an exercise of free speech follows the same line of reasoning as Hobbes' argument that the just refuser's action should be rendered ineffective by Leviathan's sword; punishment is necessary if the authority of the state is to remain inviolable. The orthodox account of civil disobedience, like *Leviathan,* is written from the perspective of what the state may tolerate if the political obligation of citizens is to remain unquestioned. In one sense, the insistence on punishment as a sign of acceptance of political obligation is more essential for contemporary writers than it is for Hobbes. Civil disobedience is based on moral and political evaluations of laws and policies, not, except indirectly, on self-preservation, and thus it contains a critical political dimension that is entirely absent from a Hobbesian polity.

This raises the broader, and more fundamental, question of whether Hobbes is not right about the character of political action open to citizens if political obligation is to remain unquestioned. This would be strongly contested by almost all present-day theorists; they argue for conditional political obligation, even though they insist that political obligation generally is unproblematic. I have argued that Hobbes' absolutism is a consequence of his extreme individualism. It might be thought that this argument in itself shows that Hobbes cannot possibly be right. A theory based on a more sociologically and anthropologically adequate individualism would have no need to subsume the political life of individuals in unconditional obedience and allow only the right of self-defence. It could encompass a liberal, constitutional form of limited government, based on conditional political obligation. Institutional recognition could be given to such political rights of citizens as voting and free speech – and, perhaps, a right to disobey. Locke's less radically individualist contract theory is often taken to give support to this claim, and the import of the critics of the very narrow, orthodox account of civil disobedience is that citizens do, or should, have such a right. For instance, attention has been drawn to the inconsistency of arguing, simultaneously, that civil disobedience is morally justified and that it must be punished (Schochet 1972).

The claim that citizens in the liberal democratic state do, or should, have a right to disobey is a claim about a moral not a legal right. If a 'law' exists then, logically, there can be no right to disobey it (legal exemptions, or conscientious objector status, can be granted, but that is a different matter). It has been suggested that a legal defence of 'conscientiousness', rather like self-defence, or insanity, should be recognized by the courts, but if a legal defence of civil disobedience is successful, however that defence may be formulated, then the apparent illegality was not what it seemed (Hall 1971). However, to argue that citizens have a moral right to disobey has implications that are unpalatable to most theorists of political obligation. If it is morally justified to exercise this right, if civil disobedience is justified in certain circumstances, then to claim that the disobedient must be punished is to reduce the notion of a 'right' to virtual meaninglessness. But punishment, as we have seen, is held to be necessary because it constitutes a recognition of the authority of the liberal state. Thus to admit a right to disobey, at least in any genuine sense of a 'right', is to pose a threat to the authority of the state.

Furthermore, 'the right to disobey' implies that citizens have a right to decide for themselves whether or not they ought to consent to the demands, or prohibitions, of the liberal democratic state. This leaves open the possibility that consent may be refused or withdrawn, and so takes seriously the idea of self-assumed obligation as consent. Such a notion of 'consent' is very different from Hobbes' identification of consent and submission under threat of violence; it also differs from the hypothetical voluntarism that infers 'consent' from various actions of citizens, whether or not they themselves interpret the actions in this way. In short, if the right to disobey is seen as more than an extension of free speech for which punishment must be inflicted, difficult questions about the basis of political obligation and its general justification begin to be raised. In particular, the question has to be faced whether political obligation can be placed on the secure footing demanded by many present-day theorists if Hobbesian absolutism and unconditional obligation is eschewed.

If theorists stop short of the limits of hypothetical voluntarism represented by Hobbes' theory, then, as Hobbes foresaw, there is always scope for potentially embarrassing questions about the justification and character of political obligation. Discussions of civil disobedience illustrate this point very well; the more narrowly that 'civil' disobedience is defined, the more it invites criticism. As the criticism becomes more radical, so the problem of political obligation in the liberal democratic state is increasingly clearly revealed. Today, it is less easy for theorists to be quite so ruthless as Hobbes in his attempt to rid voluntarism and consent of their radical implications. Nevertheless, the very fact that recent arguments are more typically liberal makes it impossible for the problem of political obligation to be completely suppressed, since it is a problem inherent in liberal voluntarism itself.

Notes

1 Another way of putting this argument is that a 'private language' is not possible; this has been a subject of discussion among philosophers under the impetus of Wittgenstein's theories. See for example Winch (1958: 33–39).
2 Cf. the comments on the capacity to make promises in Gauthier (1969: 43).
3 For a more detailed discussion (but which does not take account of the distinction between 'ought' and 'obligation') see Beackon and Reeve (1976).
4 'There could, if Hobbes is to be taken strictly, be no performative utterances in the state of nature. If, *per impossibile,* there could be performatives, they would be "void"' (Parry 1967: 251–52).
5 See, for example, Barry (1972: 51).
6 Compare Gauthier (1977: 150–57) and Taylor (1976: ch. 6).
7 See also the discussion of the 'society of sorts' that might arise between (social) individuals each acting solely on the basis of self-interest in Braybrooke, (1974).
8 For this interpretation see also Plamenatz, (1963: 125–28).
9 See Winch (1972: 250). I shall leave aside the question of how Hobbes' 'natural' individuals could ever agree who is to be authorized as Leviathan – unless he already is their conqueror.
10 See Brennan and Pateman (1979). On Hobbes' conception of the family as an artificial unit see Chapman (1975).
11 There is a large, repetitive and often tedious literature on civil disobedience. Cohen's (1971) book covers most of the topics usually discussed under this heading.
12 I have borrowed the description from James (1973). Some writers would even confine the term 'civil disobedience' to actions aimed at 'testing' the constitutional or legal status of particular laws.

References

Barry, B.M. 1972. 'Warrender and his Critics'. In M. Cranston and R.S. Peters (eds) *Hobbes and Rousseau: A Collection of Critical Essays.* New York: Anchor.

Beackon, S. and Reeve, A. 1976. 'The Benefits of Reasonable Conduct: The *Leviathan* Theory of Obligation'. *Political Theory* 4(4): 423–38.

Braybrooke, D. 1974. 'The Social Contract Returns, This Time as an Elusive Public Good'. Paper presented to the Annual Meeting of the American Political Science Association.

Brennan, T. and Pateman, C. 1979. '"Mere Auxiliaries to the Commonwealth": Women and the Origins of Liberalism'. *Political Studies* 27(2): 183–200.

Chapman, R.A. 1975. '*Leviathan* Writ Small: Thomas Hobbes on the Family'. *American Political Science Review* 69(1): 76–90.

Cohen, C. 1971. *Civil Disobedience.* New York: Columbia University Press.

Flathman, R.E. 1972. *Political Obligation.* New York: Atheneum.

Gauthier, D. 1969. *The Logic of Leviathan: The Moral and Political Theory of Thomas Hobbe.,* Oxford: Oxford University Press.

Hall, R.T. 1971. 'Legal Toleration of Civil Disobedience'. *Ethics* 81: 128–42.

Hobbes, T. 1968. In C.B. Macpherson (ed.) *Leviathan.* Harmondsworth: Penguin; first published 1651.

James, G.G. 1973. 'The Orthodox Theory of Civil Disobedience'. *Social Theory and Practice* 2: 475–98.

Macpherson, C.B. 1962. *The Political Theory of Possessive Individualism.* Oxford: Oxford University Press.

— 1968. 'Introduction'. In C.B. Macpherson (ed.) *Leviathan.* Harmondsworth: Penguin, 9–63.

McNeilly, F.S. 1968. *The Anatomy of Leviathan.* London: Macmillan.

Oakeshott, M. 1975. *Hobbes on Civil Association.* Oxford: Blackwell.

Parry, G. 1967. 'Performative Utterances and Obligation in Hobbes'. *Philosophical Quarterly* 17: 246–54.

Pateman, C. 1979. *The Problem of Political Obligation: A Critique of Liberal Theory.* Chichester: Wiley.

Plamenatz, J. 1963. *Man and Society.* Vol. 1. London: Longmans.

Rawls, J. 1971. *A Theory of Justice.* Cambridge, MA: Belknap Press of Harvard University Press.

Riley, P. 1973. 'Will and Legitimacy in the Philosophy of Hobbes: Is He a Consent Theorist?' *Political Studies,* 21(4): 500–522.

Schochet, G.J. 1972. 'The Morality of Resisting the Penalty'. In V. Held, K. Nielsen and C. Parsons (eds), *Philosophy and Political Action.* Oxford: Oxford University Press.

Taylor, C. 1976. 'Hermeneutics and Politics'. In P. Connerton (ed.) *Critical Sociology.* Harmondsworth: Penguin.

Warrender, H. 1957. *The Political Philosophy of Hobbes: His Theory of Obligation.* Oxford: Oxford University Press.

Watkins, J.W.N. 1973. *Hobbes's System of Ideas.* 2nd edn. London: Hutchinson.

Winch, P. 1958. *The Idea of a Social Science.* London: Routledge.

— 1972. 'Man and society in Hobbes and Rousseau'. In M. Cranston and R.S. Peters (eds) *Hobbes and Rousseau: A Collection of Critical Essays.* New York: Anchor.

4

IF VOTING COULD CHANGE ANYTHING, IT WOULD BE ILLEGAL (1979)[1]

'Participation' is no longer a fashionable slogan, but the fundamental problems of liberal democratic theory and practice highlighted at the beginning of the decade by demands for an extension of participation, and by the controversy between the academic defenders of empirical democratic theory and their critics, still remain unresolved. The 'stability' of the 1950s and early 1960s has now turned into a 'crisis' and, of course, democratic theory reflects this transformation; earlier celebrations of apathy have been replaced with a concern with 'overloaded' government and fears that Western liberal democracies may be becoming 'ungovernable'. Nevertheless, writers on democratic theory now have to take at least some account of the criticisms of elitist theories, and discussions of participation, as the present volume illustrates, are no longer entirely confined to a narrow concern with electoral activities. The papers in the *Yearbook* range from a study of non-voters, to investigations of attitudes to direct action (a particularly welcome development), participation in the workplace and local communities, and include a theoretical discussion of theories of mass society and a critical look at the results of research into childhood political socialisation. As in most collections the contributions are not all of the same quality, but *Participation in Politics* contains some valuable material for anyone interested in problems of participation and democracy.

Unfortunately, if readers are interested in the relationship between empirical evidence and theoretical argument, they will have to do a good deal of work themselves. The evidence presented in the papers raises some basic questions, that cannot be ignored by anyone interested in the future development of democratic theory and practice, about participation in the liberal democracies, in particular about the status of voting and its relationship to other forms of political activity. But an opportunity has been lost to indicate the wider significance of the findings. The editor has contributed a useful, general introductory essay which places discussion of political participation in historical perspective, but it includes only brief references to the content of the papers that follow. Similarly, in the longest paper by Crewe, Fox and Alt, 'Non-Voting in British General Elections 1966–Oct. 1974', which contains some striking data, the theoretical (and practical) issues raised by the evidence are largely ignored. However, the *Yearbook* is not unique in this respect. Despite the increase in empirical research now being conducted in areas that were barely considered at all, or were not seen as quite respectable a decade ago, the *critical* implications of empirical findings for liberal democratic theory still tend to be neglected.

It has long been accepted as one of the best attested findings in political science and political sociology that the characteristics of voters and electoral abstainers closely resemble those of individuals politically active or inactive in other ways: voters and the otherwise politically active tend to be from higher SES groups, male, white, over 35, married and members of voluntary associations. The findings of Crewe *et al.,* on voting run counter to this conventional picture. First, they found that persistent non-voters are very rare indeed; only 1 per cent of their respondents had failed to vote in any of the four elections covered. Seventy-two per cent voted in all four, 61 per cent in three out of four, and 73 per cent of those who did not vote in 1970 did so in the February 1974 election. The authors stress that the 'ease' of voting has been greatly underestimated in most discussions of participation. It requires minimal effort, skill and initiative, no co-operation with others, and the secret ballot protects the individual from conflict or sanctions. Therefore, the 'costs' of voting usually fall well below the point at which they would enter into a 'rational choice' calculation. There is usually a temporary and specific reason, e.g. illness, for failure to vote. Second, it was found that there were very few sociological differences between voters and non-voters. Neither class, education, nor sex (the apparent sex difference is a reflection of the greater longevity of women) nor TU membership affect turnout. Those least likely to vote are the young, the residentially mobile, occupants of privately rented accommodation (rather than council tenants) and individuals who are single, separated, widowed or divorced. The common factor linking these individuals is 'isolation from personal and national networks that by informing or exhorting exert pressure to go to the polls'. Crewe *et al.* conclude that 'it is social isolation…not social deprivation' that leads to irregular voting and (rarely) to complete abstention.

It was also found that the major feature distinguishing voters from non-voters was psychological not social. In their degree of political motivation or commitment, especially identification with a major political party, voters are more like people who are politically active in other ways than they resemble non-voters. Nevertheless, activists are a sociological minority, while non-voters are an attitudinal minority. Moreover, the differences between voters and non-voters should not be exaggerated: even the most politically uninterested citizens vote – half of them always do so. And half of the irregular voters display a fair degree of political motivation. Among the individuals who failed to vote in any of the four elections, politically committed abstention was rare. It is not usually alienation from the system that underlies persistent absence from the polls.

What is the wider significance of this evidence? The authors conclude with a discussion of the consequence of their findings for the electoral strategy of the British parties. For connoisseurs of elections, excellent criticism is provided of the widely held belief that high turnout and increases in turnout benefit the Labour Party, but the problems run deeper than party strategy. They concern the validity of the almost universally accepted belief that voting is *the* 'political' act of the citizen of a democracy. This question can be approached by considering the account of the rationality of voting suggested by Crewe *et al.* They argue that the rational choice or decision theory model can be saved because the costs of voting are usually so negligible. But their paper gives little support to this explanation of voting. Rather, their findings on the relationship between social isolation and irregular voting suggest a different explanation. They stress the high value that is placed on voting in the British political culture, and they comment that the 'benefit' of voting may derive 'from conformity to the values of the national community'. Going to the polls 'provides no tangible benefit to the individual elector either exclusively or as a member of a group'. They also refer to the finding by other investigators that most citizens appear to see voting as a civic duty. (Additionally, the proportion of both regular and occasional voters who agree that the attention that MPs and local councillors pay to citizens is 'not much' or 'none at all' is very similar, 31 per cent and 38 per cent respectively.)[2]

The difficulty here is that neither the rational choice model nor this sociological explanation captures the historical reasons why the vote has been seen as so important. Crewe *et al.* note that the suffrage came to symbolise the general right to participate in political life. This is undoubtedly true, but the vote was also seen in more than symbolic terms. It seems hardly likely that fighters for the suffrage expected the vote of any one individual to make a difference to the outcome of an election in the unrealistic manner demanded by individualist rational choice theory. Nevertheless, working class men and the women suffragists did expect that the vote would make a difference to the lives of working class people or women. The vote was a means of gaining some individual and collective control over one's life and the governmental decisions that affected it. Moreover, the liberal tradition of argument emphasises that the vote is a vital protective device to safeguard the interests of citizens. Thus, it is rational to vote if exercise of the franchise serves this instrumental function. Critics of empirical theories of democracy and their defence of apathy, including this reviewer, have argued that far from apathy of lower SES individuals and women denoting satisfaction with the system, it is a rational response to a perception that participation (including voting) is not worth it, for it is ineffective; a suggestion that received support from the conclusion of *Participation in America* that participation 'helps those who are already better off'. The evidence in the paper by Crewe *et al.* undercuts this explanation, at least for voting. Not only do the vast majority of citizens vote, but they do not appear to see the vote in instrumental terms.

Why then are so many citizens voting and voting so regularly? One of the curiosities of research into participation is that although there is now an enormous amount of information on the social, economic and psychological correlates of individual participation in electoral activities, we know virtually nothing about how citizens themselves interpret their own act of voting. The data presented by Crewe *et al.* certainly suggest that the high social and cultural value attached to voting (especially mediated through identification with a party) is central to any explanation. However, this merely raises the further question of why such a high valuation should be placed on voting, and why it should be seen as a duty, in apparent abstraction from its consequences.

In his introductory essay, Crouch notes that one result of the granting of universal suffrage was the strengthening of the legitimacy of the liberal state. It is central to the legitimating ideology of the liberal state, as Chamberlain points out in his discussion of the 'dominant values' in 'Attitudes Towards Direct Political Action in Britain', that governments are periodically elected in free, competitive elections; it is because of the existence of this specific electoral mechanism (or 'political method' as Schumpeter called it) that Western societies are 'democratic' and the interests of all their citizens are protected. Thus it appears that the rarity of electoral abstention reflects an acceptance by citizens of the 'values of the national community'. Or does it? The evidence in Chamberlain's paper about a rent strike in the London borough of Barking suggests that this is far too simple a view of the matter. His paper complements, and should be read in conjunction with Crewe *et al.*'s discussion of voting, since Chamberlain explicitly tests Parkin's hypothesis about the relation between the dominant value system and the subordinate value system of the working class.

Chamberlain found that even his (male) respondents who had not joined the rent strike did not reply in a manner that would indicate adherence to the dominant, legitimating belief that it is morally wrong to engage in direct action, when the government has been freely elected and there are legal means available to protest against decisions and pressure for change. Significantly, of the non-withholders of rent who thought that the rent increase (the cause of the strike) was *justified,* over half, 54 per cent, gave pragmatic, not moral, reasons for not joining in – they felt they had no alternative, feared eviction and so forth – and the majority were sympathetic to the strikers and did not see them merely as trouble makers and agitators. Of the non-withholders who thought the rent increase was unjustified, 93 per cent gave pragmatic reasons for their action. Moreover, a majority of both rent strikers and those who did not join in thought that either there was 'no way' for people like themselves to influence the government, or that strikes and demonstrations were the most effective method. Only 25 per cent of rent strikers and 30 per cent of non-withholders agreed that voting and other conventional channels of political activity were the most effective means of exercising influence.

Chamberlain also refers to some nationwide surveys that support his local data, including one designed to measure citizens' feelings of 'powerlessness in the face of government'. The result of this investigation was that 55 per cent of all respondents, and 61 per cent of those in manual occupations, felt 'very' or 'fairly' powerless. Chamberlain concludes that these findings indicate that 'a sizeable number of British workers do not wholeheartedly accept those themes in the dominant ideology which stress that all citizens have a reasonable say in how the country is run', and that there are 'oppositional' as well as 'accommodative' aspects of the 'subordinate' values of the working class.

Chamberlain does not tell us whether his rent strikers or non-withholders are regular voters. In the light of Crewe *et al.*'s findings, and since the rent strike was by council tenants, it is reasonable to assume that most of them are – which raises the question why; in particular because they have so little belief in the effectiveness of the franchise or in the dominant ideology which places such a high value on voting. The answer may be that in this respect working class citizens are acting as rationally as they can within the liberal democratic system. They have good reason to differentiate between local and national levels. At local level, 'unorthodox' direct action of various kinds can offer a potentially effective means of political action on specific issues. In their paper 'Participation and the Home Office Community Development Project', Smith, Lees and Topping emphasise that in almost all local communities there are issues that will provoke a sharp and rapid response from citizens, even though on the conventional (electoral) measures of 'participation' the same citizens may be characterised as apathetic and uninterested. They point out that these same communities may well be 'riven by militant industrial action, race riots or other forms of urban unrest'. Chamberlain also provides a table that lists 26 examples of direct action in Britain from 1971–75, each involving from 500 to 1,500,000 individuals (most examples involving tens of thousands). But these actions, many of which were industrial strikes, do not count as *political* participation or appear in most empirical studies, nor are they regarded as 'political' participation in the legitimating ideology of the liberal democratic state.

The conventional liberal view of what counts as (legitimate) 'political' activity is central to the problem of voting. It is extremely hard for citizens to take direct action or engage in other 'unconventional' forms of political activity at national level (unless they take action as organised workers). It is also at national level that the belief that voting is *the* 'political' and 'democratic' activity – or even duty – of citizens is most firmly held. There can be no 'democratic' government if it is not elected in a competitive election, a point that can be understood by the most politically ill-motivated citizen. So even if voting is now, as Crewe *et al.* comment, 'in reality no more than an intermittent and marginal means of political pressure', it remains necessary to produce a 'democratic' government. And what other form of 'political' participation can an ordinary citizen engage in at national level, no matter how committed, uninterested or alienated he or she may be?

An explanation of voting along these lines is far removed from the traditional liberal conception of the franchise, and hardly accords with the hopes of those who took part in the struggles to gain manhood and then womanhood suffrage. If many voters, especially from the working class, vote because there appears little else for a 'democratic' citizen to do, or because voting is regarded as a duty of citizenship irrespective of its outcome, voting has indeed become a symbolic activity and no more than a ritualistic authorisation or legitimation of a government in office. It is the ideological, not the instrumental, role of voting that is now crucial. If a high value is placed on voting 'in the national community' only because of its ideological role in the legitimation of the liberal democratic state, then the *political* character of voting becomes questionable. True, it is 'political' in the sense that it is bound up with government and the state, but there is nothing distinctively democratic about such a conception of 'political' activity and citizenship or voting. If 'political' activity is a means through which citizens collectively can protect their interests, democratically shape and control their own lives and environment, and develop their own capacities, then the 'political' status of liberal democratic voting is far from clear.

In another paper in the *Yearbook*, 'Pre-Adult Origins of Adult Political Activity: A Sour Note' (a note that needs sounding), Dowse and Hughes conclude by remarking that the label 'political activist' is only one label that can be attached to the same individual. The SES characteristics of the 'activist' are the same as those of individuals active in 'non-political' associations; it is the context that leads their actions to be called 'political'. This is not surprising when one recalls Dahl's classic description of the liberal citizen or *homo civicus* for whom voting will be, more often than not, the least efficient way of pursuing his interests and who is not therefore a natural 'political' animal. Dowse and Hughes comment that 'in defining the context political we come up against massive definitional difficulties and variety'; or, at least, we do once it is asked why *this* context and not *that* is 'political', and why 'political' activities are those surrounding liberal democratic elections and the 'legal channels' for inter-electoral pressure. Most measures of political participation in empirical investigation are both very narrow and discussed in isolation from wider social relationships. Crewe *et al.*, for example, measure participation by the following indices: following political news in the press and TV, talking about or listening to discussions of politics, and voting. But this is a very constricted view of political life, concentrating on the national level, which often appears remote and inaccessible to many citizens, especially since it is presented in the wide circulation newspapers in a sensational manner, giving readers no means of understanding why certain 'events' and 'stories' should suddenly appear in the press. At the potentially accessible local level, citizens who appear apathetic on conventional measures of 'political' awareness, and who do not vote in local elections (where turnout is very much lower than in general elections) may take part in local campaigns – especially if a community development project provides resources, contacts and meeting places – and they may also vote in local elections if a tenants' candidate stands for office (see Smith, Lees and Topping).

The most urgent task facing students of political participation and democratic theory is to take a critical look at the conventionally accepted view of what counts as 'political' participation. *Participation in Politics,* for example, includes a paper by Daniel on 'Participation on the Shop Floor', but there is no discussion of why this topic should be included in a collection about 'political' participation, or what it might mean for liberal democratic theory and practice if shop floor participation and other forms of working class industrial action were seen as 'political'. 'Political' participation, as conventionally conceived, helps the middle class members of society; it is rational for these citizens to be 'political activists' and to make use of the legal channels of political influence open to citizens (and the channels open only to the wealthy and those who give, rather than obey, orders in the workplace). A very different picture of 'political' participation from that made familiar in the political sociology and political science textbooks might appear if attention were directed away from voting and national party identification, and toward strikes, non-co-operation of all kinds, demonstrations and other 'unorthodox' activities. If discussion of political participation is to advance, and if it is to make a real contribution to the development of democratic theory, empirical investigators and theorists have to begin to look at voting in the context of other forms of political activity. Far from being paradigmatic of 'political' participation, liberal democratic voting is central to the unsolved problems of constructing a *democratic* political theory and practice.

Finally, it is rather depressing to find that two papers in the *Yearbook* explicitly discuss only male citizens, and nowhere is there any recognition that there are special problems to be tackled about the political participation of women.

Notes

1 Review of Colin Crouch (ed.), *Participation in Politics, British Political Sociology Yearbook*, vol. 3. London: Croom Helm, 1977.
2 In a footnote, however, the authors note that in the survey of the February 1974 election respondents were asked about their feelings about thirteen different aspects of life, and non-regular voters were the least satisfied on all items except one, 'the standards and values of today's society'.

5

FEMINISM AND DEMOCRACY (1983)

A feminist might dispose briskly of the subject of this essay. For feminists, democracy has never existed; women have never been and still are not admitted as full and equal members and citizens in any country known as a 'democracy'. A telling image that recurs throughout the history of feminism is of liberal society as a series of male clubs – usually, as Virginia Woolf points out in *Three Guineas,* distinguished by their own costumes and uniforms – that embrace parliament, the courts, political parties, the military and police, universities, workplaces, trade unions, public (private) schools, exclusive Clubs and popular leisure clubs, from all of which women are excluded or to which they are mere auxiliaries. Feminists will find confirmation of their view in academic discussions of democracy which usually take it for granted that feminism or the structure of the relationship between the sexes are irrelevant matters. The present volume[1] at least acknowledges that feminism might have something significant to say to democratic theorists or citizens, albeit in a token paper by a token woman writer. In the scope of a short essay it is hardly possible to demolish the assumption of two thousand years that there is no incompatibility between 'democracy' and the subjection of women or their exclusion from full and equal participation in political life. Instead, I shall indicate why feminism provides democracy – whether in its existing liberal guise or in the form of a possible future participatory or self-managing democracy – with its most important challenge and most comprehensive critique.

The objection that will be brought against the feminists is that after a century or more of legal reforms and the introduction of universal suffrage women are now the civil and political equals of men, so that feminism today has little or nothing to contribute to democratic theory and practice. This objection ignores much that is crucial to an understanding of the real character of liberal democratic societies. It ignores the existence of widespread and deeply held convictions, and of social practices that give them expression, that contradict the (more or less) formally equal civic status of women. The objection is based on the liberal argument that social inequalities are irrelevant to political equality. Thus, it has to ignore the problems that have arisen from the attempt to universalize liberal principles by extending them to women while at the same time maintaining the division between private and political life which is central to liberal democracy, and is also a division between women and men. If liberal theorists of democracy are content to avoid these questions, their radical critics, along with advocates of participatory democracy, might have been expected to confront them enthusiastically. However, although they have paid a good deal of attention to the class structure of liberal democracies and the way in which class inequality undercuts formal political equality, they have rarely examined the significance of sexual inequality and the patriarchal order of the liberal state for a democratic transformation of liberalism. Writers on democracy, whether defenders or critics of the status quo, invariably fail to consider, for example, whether their discussions of freedom or consent have any relevance to women. They implicitly argue as if 'individuals' and 'citizens' are men.

It is frequently overlooked how recently democratic or universal suffrage was established. Political scientists have remained remarkably silent about the struggle for womanhood suffrage (in England there was a continuous organized campaign for 48 years from 1866 to 1914) and the political meaning and consequences of enfranchisement. Women's position as voters also appears to cause some difficulty for writers on democracy. Little comment is excited, for example, by Schumpeter's explicit statement, in his extremely influential revisionist text, that the exclusion of women from the franchise does not invalidate a polity's claim to be a 'democracy'. In Barber's fascinating account of direct democracy in a Swiss canton, womanhood suffrage (gained only in 1971) is treated very equivocally. Barber emphasizes that women's enfranchisement was 'just and equitable' – but the cost was 'participation and community'. Assemblies grew unwieldy and participation diminished, atomistic individualism gained official recognition and the ideal of the citizen-soldier could no longer be justified.[2] The reader is left wondering whether women should not have sacrificed their just demand for the sake of men's citizenship. Again, in Verba, Nie and Kim's (1978: 8) recent cross-national study of political participation it is noted, in a discussion of the change in Holland from compulsory to voluntary voting, that 'voting rights were universal'. The footnote, on the same page, says that in both electoral systems there was 'a one man one vote system'. Did women vote? Unrecognized historical ironies abound in discussions of democracy. Feminists are frequently told today that we must not be offended by masculine language because 'man' really means 'human being', although when, in 1867 in support of the first women's suffrage bill in Britain, it was argued that 'man' (referring to the householder) was a generic term that included women the argument was firmly rejected. Another recent example of the way in which women can be written out of democratic political life can be found in Margolis' (1979: 9) *Viable Democracy*. He begins by presenting a history of 'Citizen Brown', who is a man and who, we learn, in 1920 obtained 'his latest major triumph, the enfranchisement of women'. Thus the history of women's democratic struggles disappears and democratic voting appears as the sole creation – or gift – of men.

Such examples might be amusing if they were not symptomatic of the past and present social standing of women. Feminism, liberalism and democracy (that is, a political order in which citizenship is universal, the right of each adult individual member of the community) share a common origin. Feminism, a general critique of social relationships of sexual domination and subordination and a vision of a sexually egalitarian future, like liberalism and democracy, emerges only when individualism, or the idea that individuals are by nature free and equal to each other, has developed as a universal theory of social organization. However, from the time, three hundred years ago, when the individualist social contract theorists launched the first critical attack on patriarchalism the prevailing approach to the position of women can be exemplified by the words of Fichte who asks:

> Has woman the same rights in the state which man has? This question may appear ridiculous to many. For if the only ground of all legal rights is reason and freedom, how can a distinction exist between two sexes which possess both the same reason and the same freedom?

He replies to this question as follows:

> Nevertheless, it seems that, so long as men have lived, this has been differently held, and the female sex seems not to have been placed on a par with the male sex in the exercise of its rights. *Such a universal sentiment must have a ground, to discover which was never a more urgent problem than in our days.*
> (Fichte 1881: §3.1; 439; my emphasis)

The anti-feminists and anti-democrats have never found this 'urgent problem' difficult to solve. Differential rights and status have been and are defended by appeal to the 'natural' differences between the sexes, from which it is held to follow that women are subordinate to their fathers or husbands and that their proper place is in domestic life. The argument from nature stretches back into mythology and ancient times (and today often comes dressed up in the scientific garb of sociobiology) and its longevity appears to confirm that it informs us of an eternal and essential part of the human condition. But, far from being timeless, the argument has specific formulations in different historical epochs and, in the context of the development of liberal-capitalist society, it appears in a form which obscures the patriarchal structure of liberalism beneath the ideology of individual freedom and equality.

It is usually assumed that the social contract theorists, and Locke in particular, provided the definitive counter to the patriarchal thesis that paternal and political power are one and the same, grounded in the natural subjection of sons to fathers. Locke certainly drew a sharp distinction between natural or familial ties and the conventional relations of political life, but although he argued that sons, when adult, were as free as their fathers and equal to them, and hence could only justifiably be governed with their own consent, it is usually 'forgotten' that he excluded women (wives) from this argument. His criticism of the patriarchalists depends upon the assumption of natural individual freedom and equality, but only men count as 'individuals'. Women are held to be born to subjection. Locke takes it for granted that a woman will, through the marriage contract, always agree to place herself in subordination to her husband. He agrees with the patriarchalists that wifely subjection has 'a Foundation in Nature' and argues that in the family the husband's will, as that of the 'abler and the stronger', must always prevail over 'that of his wife in all things of their common Concernment' (Locke 1967: I§§47, 48; II§82). The contradiction between the premise of individual freedom and equality, with its corollary of the conventional basis of authority, and the assumption that women (wives) are naturally subject has since gone unnoticed. Similarly, there has been no acknowledgement of the problem that if women are naturally subordinate, or born into subjection, then talk of their consent or agreement to this status is redundant. Yet this contradiction and paradox lie at the heart of democratic theory and practice. The continuing silence about the status of wives is testament to the strength of the union of a transformed patriarchalism with liberalism. For the first time in history, liberal individualism promised women an equal social standing with men as naturally free individuals, but at the same time socio-economic developments ensured that the subordination of wives to husbands continued to be seen as natural, and so outside the domain of democratic theorists or the political struggle to democratize liberalism.

The conviction that a married woman's proper place is in the conjugal home as a servant to her husband and mother to her children is now so widespread and well established that this arrangement appears as a natural feature of human existence rather than historically and culturally specific. The history of the development of the capitalist organization of production is also the history of the development of a particular form of the sexual division of labour (although this is not the history to be found in most books). At the time when the social contract theorists attacked the patriarchal thesis of a natural hierarchy of inequality and subordination, wives were not their husband's equals, but nor were they their economic dependants. Wives, as associates and partners in economic production, had an independent status. As production moved out of the household, women were forced out of the trades they controlled and wives became dependent on their husbands for subsistence or competed for individual wages in certain areas of production.[3] Many working-class wives and mothers have had to continue to try to find paid employment to ensure the survival of their families, but by the mid-nineteenth century the ideal, the natural and respectable, mode of life had come to be seen as that of the middle-class, breadwinning paterfamilias and his totally dependent wife. By then the subjection of wives was complete; with no independent legal or civil standing they had been reduced to the status of property, as the nineteenth-century feminists emphasized in their comparisons of wives to the slaves of the West Indies and American South. Today, women have won an independent civil status and the vote; they are, apparently, 'individuals' as well as citizens – and thus require no special attention in discussions of democracy. However, one of the most important consequences of the institutionalization of liberal individualism and the establishment of universal suffrage has been to highlight the practical contradiction between the formal political equality of liberal democracy and the social subordination of women, including their subjection as wives within the patriarchal structure of the institution of marriage.

It is indicative of the attitude of democratic theorists (and political activists) towards feminism that John Stuart Mill's (1970) criticism of the argument from (women's) nature, and the lessons to be learned from it, are so little known. The present revival of the organized feminist movement has begun to rescue *The Subjection of Women* from the obscurity into which Mill's commentators have pushed it, although it provides a logical extension of the arguments of his academically acceptable *On Liberty*. *The Subjection* is important for its substantive argument, but also because the ultimately contradictory position that Mill takes in the essay illustrates just how radical feminist criticism is, and how the attempt to universalize liberal principles to both sexes pushes beyond the confines of liberal democratic theory and practice.

In *The Subjection* Mill argues that the relation between women and men, or, more specifically, between wives and husbands, forms an unjustified exception to the liberal principles of individual rights, freedom and choice, to the principles of equality of opportunity and the allocation of occupational positions by merit that, he believes, now govern other social and political institutions. In the modern world, consent has supplanted force and the principle of achievement has replaced that of ascription – except where women are concerned. Mill writes that the conjugal relation is an example of 'the primitive state of slavery lasting on…It has not lost the taint of its brutal origin' (1970: 130). More generally, the social subordination of women is 'a single relic of an old world of thought and practice, exploded in everything else' (1970: 146). Mill opens *The Subjection* with some pertinent comments on the difficulty feminists face in presenting an intellectually convincing case. Domination by men is rooted in long-standing customs, and the idea that male supremacy is the proper order of things derives from deep feelings and sentiments rather than rationally tested beliefs (and, it might be added, men have a lot to lose by being convinced). Thus feminists must not expect their opponents to 'give up practical principles in which they have been born and bred and which are the basis of much of the existing order of the world, at the first argumentative attack which they are not capable of logically resisting' (1970: 128). Mill is very conscious of the importance of the appeal to nature. He notes that it provides no criterion to differentiate the subordination of women from other forms of domination because all rulers have attempted to claim a grounding in nature for their position. He also argues that nothing at all can be said about the respective natures of women and men because we have only seen the sexes in an unequal relationship. Any differences in their moral and other capacities will become known when men and women can interact as independent and equal rational beings.

However, despite Mill's vigorous attack on the appeal to custom and nature he ultimately falls back on the very argument that he has carefully criticized. His failure consistently to apply his principles to domestic life has been noted by recent feminist critics, but it is less often pointed out that his inconsistency undermines his defence of womanhood suffrage and equal democratic citizenship. The central argument of *The Subjection* is that husbands must be stripped of their legally-sanctioned despotic powers over their wives. Most of the legal reforms of the marriage law that Mill advocated have now been enacted (with the significant exception of marital rape, to which I shall return), and the implications of his unwillingness to extend his criticism to the sexual division of labour within the home are now fully revealed. Mill argues that because of their upbringing, lack of education and legal and social pressures, women do not have a free choice whether or not to marry: 'wife' is the only occupation open to them. But although he also argues that women must have equal opportunity with men to obtain a proper education that will enable them to support themselves, he assumes that, if marriage were reformed, most women would *not* choose independence.

Mill states that it is generally understood that when a woman marries she has chosen her career, like a man when he chooses a profession. When a woman becomes a wife, 'she makes choice of the management of a household, and the bringing up of a family, as the first call on her exertions…she renounces…all [occupations] not consistent with the requirement of this' (1970: 179). Mill is reverting here to ascriptive arguments and the belief in women's natural place and occupation. He is falling back on the ancient tradition of patriarchal political theory that, as Susan Okin (1979) has shown in *Women in Western Political Thought*, asserts that whereas men are, or can be, many things, women are placed on earth to fulfil one function only: to bear and rear children. Mill neatly evades the question of how, if women's task is prescribed by their sex, they can be said to have a real choice of occupation, or why equal opportunity is relevant to women if marriage itself is a 'career'. Mill compares an egalitarian marriage to a business partnership in which the partners are free to negotiate their own terms of association, but he relies on some very weak arguments, which run counter to liberal principles, to support his view that equality will not disturb the conventional domestic division of labour. He suggests that the 'natural arrangement' would be for wife and husband each to be 'absolute in the executive branch of their own department…any change of system and principle requiring the consent of both' (1970: 169). He also suggests that the division of labour between the spouses could be agreed in the marriage contract – but he assumes that wives will be willing to accept the 'natural' arrangement. Mill notes that duties are already divided 'by consent…and general custom' (1970: 170) modified in individual cases; but it is exactly 'general custom', as the bulwark of male domination, that he is arguing against in the body of the essay. He forgets this when he suggests that the husband will generally have the greater voice in decisions as he is usually older. Mill adds that this is only until the time of life when age is irrelevant; but when do husbands admit that this has arrived? He also forgets his own arguments when he suggests that more weight will be given to the views of the partner who brings the means of support, disingenuously adding 'whichever this is' when he has already assumed that wives will 'choose' to be dependent by agreeing to marry.[4]

Anti-feminist movements and propagandists in the 1980s also claim that the domestic division of labour supported by Mill is the only natural one. They would not be disturbed by the implications of this arrangement for the citizenship of women but advocates of democracy should be. Mill championed womanhood suffrage for the same reasons that he supported votes for men; because it was necessary for self-protection or the protection of individual interests and because political participation would enlarge the capacities of individual women. The obvious problem with his argument is that women as wives will largely be confined to the small circle of the family and its daily routines and so will find it difficult to use their vote effectively as a protective measure. Women will not be able to learn what their interests are without experience outside domestic life. This point is even more crucial for Mill's arguments about political development and education through participation. He writes (1970: 237) in general terms of the elevation of the individual 'as a moral, spiritual and social being' that occurs under free government, but this is a large claim to make for the periodic casting of a vote (although the moral transformation of political life through enfranchisement was a central theme of the womanhood suffrage movement). Nor did Mill himself entirely believe that this 'elevation' would result from the suffrage alone. He writes that 'citizenship', and here I take him to be referring to universal suffrage, 'fills only a small place in modern life, and does not come near the daily habits or inmost sentiments' (1970: 174). He goes on to argue that the family, 'justly constituted', would be the 'real school of the virtues of freedom'. However, this is as implausible as the claim about the consequences of liberal democratic voting. A patriarchal family with the despotic husband at its head is no basis for democratic citizenship; but nor, *on its own,* is an egalitarian family. Mill argues in his social and political writings that only participation in a wide variety of institutions, especially the workplace, can provide the political education necessary for active, democratic citizenship. Yet how can wives and mothers, who have 'chosen' domestic life, have the opportunity to develop their capacities or learn what it means to be a democratic citizen? Women will therefore exemplify the selfish, private beings, lacking a sense of justice or public spirit, that result when an individual is confined to the narrow sphere of everyday family life.[5] Mill's failure to question the apparently natural division of labour within the home means that his arguments for democratic citizenship apply only to men.

It might be objected that it is unreasonable and anachronistic to ask of Mill, writing in the 1860s, that he criticize the accepted division of labour between husband and wife when only very exceptional feminists in the nineteenth century were willing to question the doctrine of the separate spheres of the sexes. But if that objection is granted,[6] it does not excuse the same critical failure by contemporary democratic theorists and empirical investigators. Until the feminist movement began, very recently, to have an impact on academic studies not only has the relation between the structure of the institution of marriage and the formal equality of citizenship been ignored, but women citizens have often been excluded from empirical investigations of political behaviour and attitudes or merely referred to briefly in patriarchal not scientific terms.[7] A reading of *The Subjection* should long ago have placed these matters in the forefront of discussions of democracy. Perhaps the appearance of empirical findings showing, for example, that even women active in local politics are inhibited from running for office because of their responsibility for child-care and a belief that office-holding is not a proper activity for women,[8] will be taken more seriously than the feminist writings of even eminent philosophers.

The problems surrounding women's citizenship in the liberal democracies may have been sadly neglected, but the failure of democratic theorists to confront the woman and wife question runs much deeper still. Democratic citizenship, even if interpreted in the minimal sense of universal suffrage in the context of liberal civil rights, presupposes the solid foundation of a practical, universal recognition that all members of the polity are social equals and independent 'individuals', having all the capacities implied by this status. The most serious failure of contemporary democratic theory and its language of freedom, equality, consent, and of the individual, is that women are so easily and inconspicuously excluded from references to the 'individual'. Thus the question never arises whether the exclusion reflects social and political realities. One reason why there is no consciousness of the need to ask this question is that democratic theorists conventionally see their subject-matter as encompassing the political or public sphere, which for radical theorists includes the economy and the workplace. The sphere of personal and domestic life – the sphere that is the 'natural' realm of women – is excluded from scrutiny. Despite the central role that consent plays in their arguments democratic theorists pay no attention to the structure of sexual relations between men and women and, more specifically, to the practice of rape and the interpretation of consent and non-consent which define it as a criminal offence.[9] The facts about rape are central to the social realities which are reflected in and partly constituted by our use of the term 'individual'.

Among Mill's criticism of the despotic powers of nineteenth-century husbands is a harsh reminder that a husband had the legal right to rape his wife. Over a century later a husband still has that right in most legal jurisdictions. Locke excludes women from the status of 'free and equal individual' by his agreement with the patriarchal claim that wives were subject to their husbands by nature; the content of the marriage contract confirms that, today, this assumption still lies at the heart of the institution of marriage. The presumed consent of a woman, in a free marriage contract, to her subordinate status gives a voluntarist gloss to an essentially ascribed status of 'wife'. If the assumption of natural subjection did not still hold, liberal democratic theorists would long ago have begun to ask why it is that an ostensibly free and equal individual should *always* agree to enter a contract which subordinates her to another such individual. They would long ago have begun to question the character of an institution in which the initial agreement of a wife deprives her of the right to retract her consent to provide sexual services to her husband, and which gives him the legal right to force her to submit. If contemporary democratic theorists are to distance themselves from the patriarchal assumptions of their predecessors they must begin to ask whether a person can be, at one and the same time, a free democratic citizen and a wife who gives up a vital aspect of her freedom and individuality, the freedom to refuse consent and say 'no' to the violation of the integrity of her person.

A woman's right of refusal of consent is also a matter of more general importance. Outside of marriage rape is a serious criminal offence, yet the evidence indicates that the majority of offenders are not prosecuted. Women have exemplified the beings whom political theorists have regarded as lacking the capacities to attain the status of individual and citizen or to participate in the practice of consent, but women have, simultaneously, been perceived as beings who, in their personal lives, always consent, and whose explicit refusal of consent can be disregarded and reinterpreted as agreement. This contradictory perception of women is a major reason why it is so difficult for a woman who has been raped to secure the conviction of her attacker(s). Public opinion, the police and the courts are willing to identify enforced submission with consent, and the reason why this identification is possible is that it is widely believed that if a woman says 'no' her words have no meaning, since she 'really' means 'yes'. It is widely regarded as perfectly reasonable for a man to reinterpret explicit rejection of his advances as consent.[10] Thus women find that their speech is persistently and systematically invalidated. Such invalidation would be incomprehensible if the two sexes actually shared the same status as 'individuals'. No person with a secure, recognized standing as an 'individual' could be seen as someone who consistently said the opposite of what they meant and who, therefore, could justifiably have their words reinterpreted by others. On the other hand, invalidation and reinterpretation are readily comprehensible parts of a relationship in which one person is seen as a natural subordinate and thus has an exceedingly ambiguous place in social practices (held to be) grounded in convention, in free agreement and consent.

Political theorists who take seriously the question of the conceptual foundations and social conditions of democracy can no longer avoid the feminist critique of marriage and personal life. The critique raises some awkward and often embarrassing questions, but questions that have to be faced if 'democracy' is to be more than a men's club writ large and the patriarchal structure of the liberal democratic state is to be challenged. The assumptions and practices which govern the everyday, personal lives of women and men, including their sexual lives, can no longer be treated as matters remote from political life and the concerns of democratic theorists. Women's status as 'individuals' pervades the whole of their social life, personal and political. The structure of everyday life, including marriage, is constituted by beliefs and practices which presuppose that women are naturally subject to men – yet writers on democracy continue to assert that women and men can and will freely interact as equals in their capacity as enfranchised democratic citizens.

The preceding argument and criticism is relevant to discussions of both liberal democracy and participatory democracy, but particularly to the latter. Liberal theorists continue to claim that the structure of social relations and social inequality is irrelevant to political equality and democratic citizenship, so they are no more likely to be impressed by feminists than by any other radical critics. Advocates of participatory democracy have been reluctant to take feminist arguments into account even though these arguments are, seen in one light, an extension of the participatory democratic claim that 'democracy' extends beyond the state to the organization of society. The resistance to feminism is particularly ironical because the contemporary feminist movement has, under a variety of labels, attempted to put participatory democratic organization into practice.[11] The movement is decentralized, anti-hierarchical and tries to ensure that its members collectively educate themselves and gain independence through consciousness-raising, participatory decision-making and rotation of tasks and offices.

Feminists deny the liberal claim that private and public life can be understood in isolation from each other. One reason for the neglect of J.S. Mill's feminist essay is that his extension of liberal principles to the institution of marriage breaches the central liberal separation, established by Locke, between paternal and political rule; or between the impersonal, conventional public sphere and the family, the sphere of natural affection and natural relations. Proponents of participatory democracy have, of course, been willing to challenge commonplace conceptions of the public and the private in their discussions of the workplace, but this challenge ignores the insights of feminism. It is rarely appreciated that the feminists and participatory democrats see the division between public and private very differently. From the feminist perspective participatory democratic arguments remain within the patriarchal-liberal separation of civil society and state; domestic life has an exceedingly ambiguous relation to this separation, which is a division within public life itself. In contrast, feminists see domestic life, the 'natural' sphere of women, as private, and thus as divided from a public realm encompassing both economic and political life, the 'natural' arenas of men.[12]

By failing to take into account the feminist conception of 'private' life, by ignoring the family, participatory democratic arguments for the democratization of economic life have neglected a crucial dimension of democratic social transformation (and I include my *Participation and Democratic Theory* here; Pateman 1970). It is difficult to find any appreciation of the significance of the integral relation between the domestic division of labour and economic life, or the sexual division of labour in the workplace, let alone any mention of the implications of the deeper matters touched on in this essay, in writings on industrial democracy. It is the feminists, not the advocates of workplace democracy, who have investigated the very different position of women workers, especially married women workers, from that of male employees. Writers on democracy have yet to digest the now large body of feminist research on women and paid employment or to acknowledge that unless it is brought into the centre of reflection, debate and political action, women will remain as peripheral in a future participatory 'democracy' as they are at present in liberal democracies.

I have drawn attention to the problem posed by the assumption that women's natural place is a private one, as wife and mother in the home, for arguments about the educative and developmental consequences of political participation. It might be argued that this problem is much less pressing today than in Mill's time because many married women have now entered the public world of paid employment and so they, if not housewives, already have their horizons widened and will gain a political education if enterprises are democratized. In Australia, for example, in

1977 women formed 35% of the labour force and 63% of these women were married.[13] The reality behind the statistics, however, is that women's status as workers is as uncertain and ambiguous as our status as citizens and both reflect the more fundamental problem of our status as 'individuals'. The conventional but implicit assumption is that 'work' is undertaken in a workplace, not within the 'private' home, and that a 'worker' is male – someone who has his need for a clean place of relaxation, clean clothes, food and care of his children provided for him by his wife. When a wife enters paid employment it is significant for her position as 'worker' that no one asks who performs these services for her. In fact, married women workers do two shifts, one in the office or factory, the other at home. A large question arises here why members of enterprises who are already burdened with two jobs should be eager to take on the new responsibilities, as well as exercise the opportunities, that democratization would bring.

The relative importance of the two components of the wife's double day, and so the evaluation of women's status as workers, is reflected, as Eisenstein notes, in the popular use of 'the term "working mother" which simultaneously asserts women's first responsibility to motherhood and her secondary status as worker' (1980: 207–8). Again, the question has to be asked how workers of secondary status could, without some very large changes being made, take their place as equal participants in a democratized workplace. The magnitude of the changes required can be indicated by brief reference to three features of women's (paid) worklife. The sexual harassment of women workers is still a largely unacknowledged practice but it reveals the extent to which the problem of sexual relations, consent and women's status as 'individuals' is also a problem of the economic sphere.[14] Secondly, women still have to win the struggle against discrimination by employers and unions before they can participate as equals. Finally, it has to be recognized that the workplace is structured by a sexual division of labour which poses still further complex problems for equality and participation. Women are segregated into certain occupational categories ('women's work') and they are concentrated in non-supervisory and low-skilled and low-status jobs. It is precisely workers in such jobs that empirical research has shown to be the least likely to participate.

The example of the workplace, together with the other examples discussed in this essay, should be sufficient to show the fundamental importance to democratic theory and practice of the contemporary feminist insistence that personal and political life are integrally connected. Neither the equal opportunity of liberalism nor the active, participatory democratic citizenship of *all* the people can be achieved without radical changes in personal and domestic life. The struggles of the organized feminist movement of the last 150 years have achieved a great deal. An exceptional woman [Margaret Thatcher] can now become Prime Minister – but that particular achievement leaves untouched the structure of social life of unexceptional women, of women as a social category. They remain in an uncertain position as individuals, workers and citizens, and popular opinion echoes Rousseau's pronouncement that 'nature herself has decreed that women…should be at the mercy of man's judgement' (Rousseau 1911: 328). The creation of a free and egalitarian sexual and personal life is the most difficult to achieve of all the changes necessary to build a truly democratic society precisely because it is not something remote from everyday life that can be applauded in abstract slogans while life, and the subjection of women, goes on as usual. Democratic ideals and politics have to be put into practice in the kitchen, the nursery and the bedroom; they come home, as J.S. Mill wrote (1970: 136) 'to the person and hearth of every male head of a family, and of everyone who looks forward to being so'. It is a natural biological fact of human existence that only women can bear children, but that fact gives no warrant whatsoever for the separation of social life into two sexually defined spheres of private (female) existence and (male) public activity. This separation is ultimately grounded in the mistaken extension of the argument from natural necessity to child-rearing. There is nothing in nature that prevents fathers from sharing equally in bringing up their children, although there is a great deal in the organization of social and economic life that works against it. Women cannot win an equal place in democratic productive life and citizenship if they are deemed destined for a one ascribed task, but nor can fathers take an equal share in reproductive activities without a transformation in our conception of 'work' and of the structure of economic life.

The battle joined three hundred years ago when the social contract theorists pitted conventionalist arguments against the patriarchalists' appeal to nature is far from concluded, and a proper, democratic understanding of the relation of nature and convention is still lacking. The successful conclusion of this long battle demands some radical reconceptualization to provide a comprehensive theory of a properly democratic practice. Recent feminist theoretical work offers new perspectives and insights into the problem of democratic theory and practice, including the question of individualism and participatory democracy, and an appropriate conception of 'political' life.[15] It has been hard to imagine what a democratic form of social life might look like for much of the past century. Male-dominated political parties, sects and their theoreticians have attempted to bury the old 'utopian' political movements which are part of the history of the struggle for democracy and women's emancipation, and which argued for prefigurative forms of political organization and activity. The lesson to be learnt from the past is that a 'democratic' theory and practice that is not at the same time feminist merely serves to maintain a fundamental form of domination and so makes a mockery of the ideals and values that democracy is held to embody.

Notes

1   Graeme Duncan (ed.), *Democratic Theory and Practice*, Cambridge: Cambridge University Press, pp. 204–17.

2   Barber (1974: 273). The comment on citizen-soldiers is very revealing. There is no reason why women should not be armed citizens and help defend the *patrie* (as guerrilla fighters and armies have shown). However, one of the major arguments of the anti-suffragists in Britain and the USA was that the enfranchisement of women would fatally weaken the state because women by nature were incapable of bearing arms. I have commented on these issues in Pateman (1980a). Some other aspects of the patriarchal argument from nature are discussed below.

3 For amplification of these necessarily brief comments see Brennan and Pateman (1979); Hamilton (1978); Hartmann (1976); Oakley (1976: chs 2 and 3).

4 It is worth noting that Mill implicitly distinguishes between the actions and beliefs of individual husbands and the power given to 'husbands' over 'wives' within the structure of the institution of marriage. He notes that marriage is not designed for the benevolent few to whom the defenders of marital slavery point, but for every man, even those who use their power physically to ill-treat their wives. This important distinction is still frequently overlooked today when critics of feminism offer examples of individual 'good' husbands personally known to them.

5 Mill, and many other feminists, see the lack of a sense of justice (a consequence of confinement to domestic life) as the major defect in women's characters. The assertion that the defect is natural to women is central to the belief – ignored by writers on democracy – that women are inherently subversive of political order and a threat; to the state; on this question see Pateman (1980b: 20–34).

6 It need not be granted. *The Subjection* owes a good deal to William Thompson's (much neglected) *Appeal of One Half the Human Race, Women, Against the Pretensions of the Other Half, Men, to Retain them in Political, and Hence in Civil and Domestic, Slavery* (New York: Source Book Press, 1970), originally published in 1825. Thompson was very willing to question these matters in his vision of a cooperative-socialist and sexually egalitarian future.

7 For an early critique see, for example, Goot and Reid (1975); more recently, for example, Evans (1980).

8 Lee, M.M. 1976. 'Why Few Women Hold Public Office: Democracy and Sexual Roles'. *Political Science Quarterly* 91: 297–314.

9 Criminalised in the UK only in 1991 (TC and SAC, eds).

10 A detailed discussion of the paradoxical manner in which political theorists have treated women's consent, and references to the empirical evidence on which these comments are based, can be found in Pateman (1980c). In some legal jurisdictions, for example the States of New South Wales, South Australia and Victoria in Australia, rape within marriage is now a criminal offence. Legal reform is extremely welcome, but the wider social problem remains; one of the saddest conclusions I reached during my research was that rather than rape being 'a unique act that stands in complete opposition to the consensual relations that ordinarily obtain between the sexes…rape is revealed as the extreme expression of, or an extension of, the accepted and "natural" relation between men and women' (1980c: 161).

11 On the other hand, the experience of women in the 'participatory democratic' New Left was a major impetus to the revival of the feminist movement. The New Left provided an arena for political action, the development of skills, and was ideologically egalitarian – but it remained male supremacist in its organization and, especially, its personal relations: see Evans (1979).

12 For some comments on the ambiguous place of the family, see Pateman (1980b): on the wider question of public and private, see Pateman (1983).

13 A steady increase in the employment of married women has been one of the most striking features of the post-war development of capitalism. However, it is worth re-emphasizing that (working-class) wives have always been in the paid workforce. In Britain in 1851 about a quarter of married women were employed (Oakley 1976: 44). Moreover, domestic service, until the late 1930s, was a major occupation for (usually single) women. One reason that Mill is able to overlook the fundamental importance of wives' (private) childrearing duties for their public status is that middle-class mothers had other women to look after their children; similarly, upper- and middle-class suffragettes could go to prison secure in the knowledge that domestic servants were caring for their homes and children (on this point see Liddington and Norris 1978).

14 On sexual harassment, see, for example, Mackinnon (1979).

15 See, for example, the discussion in Petchesky (1980).

References

Barber, B.R. 1974. *The Death of Communal Liberty.* Princeton: Princeton University Press.

Brennan, T. and C. Pateman. 1979. '"Mere Auxiliaries to the Commonwealth": Women and the Origins of Liberalism'. *Political Studies* 27: 183–200.

Eisenstein, Z.R. 1980. *The Radical Future of Liberal Feminism.* New York: Longman.

Evans, J. 1980. 'Attitudes to Women in American Political Science'. *Government and Opposition* 15(1): 101–14.

Evans, S. 1979. *Personal Politics.* New York: Knopf.

Fichte, J.G. 1881. *The Science of Rights.* Trans. A.E. Kroeger. London: Trubner.

Goot, M. and E. Reid 1975. 'Women and Voting Studies: Mindless Matrons or Sexist Scientism'. *Sage Professional Papers in Contemporary Sociology* 1.

Hamilton, R. 1978. *The Liberation of Women: A Study of Patriarchy and Capitalism.* London: Allen & Unwin.

Hartmann, H. 1976. 'Capitalism, Patriarchy and Job Segregation by Sex'. *Signs* 1(3), pt 2: 137–70.

Liddington, J. and J. Norris. 1978. *One Hand Tied Behind Us: The Rise of the Women's Suffrage Movement.* London: Virago.

Locke, J. 1967. In P. Laslett (ed.) *Two Treatises of Government.* Cambridge: Cambridge University Press.

Mackinnon, C.A. 1979. *Sexual Harassment of Working Women.* New Haven: Yale University Press.

Mill, J.S. 1970. 'The Subjection of Women'. In J.S. Mill and H. Taylor (eds) *Essays on Sex Equality.* Chicago: University of Chicago Press.

Oakley, A. 1976. *Housewife.* Harmondsworth: Penguin.

Okin, S.M. 1979. *Women in Western Political Thought.* Princeton: Princeton University Press.

Pateman, C. 1970. *Participation and Democratic Theory.* New York: Cambridge University Press.

— 1980a. 'Women, Nature and the Suffrage'. *Ethics* 90(4): 564–75.

— 1980b. '"The Disorder of Women": Women, Love and the Sense of Justice'. *Ethics,* 91(1): 20–34.

— 1980c. 'Women and Consent'. *Political Theory* 8(2): 149–68.

— 1983. 'Feminist Critiques of the Public-Private Dichotomy'. In S. Benn and G. Gaus (eds) *Conceptions of the Public and Private in Social Life.* London: Croom Helm.

Petchesky, R.P. 1980. 'Reproductive Freedom: Beyond "A Woman's Right to Choose"'. *Signs* 5(4): 661–85.

Rousseau, J.-J. 1911. *Émile.* Trans. B. Foxley. London, Dent, 1911.

PART II

Women in political theory

6

THE SHAME OF THE MARRIAGE CONTRACT (1984)

The language of contract and contractarian arguments are presently enjoying a new lease on popular and academic life, as illustrated by the political success of the libertarian New Right and the academic success of theoretical works by Rawls and Nozick. The widespread appeal of contractarian ideas suggests that the 'movement from status to contract' regarded by Sir Henry Maine as the essence of the development of the modern, liberal world, is reaching its practical and theoretical conclusion. It has recently been argued that radical contractarianism is the ideology of our society (Gauthier 1977: 130–64), but discussions of contract and the movement from the old world of status rarely extend to the one contract into which almost everyone enters during her/his life and which is of great significance for individuals' everyday lives – namely, the marriage contract. There is, however, a long history of feminist criticism of the marriage contract, which has been renewed with the revival of the organized feminist movement, and the recent innovation of 'contract marriage' (in which the two parties freely negotiate the terms and duration of the written contract which will govern their lives together) provides another good example of the current popularity of contractarian ideas and practices.[1] The character and strength of contractarianism as ideology is perhaps better revealed by an analysis of the marriage contract than the more familiar topics of discussion. My argument has something to say about this aspect of the marriage contract but, more importantly, it is concerned with the question whether marriage is essentially contractual. The question was posed in political theory by Hegel (1952), but it is also central to two centuries of feminist debate and struggle about marriage and the marriage contract and to the problem of the alternative form of personal and sexual relationships to be supported by feminists.

In political theory, the movement from status to contract is exemplified in the development of the great conception of the social contract and the claim that the state has (or is as if it has) its origin in a contract. In the seventeenth century discussions of the social contract and the marriage contract went hand in hand, and the similarities and differences between domestic and political order were used to support competing claims about the justified exercise of authority (Shanley 1979). This candor (and level of understanding) has long since vanished and the marriage contract has been excluded from the mainstream of contemporary theoretical argument. For example, the response to John Stuart Mill's critique of the marriage contract in almost all recent standard commentaries on his work has been to ignore this part of his social and political theory. The neglect is the more striking because the basis of Mill's argument is that liberal principles, including contract, should be extended to marriage. In *The Subjection of Women* he argues that the law governing marriage is 'a monstrous contradiction to all the principles of the modern world,' and that the social subordination of women is 'a single relic of an old world of thought and practice exploded in everything else' (Mill 1970: 217, 146) – a relic, that is, of the old world of status. A major theme in feminist criticism (but not the only theme as I shall emphasize later) is that the subjection of wives is bound up with the fact that the marriage contract has never been a true contract. Much past and present feminist writing thus seems to point to the conclusion that marriage properly should be contractual. In this respect, feminism contributes to the social pressures aiding the completion of the long movement from status to contract.

There has, of course, always been opposition to contractual conceptions and arguments in political theory, but criticism has concentrated on social contract doctrine. Hegel is one of the greatest of the critics of the social contract, and he is also virtually alone in opposing the contractual conception of marriage. In paragraph 75 of the *Philosophy of Right* he declares that 'shameful' is the only word to describe an essentially contractual conception of marriage. Hegel's claim about marriage is rarely discussed. The lack of attention reflects the general neglect of arguments about conjugal relations and domestic life in the work of the classic theorists, but it also arises from a consensus that marriage, as a contractual relation, is unproblematic. On the contrary, almost everything about the marriage contract is questionable – even its existence.

Hegel has good reason to argue that a purely contractual conception of marriage is shameful. He provides the theoretical basis for a critique of present attempts to put contractarianism into practice in personal relations between the sexes, but although Hegel offers a profound philosophical and sociological critique of contractual conceptions and practices he sees only one side of the shame of the marriage contract. Indeed, he endorses the other aspect of its shamefulness which feminists have always tried to bring out into the open: that the position of 'wife' in the structure of the institution of marriage is one of ascribed patriarchal subjection or status. What is less clear in feminist arguments is the form of relationship that should replace this shameful status. It is easy to suppose that the problem is resolved if a (potential) wife and husband are able freely to negotiate, as equals, the terms of their marriage contract; the solution appears to lie in an extension of the movement from status to contract to marriage. But the elimination of this last and most deeply entrenched form of status then leads straight into the shame of a contractual conception of marriage. This, too, should concern feminists. If some important feminist arguments follow the logic of the movement from status to contract, wider feminist values and ideals and the vision of a feminist social order stand opposed to contractarianism. Feminists are right to reject Hegel's attempt to give a philosophical justification to the shame of patriarchal subjection in marriage, but they also should applaud his rejection of the shame of contractual marriage.

Feminist critiques of the marriage contract

In 1825, William Thompson laid the foundation for much subsequent feminist criticism of the marriage contract in his *Appeal of One Half The Human Race*. One of Thompson's central arguments is that it is an 'audacious falsehood' to talk of a marriage contract. The so called marriage contract lacks two vital elements of a proper contract and, Thompson argues, the deficiency means that marriage, far from being a contract, is really 'the white slave code'. A slave is an individual 'whose actions and earnings…are under the arbitrary control of another human being' (Thompson 1970: 55, 66–67) and this, he argues, is an exact description of a wife. A 'contract' entails that two parties, of equal standing, voluntarily agree to enter it, but women are forced to marry just as slaves are forced into slavery. In reply to the obvious objection that, unlike slaves, women have a choice because they can remain single, Thompson argues that social custom and law (made by men) effectively deprive women of the means to earn their living, so that unless they give up hope of a decent life they have no choice but to marry, and 'marry on whatever terms their masters have willed, or starve' (1970: 57). Secondly, the idea of a marriage contract is a falsehood because a husband and wife, unlike parties to true contracts, cannot agree to revise or alter its terms; they cannot, for example, (in 1825) agree to make the contract dissoluble. Nor, most fundamentally, can they agree to alter the position of 'wife' and 'husband' constituted through the contract. However much a man may wish to do so he cannot give up the legal powers of a husband. Thompson is careful to point out that not all husbands exercise their power to its full extent; in effect he draws a distinction between the actions of individual husbands and the power embodied in the structure of the institution of marriage. Some husbands may, as he puts it, allow their wives equal pleasure to their own. However, the wife's enjoyment depends entirely on the benevolence of her husband and what he does, or does not, *permit* her to do. If a husband chooses to forgo all his legal powers, his wife still has 'but the pleasures of the slave, however varied' (Thompson 1970: 89) because her actions are always contingent upon the permission of the husband. Thompson claims that in some ways wives are worse off than the female slaves of the West Indies. For instance, a wife has to undergo 'the gratuitous degradation' of having voluntarily to agree to her subjection when she vows obedience (Thompson 1970: 65). There is at least no pretense about the fact that female slaves are forced into slavery: there is, one might say, no talk of the slave contract.

The marriage contract is criticized less polemically, but no less forcefully, four decades later in *The Subjection of Women*. John Stuart Mill was one of the rare men who not only supported the feminist movement but attempted to put his sympathies into practice. Two months before he and Harriet Taylor were married in 1851, he wrote a statement rejecting the legal powers that he would acquire as a husband – though his rejection had no legal standing – undertaking 'a solemn promise never in any case or under any circumstances to use them.' He states that he and Taylor entirely disapprove of existing marriage law because it 'confers upon one of the parties to the contract, legal power and control over the person, property and freedom of action of the other party, independent of her own wishes and will' (Mill 1970: 45). Mill follows Thompson quite closely in many of his arguments in the *Subjection*. He, too, argues that women have no alternative but to marry. 'Wife' is the only position their upbringing and social and legal pressures realistically leave open to them, but to become a wife is tantamount to becoming a slave, and, in some ways, is worse. Mill, echoing Thompson, calls a wife the 'actual body-servant of her husband: no less so, as far as legal obligation goes, than slaves commonly so called.' He draws attention to the fact that a wife, unlike (in principle at least) a female slave, has no right 'to refuse to her master the last familiarity…[she can be] made the instrument of an animal function contrary to her inclinations' (Mill 1970: 158, 160). Mill also distinguishes between the behavior of individual husbands and the structure of the institution of marriage. He argues that defenders of the marriage law rely on the example of husbands who refrain from using their legal powers, yet marriage is designed for every man, not merely a benevolent few, and it allows men who physically ill-treat their wives to do so with virtual impunity.

Mill does not explicitly argue that the marriage contract, given its structure and consequence, is not properly a contract. Rather, he calls for reform of marriage law to bring the marriage contract in line with other contracts. He notes that 'the most frequent case of voluntary association, next to marriage, is partnership in business', but marriage compares very unfavorably with business. No one thinks that one partner in a business must be absolute ruler; nobody would enter a business partnership if that were the case. Theory and experience both confirm that the appropriate arrangement is for the conditions of partnership to be freely negotiated in the articles of agreement. Similarly, Mill argues, in marriage the 'natural arrangement' is a division of powers between husband and wife, 'each being absolute in the executive branch of their own department, and any change of system and principle requiring the consent of both.' How is the division to be made? Mill suggests on the one hand, that it will be freely agreed according to the capacities of the partners; they could 'pre-appoint it by the marriage contract, as pecuniary arrangements are now often pre-appointed' (Mill 1970: 168–69). On the other hand, as feminist critics have recently pointed out, Mill is ultimately inconsistent in his argument. When discussing the tasks of a wife he falls back on the appeals to custom and nature that he explicitly rejects earlier in the *Subjection*. Mill assumes that when women have equal opportunity in education, and marriage has been reformed so that husbands are no longer legally sanctioned slave masters, a woman, by virtue of becoming a wife, will still 'choose' to remain in the home, dependent on her husband. He thus assumes that in this fundamental matter the *content* of a freely negotiated contract would reproduce patriarchal status. However, despite Mill's reluctance to take his attack on status to its logical conclusion, the general direction of his argument is that marriage must become a proper contract.

Many of the reforms of marriage law demanded by Thompson and Mill have now been enacted. The legal position of a wife in Anglo-American jurisdictions has been transformed from that of a legal non-person, the property of her husband, to near civil equality with her spouse. Nevertheless, recent feminist argument stresses that the marriage contract still diverges in significant respects from other contracts, illustrating a striking continuity in feminist criticism over one hundred and fifty years.[2] Liberal principles, and the safeguards developed for parties to contracts in other areas, still do not fully apply to the marriage contract. Feminists emphasize two areas in particular: first, the individual right of self-protection. Usually it is held that a valid contract cannot require that one party relinquish the right of self-protection, but today, as in the nineteenth century in most legal jurisdictions, it is still deemed legally impossible for a husband to rape his wife, and wives find it hard in practice to obtain proper legal protection against other forms of physical assault by their husbands.

The second peculiarity stressed by feminists is that the marriage contract does not, like other contracts, exist as a written document that is read and then signed by the contracting parties. Individuals usually must be able to read and understand the terms of a contract before committing themselves. In contrast, in marriage, a woman and man are transformed into wife and husband through a ceremony and their speech acts within it, not literally by signing a contract.[3] Moreover, unlike other contracts, the marriage contract cannot be entered into by any two (or more) sane adults but is restricted to two individuals, who must be female and male, not related in prescribed ways, and so forth. Nor can these two, as Thompson and Mill hoped, freely negotiate the terms of their contract; they do not even have a choice between several different contracts. Couples do have some scope for making their own arrangements, but it is important to note that Thompson's point about permission remains relevant; individual variations are made within 'a relationship of *personal* dependency, the couple work out together what the husband wants [the wife] to do…within certain general parameters' (Barker 1978: 242). These 'general parameters' are set by the structure of the institution of marriage. The essential feature of the marriage contract is that only a woman can have the rights and duties of a 'wife' and only a man those of a 'husband.' In other words, the singular feature of the marriage contract is that it is a contract grounded in and maintaining status or ascription. Birth and the natural criterion of sex determine who can be a 'wife' and 'husband' and what each status entails. Today, as in 1825, the shamefulness of the marriage contract for feminists is that patriarchal status, the taken-for-granted, natural subjection of (women) wives to (men) husbands is confirmed through contract.

Barker has observed that the marriage contract 'is not in fact a contract between the spouses, but rather they agree together to accept a certain (externally defined) status' (Barker 1978: 254). Although this statement points to the crucial fact that marriage is an institution of status or ascription, it fails to capture the full shame and contradiction of the marriage contract. If the marriage contract is not, as it appears to be, a contract between two individuals, the question immediately arises whether it is a contract at all. This may seem an odd question because marriage, according to the entry under 'contract' in the *Oxford English Dictionary,* has been seen as a contractual relationship since at least the fourteenth century, and Blackstone wrote in his famous *Commentaries* in the eighteenth century, that 'our law considers marriage in no other light than as a civil contract.' But repeated references to the contractual character of marriage obscure more than they illuminate. For example, in the days of arranged marriages the contract was surely between the two (fathers of the) families, not the spouses. Now that marriage is what historians like to call 'companionate' or 'egalitarian', a voluntary matter between two individuals, rather than contracting together, the spouses are still agreeing or consenting to an externally prescribed status.

In one sense this has always been very well understood.[4] In the 1640s, 'the 'contractual' element in marriage [was] simply the consent of each party to marry the other...To contract a marriage was to consent to a status which in its essence was hierarchical and unalterable' (Shanley 1979: 79).[5] The failure to distinguish contract from consent has long been a major source of confusion in political theory, especially in discussions of the social contract. Logically, contract is the 'beginning;' consent follows subsequently. (In the case of the social contract, consent is given – it is never refused in the contract story – by the 'next generation' to the political arrangements constituted through the social contract of their fathers).[6] Ideologically, however, it is extremely useful to blur the distinction between the practices of contract and consent, and it is even more useful in the case of the marriage contract than the social contract. Almost everyone agrees that the social contract is merely an exercise in hypothetical reasoning or a political fiction, but it is never suggested that the marriage contract is a fiction. The marriage contract, it is confidently assumed, is entered into every day; it is an actual original contract for each pair of spouses. But this, as Thompson declared in 1825, is an 'audacious falsehood'. The conclusion to be drawn from the feminist critique of the marriage contract is precisely that it is a fiction. It is called a contract between a man and woman; the reality is that they consent to the patriarchally ascribed status of superior husband and subordinate wife. Or is this the reality? An examination of the status of 'wife' reveals that the feminist critique has not gone far enough. The contract is a fiction, but to replace contract with consent, the consent of *both* spouses to their status, is to perpetuate a nice piece of political mystification. The presuppositions of the status of 'wife' mean that it is not possible for a woman simultaneously to become a wife and to give consent.[7]

The social practices of contract and consent depend upon the possession of certain attributes and capacities by those engaged in them; both practices assume that participants are the 'individuals' who appeared in liberal theory when the attack on status and the movement to contract began. They are individuals who are 'naturally' free (and so can be governed only with their express agreement), who have a property in their person and capacities, and are political equals – and are men. Only during the past few years, as the organized feminist movement has begun to have an impact in academia, has attention begun to be focused on the accommodation of patriarchalism, or status, with liberalism, or contract, and the exclusion of women from the (apparently) universal categories of liberalism, including the 'individual'. The exclusion has its roots in the mutual agreement between the social contract theorists and the patriarchalists that a wife's subjection to her husband had a natural foundation.[8] The depth of contemporary belief that this is the natural order of things is most starkly revealed in the legal right of a husband to rape his wife; central aspects of what has been called the 'law of male sex right' (Rich 1980)[9] are enshrined in civil law and social practice. In other words, the status of 'wife' is based on the denial that women are (or can be) 'individuals.' If a woman is to give consent to the status she is to acquire on marriage she must – naturally – have the rights and capacities of an 'individual'. However, it is logically impossible for a 'wife' to possess these attributes because that would be simultaneously to claim that a woman is both naturally free and naturally in subjection. This contradiction is hidden under the fiction of the marriage contract and the mystification of consent; a gloss of free agreement is given to the shameful reality of the ceremonial confirmation of the ascribed, patriarchal subjection of wife to husband.

It might be objected that this extension of the feminist critique would have been all very well in 1825 or 1869 but it is misplaced in the 1980s when women are, at last, being recognized as 'individuals'. In New South Wales, for example, rape within marriage has become a criminal offense. In general, the reforms of the past decade are creating the social basis from which the marriage contract and women's consent can become a reality. The conception of 'wife', it could be argued, is changing; the movement from status to contract is finally reaching into the institution of marriage. Marriage can, at last, become a properly contractual relationship, entered into on an equal footing by women and men who mutually and freely negotiate the terms of their contract. Ascribed patriarchal status will no longer determine rights and duties. Rather than dwelling on a status already receding into the past, the objection might continue, feminists should work to universalize contract as the general form of marriage. But is this the conclusion to be drawn from the feminist critique? Is contract the way to overcome the shame of status, of patriarchal subjection, within marriage? A consideration of Hegel's claim that an essentially contractual conception of marriage is itself shameful is necessary before it can be concluded that the apparently obvious solution is also a feminist solution.

The marriage contract that transcends contract

The conception of marriage as essentially contractual is part of the theoretical stock of liberalism. Locke, for example, states that 'conjugal society' arises from a 'voluntary Compact between Man and Woman', which establishes 'such a Communion and Right in one 'mutual Support and Assistance' (Locke 1967: §78). The keystone of the contractarian view of marriage is the doctrine that individuals have 'a right in one another's bodies.' The right follows from a conception of individuals as owning the property they possess in their persons and bodies; one individual can thus have rightful access to, or sexual use of, the body of another only with the consent or agreement of, or through a contract with, the property owner. The marriage contract establishes legitimate access to the body of a spouse. Logically, the contract should provide mutually equal access, but the patriarchal fiction of the contract hides the fact that the wife is excluded from the status of an 'individual' who owns property in her person; hence, her body becomes part of her husband's property, and the husband gains an unlimited access to his wife's body and the wife no right at all.

In the *Philosophy of Right*, Hegel's critique of the contractual view of marriage is directed against Kant. Kant explicitly presents marriage as nothing more than a contract for mutual use of bodies, defining marriage as the 'union of two persons of different sex for the life-long reciprocal possession of their sexual faculties' (Kant 1887: §24; 110). Marriage, Kant argues, necessarily follows from the natural sexual attraction between a woman and man. If they wish to have 'reciprocal enjoyment' or 'reciprocal use' of their bodies then they *must* marry each other. If they do not marry, then, according to Kant, natural sexual feeling dehumanizes the couple; sexual intercourse between unmarried individuals is 'in principle…on the level of cannibalism' (Kant 1887: §31; 239). Through marriage the couple can transcend mere sexual appetite and natural inclination and enter the realm of law and reason. Although each partner acquires rightful use of the body of the other as if the spouse were no more than a piece of property, Kant argues that through marriage, in which the possession is mutual and reciprocal, each retains the status of a person. Hegel attacks Kant precisely because, in his argument, marriage is 'degraded to the level of contract for reciprocal use' (Hegel 1952: Addition to §161). Such a view of marriage is shameful.

There are two related aspects to Hegel's critique of the contractarian conception of marriage. First, it is shameful because individuals are treated as if they were nothing more than owners of their physical bodies and sexual inclinations, so eliminating other aspects of human personality. Marriage becomes merely a way of avoiding sexual 'cannibalism', or unauthorized use of bodies. Individuals then appear as if their whole beings were those of the makers of contracts and this is, for Hegel, to substitute a theoretical abstraction for the complex individuality of actual men and women. Hegel discusses contract under the heading of 'Abstract Right' in the *Philosophy of Right* and argues that to see individuals purely as makers of contracts is to see them as 'immediate self-subsistent persons' (Hegel 1952: §75), abstracted from their concrete social relationships. The perspective of contract presupposes that individuals are property owners, that each owner is recognized in this capacity by others and recognizes them in turn (that is, they each admit that others are of equal standing to themselves). The practice of contracting gives objective expression to this mutual recognition. When entering a contract two individuals 'will' or share the common goal of exchanging their property to their mutual advantage. A contract enables them to make mutual use of each other – whether they are exchanging material goods or bodies.

Second, Hegel's criticism is that an essentially contractual view of marriage eliminates the qualitative distinction between the spheres of civil society and the family. Marriage and the family are shamefully treated as if they were an extension of civil society and so constituted by, and their relationships exhausted by, contract. Hegel agrees with Kant that it is our 'objectively appointed end and so our ethical duty' (Hegel 1952: §162) to marry, and thus establish a family. The contractarian conception leaves marriage open to the pure contingency, the whim and caprice, of sexual attraction, and gives rise to a superficial understanding of the marriage contract as merely the public recognition and regulation of natural sexual inclination. Hegel argues that, on the contrary, a specific form of ethical life and association, that is, the family, is created through the marriage contract. The family is the most 'immediate' dimension of ethical life, where individuals are members of an undifferentiated unity, or an association based on 'love, trust, and common sharing of [the partners'] entire existence.' The family has its origins in contract because marriage begins in contract; Hegel does not dispute this. However, Hegel claims that the marriage contract is a *unique* contract 'to transcend the standpoint of contract' (Hegel 1952: §163). One of the major theoretical aims of the *Philosophy of Right* is to show that transcendence of the standpoint of contract is necessary for the existence both of the family and the sphere of civil society. To fail to distinguish the contrasting principles of association of the two spheres is to fail to comprehend the social conditions for the existence of contract itself.

Hegel's critique of contractarian marriage is part of his much wider critique of liberal, abstract individualism, and thus goes deeper than an attack on its bleak view of individuals and their conjugal relations. The shame of contractual marriage arises from a lack of understanding of the social presuppositions of the sphere of contract. In order to enter a contract men must be 'individuals' with a certain consciousness of themselves and their social relations (as property owners, equals, bearers of rights). But this, Hegel emphasizes, is only one dimension of social life and consciousness, and it is *because* it is a dimension, not the whole, that the contracts can be made. Any single contract presupposes the rule that the contracts must be kept, a rule involving trust and fidelity (which are constitutive of the bonds of family life). A single contract is possible, and individuals understand what it entails, only because it is part of the wider practice of contracting, which is constituted by the rule that contracts are binding. The social practice of contracting depends on an intersubjective understanding of what a contract is, and Hegel's discussion shows how the liberal conception of men as essentially makers of contracts both abstracts from, yet simultaneously takes for granted, this intersubjective understanding. 'Contract' is socially meaningful precisely because consciousness is informed by conceptions and social relationships that are non-contractual. This wider consciousness cannot be developed within the sphere of contract itself.

Hegel's important argument about the social basis of contract can partly be expressed by distinguishing the 'individual', who appears in abstract guise in liberal theory, from the individuality of actual women and men, a distinction crucial for an understanding of love as the principle of association of marriage and the family. To enter the marriage contract the spouses must be 'individuals' conscious of the meaning of the social practice of contracting. However, the marriage contract 'transcends the standpoint of contract', which implies that the wife and husband are not merely 'individuals'. Their individuality and consciousness must be developed in spheres other than that of contract if the marriage contract is to have its unique status. Without this wider and richer individuality they would remain trapped at the level of contract (indeed, strictly, 'contract' would be meaningless to them), marriage could not transcend its contractual origin and they would have no comprehension of love. Hegel states that love is 'the most tremendous contradiction' (Hegel 1952: Addition to §158). It is contradictory because the lovers' first impulse is to want to obliterate their individuality in total unification with the loved one. In opposition to this desire, it is discovered that it is through the relationship with the beloved that individuality is strengthened and knowledge of the self as an autonomous person is gained. Love thus both unifies and differentiates; differentiation and individuality are created within the complex unity created by the bonds of love. The contradiction of love can be overcome by the mutual recognition that lovers give each other, through which each gains a deeper sense of their own autonomy. The social basis of love is strengthened by the dialectic of unification and differentiation, but none of this is possible within contractarian relations. In the latter, the spouses see each other from one perspective only, that of the mutual advantage of property owners, and no development of individuality can take place since the self is subsumed within the 'individual' contract-maker. The bond between these selves can only be that of mutual use – yet even this bond is illusory as it lacks the trust and faith necessary for its creation.

Before attempting to discuss the significance of Hegel's argument for feminist critiques of the marriage contract, it must be emphasized that his contract to transcend contract fails to overcome the shame of patriarchal subjection within marriage. The central place of mutual recognition in Hegel's account of love suggests that his argument is universal, that it includes both sexes. In fact, it applies only to men.[10] Hegel's claim that he has given 'ethical significance' to the 'difference in the physical characteristics of the two sexes' (Hegel 1952: §165) is baseless; he sets women irrevocably outside of ethical life and so strips his theory of its necessary universal foundation. Struggle and 'self-redemption' are necessarily required from men, outside of the family, in the development of their consciousness and individuality, but Hegel insists that women find their 'substantive destiny' purely within the family. His patriarchalism blinds him to the fact that he has thus divided and separated the sexes not, as he claims, differentiated while uniting them. He thus destroys the grounding of his theory. From inside the family, the sphere of 'immediacy', women can never develop the consciousness of 'particularity' (that of the 'individual') required if they are to enter a (marriage) contract. Nor can they develop the individuality necessary to give to and receive from a husband the recognition on which the dialectic of love and, hence, the bonds of the sphere of marriage and the family depend.

Hegel's unique marriage contract turns out to be just as much a patriarchal fiction as the mundane contracts of Locke or Kant. In one important respect Hegel also follows Kant rather than criticizing him. Kant makes much of the 'relation of

EQUALITY' in marriage between husband and wife, 'as regards the mutual possession of their Persons, as well as of their Goods' (Kant 1887: §26; 111). However, this
is a mere appearance of equality. Kant rejects the suspicion that there is something
contradictory about combining equality with the legal recognition of the husband
as master. He states that this 'cannot be regarded as contrary to the natural Equality
of a human pair, if such legal Supremacy is based only on the natural superiority of
the faculties of the Husband compared to the Wife…and if the Right to command
is based merely upon this fact' (1887: 112).

Hegel's argument also attempts to combine equality with the right of command
of the husband. His discussion suggests that, because marriage begins in a contract,
the equal exchange that (it is claimed) takes place in other contracts also obtains
between husband and wife and they thus recognize each other as equals. Indeed,
the contractarian conception of marriage explicitly implies that such an exchange
occurs; the spouses exchange the property in their persons and equality of access
to each other's body is established. However, I have already noted that the
status of 'wife' means that such an exchange is impossible; rather the husband
becomes owner of and master over the body of his wife. This reality is masked in
Hegel's critique of the abstraction of the standpoint of contract because he sees no
contradiction in a contract between a man who is an 'individual' and a woman
who is by nature unable to develop the capacities of an 'individual'. If there is
any exchange embodied in the contract it consists of an exchange of obedience
by the wife in return for protection by her husband[11] – except that no protection
is afforded to a woman with the status of 'wife'. The contractarian conception of
marriage and Hegel's unique marriage contract are both covered in shame.

Contract, love and friendship

The appeal of (properly) contractual marriage as a solution to the shame of the
patriarchal subjection of wives is hardly unexpected when women have only so
recently won major advances in the struggle for practical social recognition as 'individuals.' The solution also has popular, commercial backing in numerous advice
books on marriage and sexual matters.[12] However, because women are finally
being admitted as 'individuals', the full implications of contractarianism, or the full
implications of completing the movement from status to contract, are becoming
apparent. The theoretical implications were spelt out in Hegel's philosophical and
sociological critique of the standpoint of contract and abstractly individualist liberalism. To attempt to replace status by contract alone is to assume that the example
of a single contract can be generalized so that social life as a whole is constituted
through contract, or is a series of mutually advantageous exchanges between individuals. The argument of the *Philosophy of Right* is that this assumption is incoher-
ent, and that the movement from status to contract cannot be taken to its logical
conclusion. The standpoint of contract is unable to provide a coherent basis for
social order. Without extra-contractual social relations and consciousness, which
are explicitly rejected by the standpoint of contract, contract itself is impossible.

Hegel's general critique of contract might seem far removed from feminist attacks on the marriage contract. Yet, when feminists point to the divergences between the marriage contract and other contracts this inevitably suggests (in the absence of argument to the contrary) that they are looking to a contractarian alternative. Feminism thus appears to lie firmly within the logic of the movement from status to contract. But if this is the case, feminists are relying on a theoretical perspective that, ultimately, can give no grounding for a feminist social order, and on a conception of social and sexual relationships with practical implications that run counter to central values and ideals of feminism.

Despite the enormous theoretical strength of the Hegelian critique of the abstract basis of contract doctrine, general theoretical argument has done little to impede the spread and consolidation of contractarianism. However, this is not surprising, since contractarianism is not a purely theoretical matter. 'Contract' originated in a revolutionary challenge to traditional ties of status between males, and contractual conceptions helped constitute the institutions of the new, liberal society. But contractarianism is also the ideology of our society and, as the example of the marriage contract reveals, contract does not merely reflect but, more importantly, obscures the patriarchal structure of domination of liberalism. Feminists have noted, for example, that the advocates of 'contract marriage' ignore the fact that it is open only to a few well-educated, professional women to negotiate as equals with men to draw up a mutually advantageous contract. The patriarchal structuring of the occupational hierarchy means that most women in the paid labor force earn considerably less than men, so they lack the power to bargain for a contract with an egalitarian content. Such practical objections and wider theoretical critiques nevertheless do little to detract from the success of contract as ideology; 'questions about the theoretical coherence of contractarianism need not affect its ideological coherence, except insofar as they become questions in the minds of its adherents' (Gauthier 1977: 156). Examples of times and places when questions have been asked can be found in the history of the socialist and feminist movements, but this has not been sufficient to develop a general, popular questioning consciousness. The revival of the organized feminist movement offers the possibility that 'questions in the mind' could become widespread precisely because feminism is the political movement concerned with the way in which the structure of our individuality and personal lives is an integral part of the structure of liberal-patriarchal institutions. The theoretical and practical problems of the standpoint of contract are thus raised in their most acute form.

One of Hegel's objections to the view that marriage is no more than a contract is that it leaves marriage at the mercy of the whims and capricious wills of the contractors. Similarly, Durkheim, who also argues that 'a contract supposes something other than itself', emphasizes that the bond created by contract is both external and of short duration; it leads to 'transient relations and passing associations' (Durkheim 1964: 381; 204). A contract of mutual advantage and reciprocal use will last only so long as it appears advantageous to either party. A new contract with a different partner, will always appear as a possible and enticing alternative. The way in which popular advice books present divorce illustrates this very well; divorce is seen as something that can be 'pre-considered in terms of personal upward mobility, with stress…on what lies ahead that may be incorporated into a new and better image.'[13] A contract of mutual use could specify that the contractors will become parents – but how exactly do contractarians see the relation of child to parents? Hobbes was the only classic contract theorist willing to sweep away the last stronghold of status and take contract to its logical conclusion. He interpreted the dictum that we are 'born free and equal' quite literally and argued that the relation of child to parent was conventional or contractual. A consistently contractual conception of marriage must hold that, immediately children reach the age (however young that may be judged to be) at which they are capable of making a contract with their parents, they should do so. Or, if the parents cannot offer a sufficiently advantageous contract, the child must be free to contract with other adults. This view may have its attractions when contrasted with the idea that parents have a property in their children, but it is extremely doubtful whether the transitory, external bonds of mutual use and advantage between adults, and between adults and children, could provide the necessary social foundation for children to develop a secure self-identity and individuality, even a self that is purely the self of a contractor.

The social conditions within which human beings can develop and flourish are formed by the non-contractual relationships that contractarianism attempts to eliminate. There is no place for love within the standpoint of contract, unless, that is, it is reduced to no more than sexual inclination and satisfaction. For Kant, marriage *is* the right to another's body or the reciprocal use of the property in a spouse's person. This chill reductionism is illustrated in a recent example of the way in which 'radical contractarianism has come more and more to dominate our thoughts and actions' (Gauthier 1977: 159). An economic account of marriage claims that love is a 'particular non-marketable household commodity' (Becker 1974: 12). – which can thus enter into the calculation of mutual advantage when entering the marriage contract. Love, in the sense of bodily use, is clearly marketable, or it could not form part of the contract, and one does not have to believe that sexual pleasure is somehow inherently immoral, or that it can never on occasions be proper to seek no more than sexual pleasure, to agree with Hegel that there is something shameful about this idea of marriage. The widespread marital and non-marital use of women's bodies has led feminists to claim that 'the sexual revolution is not our revolution' (Diamond 1980: 701); it may thus seem puzzling that there is also a long history of feminist criticism of love.

Feminists have attacked love since at least 1792 when Mary Wollstonecraft stated that she would commit 'high treason against sentiment and fine feelings' by writing disrespectfully of love (Wollstonecraft 1975: 27). Feminists have strongly criticized both the marriage contract which gives the husband unlimited access to the body of his wife, and romantic love, a particular form of love, or ideology of sentiment, that helps maintain the fiction of the marriage contract and obscure the reality of the patriarchal subjection of wives. In earlier feminist critiques of marriage and love, friendship is seen as the alternative, egalitarian basis for conjugal relations. Recent writers usually refer to love rather than friendship, although it has been suggested that if marriage is seen 'non-instrumentally' then it is 'a gesture of friendship' (O'Driscoll 1977). The contemporary feminist non-romantic view of love is sketchily presented, but it has some striking similarities to the earlier idea of friendship between wife and husband. Shanley has recently argued that Mill's *Subjection of Women* is fundamentally concerned not with legal reform but 'the hope of establishing friendship in marriage' (Shanley 1981: 229). Mill's criticism of marriage displays the ambiguity characteristic of his social and political thought as a whole. If one strand of his argument suggests that marriage as a proper contract is the solution to the slavery of wives, he also offers hints of another conception of marriage. He looks to a relationship no longer based 'in the instinct of individuals for self-protection, but in a cultivated sympathy between them,' a relationship which would be a 'school of sympathy in equality, of living together in love, without power on one side and obedience on the other' (Mill 1970: 174, 175). At the end of the *Subjection,* when Mill turns to the 'ideal of marriage,' his discussion echoes Mary Wollstonecraft, for he writes of friendship, not love. A sympathetic association between the sexes will, he argues, lead to 'a real enriching of the two natures.' Mill notes that such enrichment can now occur between friends of the same sex, and in marriage, too, 'a foundation of solid friendship' could provide the basis for 'that best kind of equality, similarity of powers and capacities with reciprocal superiority in them' (Mill 1970: 234, 235).

Shanley notes that Mill's ideal does not encompass 'the possible enhancement which sexuality might add to marital friendship' (Shanley 1981: 243). Both Wollstonecraft and contemporary feminists emphasize this enhancement, but without falling back on the contractarian view of marriage as an exchange of property and use of bodies. While rejecting the corrupt emotion of romantic love, born of domination and subjection, contemporary feminists see (real) love rather as Wollstonecraft saw friendship. They argue that love is possible only between equals, and refer to the mutual enrichment and enlargement of personality which love can bring, and the mutual esteem and respect on which it is based.[14] Thus the feminist alternative to the fiction of the marriage contract is a relationship resembling Hegel's non-contractual love. It is significant that we have no word for such a relationship. 'Marriage' is too inextricably tied to the past of fiction and patriarchal subjection to be used for a sexually egalitarian partnership; I shall refer to the latter as personal association. Perhaps it does not matter in the end whether the bond constitutive of personal association is called love or friendship. (The earlier feminist theorists may have turned to 'friendship' because philosophers have traditionally claimed that women naturally lacked the capacities that would enable them to be men's friends.) Hegel's dialectic of love, which has nothing romantic about it and which includes sexual passion, is, despite his patriarchalism, a crucial source for the development of a feminist theory and practice of personal association in which the bond of love and mutuality enables two individuals to 'recognize' each other and enrich their union and individuality. However, a question remains about the creation of this bond. Perhaps, as Hegel argues, the marriage contract (its shameful past behind it) could find its rightful place as the public acknowledgment of the mutual trust, respect and love of the partners or friends; marriage would still be the contractual origin of a non-contractual association.

Beyond status and contract

Hegel claims that the marriage contract is a unique contract which transcends the practice of contracting. But why, it may be asked, introduce anything so paradoxical: why is it necessary for contract to enter into a non-contractual sphere of life? Hegel's reason for retaining the marriage contract is to ensure that individual freedom, in the sense of 'particularity', or the 'individual' aspect of individuality, finds a place in all spheres of the ethical life of the community. His attempt founders with his separation of the sexes, but it is important to draw attention to the assumption underlying his argument: that a fundamental aspect of freedom can find expression only through contract. The assumption means that personal freedom becomes bound up with contract and hence with the abstract idea of the 'individual'. Valuable dimensions of personal freedom are then interpreted in one particular way, which appears as the only plausible interpretation. Bodily integrity, control of our bodies, is central to personal autonomy, to the ability to say 'yes' and 'no' and decide for ourselves how our personal lives will be ordered, and it appears that, if this dimension of freedom is to be given its proper weight, women and men must be seen as 'individuals' and their relationships must take a contractual form. The alternative to a husband's patriarchal right to his wife's body thus appears to be the extension to women of ownership of the property in their persons. It seems that freedom necessarily entails ownership of the property in one's self and attributes, and that there are no alternative interpretations of personal autonomy; the shame of patriarchal subjection is replaced by the shame of contract and the ideology of contractarianism remains unquestioned.[15]

Attempts by critics of contract and abstract individualism to formulate a conception of the person as an essentially social being, with a developing and complex individuality, have invariably failed to break free of patriarchal assumptions, and are thus of limited assistance to feminist theorists. At best, conjugal relations and the physical reproduction of the next generation have been disregarded in discussions of freedom, autonomy and individuality. Against this theoretical background, and in the face of the many practical ways in which women have been and continue to be denied bodily integrity, the claim that women, too, own the property in their persons and thus have right of control over their bodies is of obvious importance. The crucial question, though, is whether feminism can go beyond this view and develop a non-contractarian conception of autonomy and bodily integrity. This difficult task remains to be completed, but while feminist theorists can draw upon the insights of the great critics of the standpoint of contract, a feminist conception of individuality will differ from previous formulations because it will be both egalitarian and grounded in the fact that humankind has two bodies – and only women's bodies become pregnant. In a personal association, ascription or status will no longer determine the activities of the partners, so that childrearing will cease to be the responsibility of women alone, but it does not follow that the meaning of bodily integrity and autonomy will be exactly the same for women as for men. Bodily integrity for women can never be separated from the question of physical reproduction, so that, as Petchesky has pointed out (Petchesky 1980), a tension will always exist between autonomy and mutuality.

However, it might still be argued that, even though the abstractions of the standpoint of contract have been replaced by a social conception of individuality and mutuality, personal association can still, as Hegel claims, begin in a contract. I earlier remarked upon the failure by political theorists to distinguish consent from contract, and Hegel's argument about personal freedom and contract foreshadows a much wider contemporary tendency to identify with contract the many different ways in which women and men can freely make agreements and so bind themselves into the future. It is usually assumed that contracting exemplifies such activities, which provides a clear indication of how far the movement from status to contract and the consolidation of the ideology of contractarianism have advanced. The identification of, for example, agreeing, consenting, assenting, and promising with contract systematically shuts off exploration of non-contractual conceptions of social relationships and their political significance, and identifies the social creativity of free agreement with contract. Once contract is distinguished from other ways of agreeing and making commitments, it becomes clear that there is no necessity for personal association to have its origins in a contract. On the contrary, personal association begins in a promise. A contract of mutual use or an exchange of property in bodies excludes the trust and love that are fundamental to personal association, whereas a promise presupposes fidelity. I have discussed elsewhere the way in which promising rather than contract exemplifies the social creativity made possible through the practice of free agreement,[16] and it is by making a *promise that* two autonomous, loving partners can create a new relationship between themselves that mutually binds them into the future. Their voluntary, reciprocal commitment (or obligation) is the concrete, public expression of their love. By creating a personal association they constitute the bonds of mutuality within which they can maintain and enhance their autonomy and individuality through the dialectic of love.

The creation of a personal association does not, however, take place in social abstraction, nor do women and men exist only as members of personal associations. Personal association is one dimension of social life and can be fully understood only in the context of its place in a wider communal whole (just as Hegel's conception of the family is integral to the social whole of family-civil society-state). Differentiation, individuality and mutuality within personal association reflect the wider social context of a differentiated community. The liberal conception of the property-owning 'individual' attempts to separate individuality from sociality and mutuality. The assumption underlying this attempt is that all social ties are of the same kind; all dimensions of social life are constituted by contract. In this respect, contract is not so much a movement from status as its negation or mirror image. The undifferentiated social bonds of a hierarchy of ascription are replaced by the undifferentiated, universal bond of contract. One of Hegel's profoundest insights and greatest theoretical legacies is the conception of a differentiated social order in which the various spheres of social life each rest on their own principle of association, or, to use Rawls' terminology, each has its own virtue. Love and promising are the virtues of personal association, but this is only one dimension of social life and other forms of association are grounded in their own principles or morality. Moreover, the mutuality of personal association presupposes that the social conditions exist, or are being created, that enable autonomous partners to enter into this commitment. Women and men cannot maintain their autonomy and individuality within personal associations if they are not also full and equal members of economic associations and equal citizens in political life. The transformation of marriage into feminist personal association thus presupposes, and is presupposed by, a similarly radical transformation of the patriarchal social structure of our economic and political life. The implications of this wider social transformation lie outside the scope of this essay, but a brief comment must be made about the conception of a differentiated social order.

I have argued that contract is unnecessary in personal life to give expression to autonomy and individuality. There is no need to introduce the mysteries of contracts that transcend contract. However, Hegel argues that contract is the virtue or principle of association of a specific sphere of social life; contract finds its proper place in civil society or economic life. This raises the complex (and virtually uncharted) question of what 'differentiation' involves. Must the principles of association that constitute a differentiated social order be contrasting or even opposing principles, in the manner in which love and promising stand in opposition to contract, or is it possible to have a social whole of nor-contractual, yet differentiated, principles? In *The Problem of Political Obligation* (Pateman 1979), I argued that (non-contractual) political obligation is the virtue of participatory democratic political life, and the political counterpart of promising. The non-contractual counterparts of love and mutuality are community and solidarity,[17] but the problem remains whether, if contract is rejected in personal and political life, a vital aspect of personal and collective freedom is also being rejected. Liberalism, of course, insists that contract is necessary and liberals find support today from the advocates of market socialism. The difficulty here is that little discussion is available of potential alternatives to the authoritarian structure of the command economy on the one hand, and contract, whether embodied in the capitalist or socialist market, on the other. This closure of possibilities resembles the alternatives of patriarchal subjection or contract found in discussions of the marriage contract. There is a parallel failure to recognize the significance of the critique of the standpoint of contract for the democratic restructuring of economic life, or that status, instead of being negated, might be transcended. If the argument has any force that autonomy in personal and political life can be upheld and furthered – indeed, can only be universalized – within a non-contractual association, then it does not seem implausible to suggest that a similar non-contractual alternative may be available in economic life. The major conclusion to be drawn from a critique of the shame of the marriage contract is that the theory and practice of a feminist social order lies beyond both status and contract.

Notes

1 On contract marriage see, e.g., Weitzman (1974).
2 For the argument in the text see Ketchum (1977) and Barker (1978). For a discussion of the empirical evidence on the deleterious effects of marriage for women, see Bernard (1974). Another contemporary feminist argument about the marriage contract is that it is really a labor contract through which husbands appropriate the unpaid work of their wives; see Delphy (1976).
3 In Australia, marriage celebrants now give potential spouses a leaflet, 'Marriage and You', issued by the Attorney General's Department, when they give notice of marriage. The leaflet 'tells you (1) something of what it means to be married; (2) the duties of marriage; (3) about pre-marital education…(4) about pre-marital counselling…' (I am grateful to Marian Sawer for providing me with a copy of the leaflet). Strictly, a man and woman become 'husband' and 'wife' after performing a speech act *and* having sexual intercourse. The 'marriage license' is not so much a contract as a licence from the state and/or church to have sexual intercourse and procreate. A priest recently refused to perform a marriage ceremony for a partially paralyzed man in Chicago because he was unable to have sexual intercourse; report in *Sydney Morning Herald,* 28 January 1982. See the text below for comments on the bodily integrity of wives.
4 In 1888 an American judge stated that 'when the contracting parties have entered into the married state, they have not so much entered into a contract as into a new relation, the rights, duties and obligations of which rest not upon their agreement, but on the general law of the State…it was of contract that the relation should be established, but being established, the power of the parties as to its extent or duration is at an end' (McWalter 1973: 608).
5 In the seventeenth century 'contract seems to have been used more as a formal explanation of how people entered relationships than as a definition of the nature and content of these stations' (Schochet 1975: 82).
6 The distinction between contract and consent, and its relevance for social contract theory and arguments about political obligation, is explored in detail in Pateman (1979).
7 The question of women and consent is discussed in more detail in Pateman (1980).
8 On this agreement see Brennan and Pateman (1979).
9 Social beliefs about the proper status of women are also well illustrated by the fact that in November 1979 in Dublin it was still possible for a husband to sue successfully for damages under the law of 'criminal conversation' if his wife committed adultery. Report in *New Statesman,* 2 May 1980.
10 My comments in this paragraph have benefited from Mill (1979).
11 For the argument that this is the paradigmatic form of exchange in liberalism, see Pateman (1979).
12 On the advice manuals see Ross (1980); also Ehrenreich and English (1978).
13 Cited in Ehrenreich and English (1978: 276; from Newberger and Lee (1975)). Another writer comments: 'How better to alienate individuals from their identities than to treat them as business associates in a contract entered into exclusively on the basis of benefits received – entered into solely to enhance the private interests of the contracting parties…The real point of the modern marriage contract is to anticipate and provide for divorce…' Barber (1975: 62–63).
14 See, for example, Greer (1971: esp. 139–245); and Firestone (1971: chs 6 and 7); compare de Beauvoir 1972: part VI, sect. 2).
15 One consequence of the view that women have a property in their persons and bodies is that their right to sell their bodies in the market is established. I have criticized a contractarian defence of prostitution in Pateman (1983).

16 Promising and its creative potential is discussed in detail in Pateman (1979: chs. 1 and 2). There are circumstances in which promises, though binding, may justifiably be broken. Similarly, there will be circumstances in which personal associations will be dissolved. It does not seem fruitful to advocate greater legal, or state, impediments to ensure a longer-lasting (reformed) marriage as Barber (1975: 143–44) suggests.

17 Solidarity is not precisely right, since it is extremely doubtful if 'solidarity', 'comradeship' and similar terms include women. Women are usually auxiliaries to the male comrades and spectators of their solidarity. That it is so hard to find political concepts that encompass both sexes reflects the masculine character of the political itself, analyzed by Nancy Hartsock in Stiehm (1984: 123–50).

References

Barber, B. 1975. *Liberating Feminism*. New York: The Seabury Press.

Barker, D.L. 1978. 'The Regulation of Marriage: Repressive Benevolence'. In G. Littlejohn, B. Smart, J. Wakeford and N. Yuval-Davis (eds) *Power and the* State. London: Croom Helm.

Bernard, J. 1974. *The Future of Marriage*. New York: Bantam Books.

Brennan, T. and C. Pateman 1979. '"Mere Auxiliaries to the Commonwealth": Women and the Origins of Liberalism'. *Political Studies* 27(2): 183–200.

Delphy, C. 1976. 'Continuities and Discontinuities in Marriage and Divorce'. In D.L. Barker and S. Allen (eds) *Sexual Divisions and Society*. London: Tavistock, London.

Diamond, I. 1980. 'Pornography and Repression: A Reconsideration'. *Signs* 5(4): 686–701.

Ehrenreich, B. and D. English. 1978. *For Her Own Good: 150 Years of the Experts' Advice to Women*. New York: Anchor Press.

Gauthier, D. 1977. 'The Social Contract as Ideology'. *Philosophy and Public Affairs* 6(2): 130–64.

Hegel, G.W.F. 1952. *Philosophy of Right*. Trans. T.M. Knox. Oxford: Oxford University Press.

Kant, I. 1887. *The Philosophy of Law*. Trans. W. Hastie. Edinburgh: T & T Clark.

Ketchum, S.A. 1977. 'Liberalism and Marriage Law'. In M. Vetterling-Braggin, F.A. Elliston and J. English (eds) *Feminism and Philosophy*. Adams, NJ: Littlefield.

Locke, J. 1967. 'Second Treatise of Government'. In P. Laslett (ed.) *Two Treatises of Government*. Cambridge: Cambridge University Press.

McWalter, K.G. 1973. 'Marriage as a Contract: Towards a Functional Definition of the Marital Status'. *Columbia Journal of Law and Social Problems* 9.

Mill, J.S. 1970. 'The Subjection of Women'. In J.S. Mill and H. Taylor (eds) *Essays on Sex Equality*. Chicago: University of Chicago Press.

Mill, P.J. 1979. 'Hegel and 'the Woman Question': Recognition and Intersubjectivity'. In L. Clark and L. Lange (eds) *The Sexism of Social and Political Theory*. Toronto: University of Toronto Press.

Newberger, H. and M. Lee. 1975. *Winners and Losers*. New York: Signet.

O'Driscoll, L. 1977. 'On the Nature and Value of Marriage'. In Vetterling-Braggin, M., F.A. Elliston and J. English (eds) *Feminism and Philosophy*. Adams, NJ: Littlefield.

Pateman, C. 1979. *The Problem of Political Obligation: A Critique of Liberal Theory*. Chichester: Wiley.

— 1980. 'Women and Consent'. *Political Theory* 7(2): 149–68.

— 1983. 'Defending Prostitution: Charges Against Ericcson'. *Ethics* 93(3): 561–65.

Petchesky, R.P. 1980. 'Reproductive Freedom: Beyond "A Woman's Right to Choose"'. *Signs* 5(4): 661–85.

Rich, A. 1980. 'Compulsory Heterosexuality and Lesbian Existence'. *Signs* 5(4): 631–60.

Ross, E. 1980. '"The Love Crisis": Couples Advice Books of the Late 1970s'. *Signs* 6(1): 109–22.

Schochet, G.J. 1975. *Patriarchalism in Political Thought*. Oxford: Blackwell.

Shanley, M. 1979. 'Marriage Contract and Social Contract in Seventeenth Century English Political Thought'. *Western Political Quarterly* 32(1): 79–91.

Shanley, M.L. 1981. 'Marital Slavery and Friendship: John Stuart Mill's *The Subjection of Women*'. *Political Theory* 9(2): 229–47.

J. Stiehm (ed.) 1984. *Women's Views of the Political World of Men*. New York: Transnational.

Thompson, W. 1970. *Appeal of One Half the Human Race, Women, Against the Pretensions of the Other Half, Man, to Retain them in Political, and Thence in Civil and Domestic, Slavery*. New York: Source Book Press; originally published 1825.

Weitzman, L. 1974. 'Legal Regulation of Marriage: Tradition and Change'. *California Law Review* 62: 1249–78.

Wollstonecraft, M. 1975. *A Vindication of the Rights of Women*. New York: Norton.

7
SEX AND POWER (1990)

Catherine MacKinnon is one of the most controversial feminist theorists writing at present. Both her arguments and her campaign against pornography arouse strong feelings. MacKinnon's sharp sallies, barbed aphorisms, and engaged, sometimes passionate, but important and thought-provoking arguments in *Feminism Unmodified* will add plenty of fuel to the flames. Some of her arrows are directed at feminists, in particular those who occupy positions of influence in law or universities but who 'collaborate' in women's subjection (1987: ch. 15). The book contains sixteen speeches delivered between 1981 and 1986, together with an introduction and afterword. Many of the speeches, MacKinnon states, are published in the form in which they were delivered, and occasionally interjections from the audience are included; there is an immediacy about the prose not often encountered in political philosophy or jurisprudence. There are seventy-five pages of footnotes and references to legal cases.

In the introduction, MacKinnon singles out three themes that unify the book: sexuality, gender, and pornography. Six chapters of *Feminism Unmodified* are devoted to pornography, and MacKinnon also refers to it throughout the book. She also discusses the question of equality and difference, currently a subject of intense debate among feminists; launches a vigorous attack on liberal approaches to law and feminism and the associated conceptions of objectivity, universality, gender neutrality, and privacy; and presents some firm views on epistemology and the character of feminist theory. There are also chapters on a case brought by a Native American woman against her tribe and on women and sport.

The title of the book reflects MacKinnon's rejection of feminism that is modified by additions such as 'liberal' or 'socialist'. Feminism is frequently divided into liberal, socialist (or Marxist), and radical varieties. Such classifications are more misleading than helpful in current political conditions, but, more important, the modifiers imply that feminism cannot stand alone and is always dependent on another theory for a mode of inquiry and major arguments. As MacKinnon noted in one of two earlier papers (the argument of these is drawn on and amplified at various points in *Feminism Unmodified*) feminism is often seen 'not as a systematic analysis but as a loose collection of factors, complaints, and which are merely descriptive of women's misfortunes (MacKinnon 1982: 528; 1983). Part of MacKinnon's aim in the book is to show that feminism – unmodified – is a powerful explanatory political theory in its own right. A properly feminist theory must be unmodified because other political theories repress or ignore the problem addressed by feminism – the political problem of men's power over women. Modified feminism, reliant upon the very theories that systematically obscure the problem of men's power, must be replaced by what MacKinnon calls 'the dominance approach' (1987: 40).

I share MacKinnon's view of the distinctive contribution of feminist theory. Contemporary feminism has revealed a problem that was once discussed in political theory – in the pages of the social contract theorists, for example, or by the so-called utopian socialists – but that is now treated by mainstream political theorists as falling outside their proper concerns. The prevailing assumption is that the relation between the sexes is a matter of nature and irrelevant to politics. The claim that men exercise jurisdiction over women by virtue of their natural capacities, as a consequence of the natural difference between the sexes, was advanced by the contract theorists in order to head off the revolutionary implications for sexual relations of the doctrine of natural freedom and equality. Men's domination of women was thus placed outside the criticism and controversy that surrounded the justification of other forms of rule.[1]

Ironically, this exclusion, which began as an explicitly political strategy, is now accepted by contemporary theorists as a valid limitation on the scope of political inquiry. They do not, therefore, ask any questions about why the characters of women and men are seen in a specific manner, or question the construction of the difference between the sexes as the political difference between freedom and equality (for men) and subjection (for women). Men's power over women is precisely the problem with which feminism has been concerned since the late seventeenth century, but feminist writers have never been included in the canon of political theory, and feminists today are only slowly recovering the tradition of feminist thought. MacKinnon's insistence that feminism deals with a specific problem, through an approach distinct from other political theories, is thus welcome. Her elaboration of unmodified feminism is not, however, without some fundamental difficulties.

The difficulties become apparent in MacKinnon's discussion of the seemingly irresolvable dilemma about equality and difference. The standard view sees the issue as one of sameness and difference between the sexes: either men and women share a common humanity (they are the same, therefore equal) so that laws and institutions should be gender neutral; or women's difference from men requires laws and institutions that recognize that women need special treatment or protection (they are not the same, or equal). Such an approach, as MacKinnon points out, requires a standard or yardstick against which equality can be measured, so that those who are equal (the same) can be treated in the same fashion; problems of classification and discrimination thus predominate. The familiar difficulty then arises that equality, universality, and neutrality, or the absence of discrimination, quickly come into conflict with efforts to promote equality for groups of people, for example, women. The special classification required and the special (different) treatment demanded to foster equality for a whole category of individuals can only appear from this perspective as discrimination and as antithetical to equality.

But the problems go deeper than this. Feminists, including MacKinnon, have observed that the standard for equality between the sexes is made in the male image. Ostensibly gender neutral laws and policies implicitly embody a masculine standard against which women are measured. At the beginning of the modern period, political and civil 'equality' was constructed as a relationship between men, between the 'individuals' who possessed the natural capacities to enjoy this standing in public life. After all, women are the 'different' sex, not men. The question is always that of women's equality with men (the standard) and, since women, who are different from men, are involved, the problem of equality versus difference – protection, special treatment, discrimination – will therefore arise over and over again.

Special or protective treatment for women has long been a vexed question within feminism, but only since the 1970s, with the advent of 'gender neutral' legislation, have the problems with equality become fully clear. They have been revealed with particular clarity in the United States, where individualism of a singularly radical, asocial character, fosters the assumption that any acknowledgment at all of women's difference from men is inimical to equality (the sameness of individuals). For example, MacKinnon cites the curious legal contortions in the United States over pregnancy and women workers. Men cannot become pregnant, but can equality be maintained if women's difference in this respect is recognized in legislation? The American Civil Liberties Union argued against provisions for maternity leave and subsequent job security on the grounds that this penalized male workers, gave pregnant women 'rights not enjoyed by other workers', and so caused hostility (1987: 242, n. 18). But 'other workers' that is, men, do not become pregnant, so there seems no way out of the equality/difference dilemma.

MacKinnon argues that to see the problem as one of equality and difference is a fundamental mistake. First, she argues that *inequality,* the power that men exercise over women, not equality is the issue for women. Second, MacKinnon denies that sexual difference is the problem. She criticizes both those who assume that sexual difference is a matter of nature so that the meaning of manhood and womanhood can be determined by direct scrutiny of natural or biological characteristics, and those who appeal for a reevaluation of difference, of women's different voice and women's special attributes and tasks. She argues that there is no natural difference between men and women that lies repressed beneath existing social relations or that requires reevaluation. There is only power. 'Men' and 'women', 'sex' and 'sexuality', as these terms are presently understood, are brought into being through men's domination of women. 'There would be no such thing as what we know as the sex difference – much less would it be the social issue it is or have the social meaning it has – were it not for male dominance' (1987: 51).

MacKinnon's solution to the dilemma of equality and difference is, therefore, to deny that either term is relevant. At this crucial point, however, MacKinnon's argument lacks historical depth and an appreciation of the paradoxes and contradictions of women's position. To be sure, few discussions of equality take account of the structure of inequality of sexual relations, but that is not to say that women's position can be understood without recognizing that women are both equal and subordinate, both free and subject, both citizens and yet not citizens in the same way as men. By dismissing both equality and difference, MacKinnon is unable to ask any questions about the relationship between these two categories and how they have been constructed as opposites.

Equality and difference are not necessarily opposed, but, historically, this is how the categories have developed. Thus, any acknowledgment of women's bodily difference from men can only appear as an attempt to pull back into the sphere of equality matters that equality must exclude. At best, from within the existing construction of the categories, recognition of difference can be seen as an exception, as 'special' treatment or 'protection' but not as part of equality. A consideration of how the problem of men's power emerged and was repressed in modern political theory indicates that the meanings of equality and difference are mutually dependent. Men's equality depends upon the political significance accorded to sexual (women's) difference. Women's bodies are such that they lack the attributes of the equals who can participate in public life; yet, at the same time, women's political incorporation has also been determined by that bodily sexual difference – as much of MacKinnon's discussion illustrates. The question has never been whether sexual difference is politically relevant but, rather, how that difference is to be given political expression.

Indeed, the claim that sexual difference is nothing more than an artifact of men's power sits very oddly with much of the discussion of *Feminism Unmodified*. MacKinnon's major claim, which distinguishes her position from many other feminist approaches, is that what is at issue in the present structure of social relations is *sexual* subordination. It is sex and sexuality – sexual power – and not, as many other feminists have argued, reproduction, or mothering, or domestic labor, or men's control of women's labor power, or the law of the father, that lies at the center of women's subordination. MacKinnon's insistence that women's subordination to men is different from the subjection of other groups or categories of people because it is sexual in character is the most important contribution of *Feminism Unmodified*. The cornerstone of men's claim to jurisdiction over women is that they have right of sexual access to women's bodies. This is, I have argued, the right established through the (story of the) sexual contract at the same time that the right of jurisdiction by the state over individual citizens is established through the social contract. But it does not follow that sexual difference is nothing more than an artifact of men's domination of women.

MacKinnon may not have argued in this fashion if she had not used the now ubiquitous terminology of 'sex' and 'gender'. 'Gender' was introduced by feminists to combat the patriarchal claim that nature has decreed women's place. 'Sex' was declared the province of nature, of biology, of physiology, and bodily differences between women and men. 'Sex', or the natural male and female forms, was separated from 'gender', or the social constructions and meanings that constitute the masculinity and femininity of 'individuals'. There were good political reasons for such a terminological strategy in the early days of the revival of the organized feminist movement in the late 1960s, and the assumption underlying the sex/gender distinction, that the body is socially and politically neutral, fits in with the language of 'sex roles' of the period. These roles were assumed to be entirely conventional, determined by 'socialization' or education; that is to say, they were the roles of genders, not embodied sexes, and feminism could hold out the promise of education and social reform that would lead to a gender neutral world.

The fundamental problem with this language is that the body is not politically neutral or neuter. Humankind has two bodies – and the bodies of women and men have very different social and political significance. Men do not exercise power as, or over, a 'gender', but over embodied women; men, as MacKinnon argues, exercise power as a sex, and wield sexual power. This is not to say that what it is to be a man or woman is derived from some essential, timeless facts of nature. Nature, bodies, biology, sex, always have a social and political meaning; but, at the same time, human beings share natural bodies with the animals, subject to the natural processes of birth, growth (appropriate to their sex), and death. The implicit assumption of arguments about 'gender' is that sex (nature) is infinitely malleable, that it poses no limits, so that 'gender' can be anything at all, or nothing at all, if we so desire. In short, it is an argument about the conquest of nature. Many feminists have become increasingly anxious about the implications for women of men's project to conquer nature, especially since the development of the new reproductive technologies. But there are few signs yet of the necessary rethinking of the sex/gender dichotomy, although many other elements of the series of oppositions that express the division between nature and civilization (such as private/public, emotion/reason, love/justice, difference/equality, feminine/masculine) have come under feminist scrutiny.

MacKinnon's use of 'sex' and 'gender' is exceedingly confusing. She states, for example, that from the perspective of the dominance approach, 'the only real question is what is and is not a gender question' (1987: 43), that gender is only 'ascriptively' tied to bodies (1987: 234, n. 26), and that the social meaning of difference is 'gender-based' (1987: 51). Yet she also says that she uses 'sex and gender relatively interchangeably' (1987: 263, n. 5). The confusion is not surprising when MacKinnon's major thesis, that men's power is sexual power, makes little sense translated into 'gender'. For example, maternity leave is an issue because only women become pregnant and they do so as a result of sexual intercourse with men. Again, MacKinnon notes that not all men, all the time, have power. Sometimes men are used sexually by other men as if they were women. Typically these are young boys or men in prison, that is, men who, by virtue of their youth or incarceration lack power. Yet, as MacKinnon states, even men in such a position do not 'experience or share the meaning of being a woman' (1987: 234, n. 26). They remain men. They experience their violation as embodied men, with all that the embodiment entails for their political position as a sex.

Consider, too, MacKinnon's discussion of abortion. She notes that the Playboy Foundation has always provided funds to support abortion rights, and she argues that the reason is that abortion sets up an 'equality' between men and women. Here, the language of 'gender' comes into play: abortion can be seen as an attempt to render sexual difference irrelevant in the name of gender equality. Women can engage in sexual activity in exactly the same way as men without having to take account of the (natural) consequence, pregnancy, that can ensue for the gender who happen to have women's bodies. Such gender equality means that there is no good reason for one gender to refuse the sexual advances of the other – hence Playboy's interest in abortion. MacKinnon's argument about abortion, however, is about sex and sexual power. She argues that virtually everyone involved in the controversies over abortion, activists and philosophers alike, have ignored the fact that sexual intercourse precedes pregnancy. The relations between women and men within which intercourse takes place are, therefore, also ignored.

Under conditions of men's domination, MacKinnon argues, abortion 'facilitates women's heterosexual availability' and 'frees male sexual aggression' (1987: 99). Abortion can make it all the harder for women's refusal of consent to be treated seriously, but this is not to say, as MacKinnon's statements imply, that abortion in itself 'frees' men's aggression. The incidence of backyard abortions suggests that much the same problem about consent existed when abortion was illegal. MacKinnon also exaggerates by claiming that 'virtually every ounce of control' that women have gained from legal reform 'has gone directly into the hands of men – husbands, doctors, or fathers' (1987: 101). If men have exclusive control over (legal) abortion and if it redounds to their sexual advantage, then there would seem to be no reason why abortion should be so controversial, or why, as MacKinnon emphasizes, its legal status should be so insecure and under constant attack.

That legal reforms are under threat has been clearly demonstrated since MacKinnon made these speeches. *Roe v. Wade,* the case which legalized abortion in the United States, has not yet been attacked directly, but in July 1989 the Supreme Court opened the way for state legislatures to restrict women's access to abortion (and so encouraged anti-abortionists elsewhere to increase their pressure for similar restrictions). In a majority verdict, the Court upheld as constitutional a Missouri act which prohibits the use of public facilities for, and participation of public employees in, abortions. In an argument that reaffirmed what has usually been the case – that money is what counts for access to safe abortions – the Court stated that the restriction was merely upon 'a woman's ability to obtain an abortion to the extent that she chooses to use a physician affiliated with a public hospital'.[2] Abortion might thus seem to be a matter that political philosophers should consider in their long controversy about whether or not the provision of public facilities and welfare is required if the worth and dignity of democratic citizenship is to be upheld. Yet abortion is rarely discussed in this way. Indeed in the United States, far from any connection being drawn between access to abortion and women's standing as citizens, the ruling in *Roe v. Wade* was that legal prohibition of abortion violated the constitutional right to privacy.

Privacy, MacKinnon states, includes protection against unwarranted governmental intrusion into 'individual bodily integrity, personal exercise of moral intelligence, and freedom of intimacy' (1987: 97). MacKinnon asks whether the privacy doctrine actually applies to women. Her conclusion is that it does not; 'privacy' in this context means the protection of men's right of sexual access to women's bodies, whether or not in any instance the woman consents. For two decades feminists have drawn attention to the many ways in which the separation of 'private' life from the 'public' world has denied women right of protection and bodily integrity, and how, at the same time, government and the law have reached across into the privacy of the home to uphold men's power and privilege as a sex. 'Privacy' for women, as MacKinnon stresses, means something different than it does for men. A defense of abortion in terms of privacy avoids the question whether enforced motherhood is a matter not of privacy but of public citizenship. Feminists might ask how it is, when enforced labor was long ago deemed incompatible with free democratic citizenship, that so many popular and official voices see no contradiction between the enforced labor of motherhood and women's standing and dignity as citizens.

MacKinnon's arguments will appear most peculiarly American to readers in other countries in her extensive discussion of pornography. In Australia and Britain, for example, feminists are certainly critical of pornography, but the subject has neither been as central to feminist concerns nor aroused the passions and divisions among feminists that it has in the United States. One reason for this difference is undoubtedly that only the United States has the First Amendment, and only there has pornography been defended so strongly on the grounds of free speech. Another reason, exemplified in MacKinnon's speeches, is that American feminists have been much more willing to insist that pornography is a major, or even the major, *causal* factor in women's subordination than have British or Australian feminists. The latter are less likely to see pornography as an independent causal factor than as one part of a wider sex industry that reflects and reinforces a structure of masculine power.

MacKinnon argues that pornography, when seen from a feminist perspective, allows us to understand the meaning of sex and sexuality in a system of male dominance. In pornography, domination, submission, force, and violence are eroticized. 'Sex' is eroticized domination. The sex portrayed in pornography is not merely deviant or perverted, but an exposure of the reality of the structure of sexual relations. 'Sex' is usually assumed to be consensual. Thus, when pornography depicts coercion, the assumption is that it is not about sex but violence. MacKinnon vigorously contests the comfortable belief that sex can be sharply demarcated from coercion, force, and violence. This is another valuable aspect of her argument. The separation between freedom and submission becomes difficult to sustain once sexual relations cease to be parceled out into discrete boxes, with 'sex,' that is, consensual intercourse, in a box of its own and rape, prostitution, pornography, and the rest also neatly boxed away and declared to be different from 'sex'. Once the relationship between all these features of sexual life is considered, the place of consent in any meaningful sense (i.e., a sense which recognizes women's right to refuse men sexual access) becomes increasingly hard to discern.

MacKinnon argues that pornography, together with rape, sexual harassment, and other forms of sexual abuse of women, 'form a distinctive pattern: the power of men over women in society' (1987: 5). She repeats a series of facts in several speeches: 44 percent of American women have been raped or faced an attempted rape; 43 percent of girls under eighteen have been sexually abused; 85 percent of working women report being sexually harassed during their working lives; between 60 and 70 percent of murdered women were killed by a husband, lover, or ex-lover. Such matters are not easy to quantify, but it is not the precise percentages that are so important for MacKinnon's argument as the fact, now confirmed by a large body of empirical evidence from the Anglo-American countries, that very large numbers of sexual assaults by men against women occur every year.

Political theorists and moral philosophers place very high value on consent as a constitutive principle of democracy, but there is remarkably little discussion in the mainstream literature about the significance of such facts for consent and, hence, for women's standing as citizens. Or, indeed, about the fact that, in Britain, husbands still retain the legal right to rape their wives.[3] Empirical evidence shows that the courts, as well as men in general, have great difficulty in distinguishing enforced submission from consent.[4] Judges sometimes make very plain that what 'sex' means is the right of men to sexual access to women, irrespective of consent. In a recent case in Britain, for example, a judge merely placed on probation a man who sexually assaulted his mentally retarded twelve-year-old step-daughter, because, the judge said, his wife's pregnancy led 'to a lack of sexual appetite in the lady, and considerable problems for a healthy young husband.'[5] Nor is the demand that women's bodies should be on sale as commodities in the capitalist market seen as peculiar or problematic in itself (the problem is invariably seen as a question of the psychology of the prostitute).

MacKinnon also presents a threefold argument against the view that pornography is merely an example of free speech. First, she criticizes the claim that pornography is comparable to the expression of minority opinion. Pornography is a huge business; MacKinnon cites a figure of eight billion dollars per year. If the worldwide sex industry, including prostitution, sex tours, and so forth, were taken into account the scale of this branch of capitalism is clearly vast. Second, MacKinnon argues that what is at issue in pornography is not speech but silence. The framers of the First Amendment, she argues, assumed that free speech existed. Their concern was to prevent governmental infringment of this right. But men's and women's speech is not equally free. Men's speech is authoritative and women's words are discounted; women have been silenced. But this is hardly so true as it once was, and women have never been completely silenced. Feminists in the nineteenth century were well aware of the problem of sexual abuse, but their words were not sufficient to ensure that 'wife torture,' as they sometimes called one aspect of the question, was treated as a real, serious problem. Since the current revival of the women's movement, women have begun to gain a wider hearing about rape and other forms of assault, even if there is a very long way to go. Still, MacKinnon rightly emphasizes that women's speech is not extended through pornography, which both literally and figuratively portrays women as either unable to speak or in no need of speech, except for the word 'yes'.

MacKinnon's third argument attacks the view that pornography is harmless and, therefore, deserves all the legal protection accorded to freedom of speech. Speech that causes harm is usually excluded from protection. MacKinnon begins by taking issue with the liberal interpretation of the First Amendment that separates words and pictures from action and then claims that only the latter can inflict harm. One example she gives is of a sign saying 'whites only'; she asks 'is that the idea or the practice of segregation?' (1987: 156), and certainly there are many performative utterances which are actions through the medium of words. MacKinnon argues that pornography is an act, repeated over and over again. She states, for example, that 'male power makes authoritative a way of seeing and treating women, so that when a man looks at a pornographic picture…the *viewing* is an *act,* an act of male supremacy' (1987: 130). Or again, pornography is the 'quintessential social act' in a system of male dominance (1987: 154). But however pornography is character-ized, as speech or action, the crucial question is whether it is harmful. The general view seems to be that it is not – unpleasant perhaps, or distasteful, but not harmful.

MacKinnon's reply is that conventional approaches to pornography cannot find the harm because they always look in the wrong place. When pornography is seen as a question of the application of an abstract, politically neutral definition of obscenity, or as a question of the morality of the portrayal of sexual activity, then no harm can be discerned. The harm only becomes apparent when pornography is seen as a problem about political power and the portrayal of the sexual assault of *women*. MacKinnon refers to at least three different ways in which pornography harms women. The first is the least contentious; evidence from criminal cases shows that some assaults are directly prompted by pornography (and – for what this kind of thing is worth – laboratory experiments have shown that men's attitudes to women change for the worse through exposure to pornography). The second form of harm is that real women have been photographed to make pornographic pictures and films, and they are sometimes physically forced to perform the acts, or, more indirectly, economic coercion is involved since the sex industry pays bet-ter wages than most occupations open to women. The women are harmed twice over: through their coercion and through their bodily involvement and subsequent representation of their sexual degradation.

The third example of harm is the most controversial: pornography causes harm to all women because it is the cause of the sex difference. Pornography, MacKinnon states, 'turns sex inequality into sexuality and turns male dominance into the sex difference' (1987: 3), and 'pornography institutionalizes the sexuality of male supremacy' (1987: 148). I have already criticized MacKinnon's argument that the sex difference is merely an artifact of power, and I do not find her argument convincing when the power is held to be that of the pornographer. MacKinnon refers to the need for a new theory of social causality, but two decades of feminist theorizing have provided some adequate means to understand pornography. The really difficult problem is achieving the social change necessary to create freedom for women. At one point MacKinnon dismisses critics who argue that women's subjection predates pornography, so pornography cannot be the cause, by accusing them of believing that any action against pornography will be of no assistance to women. They need believe no such thing.

Fully to understand how pornography harms women, an understanding is also required of the social, economic, and intellectual changes that aided the transformation of the private collections of the upper classes and the furtive trade in 'dirty books' (or postcards) into 'porn', into part of the worldwide mass marketing of sex, that is, women, as a capitalist commodity. MacKinnon says nothing about how pornography has become such a major industry in recent years. The sex industry could not have developed if the meaning of sexual difference had not already been established as the political difference between men's freedom and women's subjection, and 'sex' had not already meant men's mastery. I have tried to chart some of the most important elements in the development of these meanings in Pateman (1988). Pornography is now a major mechanism through which these meanings are reinforced and transformed in their contemporary guises.

Some of MacKinnon's statements suggest that she is concerned with meaning rather than cause. For instance, she says that 'the way pornography produces its meaning constructs and defines men and women as such' (1987: 173). Or consider her claim that the fundamental question is 'the mechanism of social causation by which pornography *constructs* women and sex, defines what 'woman' means and what sexuality is, in terms of each other' (1987: 161); or, 'pornography codes how to look at women, so you know what you can do with one when you see one' (1987: 173). And, in pornography, what men can do when they have one of us has no limits. Women are represented as freely available for sexual use, whether or not they are willing, and violence, degradation, and humiliation are represented as sex; the meaning of womanhood is proclaimed to be sexual submission. MacKinnon notes that, at heart, none of us believes that the woman represented in pornography is ourselves; sadly, she is. The emergence of the sex industry and the representation of sex as women's (enforced) submission is a major obstacle to women's autonomy, political equality, and citizenship. Perhaps, as MacKinnon says, opening up the graphic portrayal of the sexual subjection of women to public scrutiny is a mistake. One can only hope so.

Some feminists have accused those hostile to pornography of being 'antisex'. The same accusation was made in the past against feminists concerned about the character of sexual relations, especially if they saw chastity as the only way for women to maintain their freedom and integrity. The charge is curiously misplaced. The feminist critics are not against sexual enjoyment; on the contrary, their goal is a structure of relations within which women can freely and autonomously enter into consensual sexual activity. They wish to see a society in which women can withhold as well as give consent and in which enforced submission is seen as a crime not 'sex'. The problem remains of how to undermine the representation of women (sex) in pornography. Some feminists have turned to arson against pornography stores, and much has been written, many speeches made, and gatherings held. MacKinnon has made a very controversial attempt to provide a legal remedy in the ordinance that she and Andrea Dworkin drafted for the city of Minneapolis. The ordinance, which treated pornography as a violation of women's civil rights and allowed (civil) action by victims and against trafficking, is discussed and defended in *Feminism Unmodified,* and copious legal citations are provided. In Australia, customs regulations have been used to prohibit imports of the most sadistic material and pornography involving children. Use of law, of course, brings its own problems, such as black markets, smuggling, and the well-known problems of defining 'pornography', but perhaps the law is a necessary recourse for women given the scale of the industry.

MacKinnon's book is lively, very provocative and, by and large, easy to read, although I would no doubt have followed some sentences more easily as a member of the audience when the speeches were delivered than as a reader ('pornographed' [1987: 128] is an unnecessary addition to the language). MacKinnon concentrates relentlessly on some unpleasant facts about power and sexual relations, facts which do not usually figure very largely in philosophical discussions. But anyone concerned about freedom, justice, equality, and democracy needs to think very hard about those facts and MacKinnon's powerful speeches.

Notes

1 These questions are discussed in Pateman 1988; 1989a; Pateman and Shanley 1991.
2 Excerpted from the U.S. Supreme Court decision as quoted in the *New York Times* 4 July 1989.
3 Criminalised in the UK only in 1991 (TC and SAC, eds).
4 See, e.g., Estrich (1987); Pateman (1980; 1989b); MacKinnon (1983) discusses consent.
5 Shyama Perera, 'Mackay Orders Abuse Case Report', *Guardian,* 1 December 1988.

References

Estrich, S. 1987. *Real Rape.* Cambridge, MA: Harvard University Press.

MacKinnon, C.A. 1982. 'Feminism, Marxism, Method, and the State: An Agenda for Theory'. *Signs: Journal of Women in Culture and Society* 7: 515–44.

— 1983. 'Feminism, Marxism, Method, and the State: Toward Feminist Jurisprudence'. *Signs:* 635–58.

— 1987. *Feminism Unmodified: Discourses on Life and Law.* Cambridge, MA: Harvard University Press.

Pateman, C. 1980. 'Women and Consent'. *Political Theory* 8: 149–68.

— 1988. *The Sexual Contract.* Cambridge: Polity.

— 1989a. '"God Hath Ordained to Man a Helper": Hobbes, Patriarchy and Conjugal Right'. *British Journal of Political Science* 19: 445–63.

— 1989b. *The Disorder of Women: Democracy, Feminism and Political Theory.* Cambridge: Polity Press.

Pateman, C. and M.L. Shanley (eds). 1991. *Feminist Interpretations and Political Theory.* Cambridge: Polity.

8

EQUALITY, DIFFERENCE, SUBORDINATION

The politics of motherhood and women's citizenship (1992)

The feminist movement and feminist scholarship are frequently seen as divided between the advocates of equality on the one side and the advocates of sexual difference on the other. Some feminists are presented as demanding equality in the sense of the identical treatment of women and men, and others as demanding that the distinctive characteristics and activities of women should be given special consideration, and it appears that women are forced to choose, and have always been forced to choose, between the two. As Joan Scott has commented:

> When equality and difference are paired dichotomously, they structure an impossible choice. If one opts for equality, one is forced to accept the notion that difference is antithetical to it. If one opts for difference, one admits that equality in unattainable.
>
> (Scott 1988: 172)

This perception of the relation between 'equality' and 'difference' is not unique to the United States; but an extremely individualist political culture combined for long periods with a conservative Supreme Court has meant that a choice between equality and difference is often posed more sharply than in, say, Britain or Australia. One of the most recent examples is the verdict in the *Sears* case, in which the claim of the Equal Employment Opportunity Commission that a preponderance of men employed in commission sales resulted from discrimination against women workers was rejected in favour of the argument of Sears, Roebuck that this was the consequence of differences in the interests and voluntary choices of women and men.[1]

A common interpretation of the history of women's struggle for citizenship, and especially for the suffrage, is that it was simply a campaign for equality, for the 'rights of men and citizens' to be extended to women. This view misunderstands the way in which our predecessors fought for citizenship. From at least 1792, when

Mary Wollstonecraft's *A Vindication of the Rights of Woman* was published, women have demanded both equal civil and political rights, and that their difference from men should be acknowledged in their citizenship. Most suffragists, for example, argued that womanhood suffrage was required as a matter of justice and to make government by consent a reality, and also that the distinctive contribution that they could make to political life as women was a major reason why they should be enfranchised. A rift in the feminist movement opened up in the inter-war years in the United States and Great Britain over the question of protective legislation for women workers and welfare measures for mothers and children; supporters of the Equal Rights Amendment and 'equal rights' were arrayed on the one side and the advocates of social reform and the New Feminists on the other. The rift was very real and the controversy sometimes heated. Nevertheless, positions on both sides were not as clear cut as the simple opposition between 'equality' and 'difference' suggests. Indeed, it is often overlooked that since all those involved had supported women's suffrage, the argument was carried on against the background of unanimous support for one very important aspect of 'equality'.

Nor was there a clear division between working-class proponents of 'difference' and 'protection' and middle-class demands for 'equal rights'. Some women workers in Britain opposed protective legislation because it excluded women from various areas of employment, and some women trade unionists and women workers supported the National Women's Party (NWP) which led the fight for the ERA in the United States. Moreover, the NWP insisted that it was not against protective legislation if it applied to both sexes; and its leader, Alice Paul, stated, for example, that women were 'the peace-loving half of the world and the home-making half of the world' (cited in Bacchi 1990: 45). In Britain, 'equality' feminists in the Open Door Council also supported protective legislation that applied to men and women, and were in favour of maternity benefits for women workers (Smith 1990). From the other side, members of the Women's Bureau in the United States, who opposed the ERA, tried to secure equal-pay legislation, and the New Feminists in Britain saw family allowances as a means to reduce a wife's dependency on her husband, that is, as a means of increasing 'equality'. Blurring the opposition even further, the Six Point Group demanded, 'alongside equal pay, that "[T]he economic value of the work of women in the home must be recognized"' (cited in Bacchi 1990: 66).

These examples should be sufficient to indicate that even when 'equality' and 'difference' have been associated with two wings of the feminist movement, the politics of the feminist movement is a good deal more complex than is often suggested. I want to investigate, in an exploratory fashion, another aspect of this complexity: what I shall call the politics of motherhood. The fact that only women have the capacity to become pregnant, give birth and suckle their infants is the mark of 'difference' *par excellence*. Childbirth and motherhood have symbolized the natural capacities that set women apart from politics and citizenship; motherhood and citizenship, in this perspective, like difference and equality, are mutually exclusive. But if 'motherhood' represents all that excluded women from citizenship, motherhood has also been constructed as a political status. Motherhood, as feminists have understood for a very long time, exists as a central mechanism through which women have been incorporated into the modern political order. Women's service and duty to the state have largely been seen in terms of motherhood, and to begin to examine the politics of motherhood it is necessary to see how women's duty is connected to men's service to the state as workers and soldiers.

Women's inclusion into the political order needs special emphasis, since it is often assumed that the problem of women's citizenship is one of exclusion. A major reason for the complexity of women's political status is that it has never been a matter of mere exclusion. Women's political standing rests on a major paradox; they have been excluded and included on the basis of the very same capacities and attributes. Feminist theorists have shown how political constructions of what it means to be a man or a woman are central to conceptions of the well-ordered polity. In my own work I have examined how the classic contract theorists presented sexual difference as the political difference between freedom (men) and subordination (women). Women were held by nature to lack the characteristics required for participation in political life, and citizenship has been constructed in the male image (Pateman 1988).[2] Women, our bodies and distinctive capacities, represented all that citizenship and equality are not. 'Citizenship' has gained its meaning through the exclusion of women, that is to say (sexual) 'difference'.

But this is only part of the story of the development of modern patriarchy. The classic theorists did not completely exclude women from the political order, from 'civil society'. The creation of modern patriarchy embodied a new mode of inclusion for women that, eventually, could encompass their formal entry into citizenship. Women were incorporated differently from men, the 'individuals' and 'citizens' of political theory; women were included as subordinates, as the 'different' sex, as 'women'. They were incorporated as men's subordinates into their own private sphere, and so were excluded from 'civil society' in the sense of the public sphere of the economy and citizenship of the state. But this does not mean that women had no political contribution to make and no political duty to perform. Their political duty (like their exclusion from citizenship) derives from their difference from men, notably their capacity for motherhood.

The eighteenth-century doctrine of republican motherhood provides an illustration of the multiple layers of meaning of motherhood as a political status. The political theory of civic republicanism emphasized active political participation by citizens imbued with civic virtue, who were also capable of bearing arms. Republican citizens were thus men and soldiers – but what of women? They were to be the subordinate companions of citizens, but with their own political task; they were to be republican mothers. In America, a republican mother was excluded from citizenship, but she had a crucial political part to play in bearing and rearing sons who embodied republican virtues. She remained an auxiliary to the commonwealth but an auxiliary who made a fundamental political contribution (Kerber 1980). During the French Revolution – when the 'rights of men and citizens' were first proclaimed – women's political rights and activities were suppressed and their place declared to be that of republican mothers (Landes 1988: esp. ch. 4).

Why should the republican mother not be a citizen? There was, from a feminist perspective, no rational reason at all. Women would express their citizenship, in part at least, through motherhood. From the 1790s onwards, the demand was made that women's private duty should become part of citizenship. A century after the French Revolution, in the 1890s and early 1900s, as Karen Offen has shown, a 'familial feminism' was predominant in France (Offen 1984: 665–66). Feminists argued that the state should support women in their duty as mothers and improve the material conditions of motherhood, and that those who performed this national task should be granted the standing and rights of citizens.

This argument had been made during the period of the French Revolution by Mary Wollstonecraft. As I noted above, Mary Wollstonecraft argued simultaneously for equality and the recognition of difference. She called for equal civil and political rights for women and their economic independence from their husbands – stating, 'Let woman share the rights and she will emulate the virtues of man' – and, at the same time, for women's citizenship to be expressed differently from men's. Women had a 'peculiar destination' as mothers, and their equal citizenship would be expressed through their motherhood. She wrote that, 'speaking of women at large, their first duty is to themselves as rational creatures, and the next, in point of importance, as citizens, is that, which includes so many, of a mother'. She hoped that the day would come when men would be despised if they were not active citizens; 'and while he was employed in any of the departments of civil life, his wife, also an active citizen, should be equally intent to manage her family, educate her children, and assist her neighbours' (Wollstonecraft 1975: 145–46, 189, 194).

The problem with this feminist strategy is that it remains impaled on the horns of what I have called Wollstonecraft's dilemma. The dilemma arises because, within the existing patriarchal conception of citizenship, the choice always has to be made between equality and difference, or between equality and womanhood. On the one hand, to demand 'equality' is to strive for equality with men (to call for the 'rights of men and citizens' to be extended to women), which means that women must become (like) men. On the other hand, to insist, like some contemporary feminists, that women's distinctive attributes, capacities and activities be revalued and treated as a contribution to citizenship is to demand the impossible; such 'difference' is precisely what patriarchal citizenship excludes.

Contemporary arguments about the re-evaluation of women's capacities, especially motherhood, also raise another question: namely, how is 'motherhood' to be understood? Does 'motherhood' refer only to the relation between mother and child; or does 'motherhood' also refer to women's standing in the political order? One feminist argument, especially influential in the United States, treats motherhood in the former sense and focuses on 'maternal thinking'.

Sara Ruddick argues that all thought is a response to social practice; in this case, the practice or discipline of motherhood. Maternal thinking grows out of a mother's concern for the child's preservation, growth and acceptability (will the child be an 'acceptable' member of society?) and is centred around 'attentive love' (Ruddick 1981: 227). The notion of maternal thinking does not involve a simple return to an argument from (women's) nature. Ruddick insists that 'maternal' is a social category, so that men, if they care for others, can be maternal thinkers. She argues that the conditions of women's motherhood have largely been defined by men, thus maternal thinking is always open to determination by the dominant culture and, hence, to inauthenticity. Maternal thinking has to be transformed by feminist consciousness, and then, Ruddick argues, 'the self-conscious inclusion of maternal thought in the dominant culture will be of general intellectual and moral benefit'. Once maternal thinking is brought into 'the public realm' the care of children can become 'a work of public conscience and legislation' (Ruddick 1981: 226). Similarly, Jean Elshtain claims that, 'were maternal thinking to be taken as the base for feminist consciousness, a wedge for examining an increasingly overcontrolled public world would open immediately' (cited in Dietz 1985: 23). The task for feminists, Ruddick states, is to formulate a 'theory of justice shaped by and incorporating maternal thinking' (Ruddick 1981: 226).

An argument based on the 'difference' symbolized by motherhood has inevitably provoked a response from an advocate of 'equality'. Mary Dietz argues that maternal thinking reinforces the split between private and public. Maternal thinking is not political; it arises from a relationship between unequals (the mother and child) that is 'intimate, exclusive, and particular', and is thus opposed to democratic citizenship which is 'collective, inclusive, and generalized'. The bond between mother and child is quite different from the bonds of citizenship. To argue that maternal consciousness can be a basis for feminism and citizenship is to look at political life from the wrong way round. Only when women act as citizens, not mothers, can the policies advocated by feminists be implemented. Dietz concludes that 'accordingly, the values [feminists] must defend are not as such maternal (the growth and preservation of children) but political (freedom, equality, community power)'. Feminists should not reduce women's identity to the single dimension of 'mother', but should endeavour to '[nurture] the reality of women as, in large part, citizens' (Dietz 1985: 20).

The debate therefore continues to oscillate between 'difference' (maternal thinking should be valued and brought into the political arena) and 'equality' (citizenship not motherhood is vital for feminists) and so remains caught in Wollstonecraft's dilemma. There are also other problems when 'motherhood' is seen only in terms of the mother-child relation. For instance, attention is deflected from the structure of sexual relations and the meaning of 'sex' in contemporary society; in other words, little consideration is given to the context in which women become pregnant.[3] Instead, attention becomes focused on 'motherhood' as part of 'the family', the private sphere, and motherhood appears as either non-political or outside politics, and two solutions to women's predicament present themselves. One popular proposal is for 'shared parenting' within the family; men must be encouraged to be 'mothers'. But as Lynne Segal has commented rather sharply: 'watching childbirth, pushing prams, putting children to bed, many men now relate sensitively to women and children in ways unthinkable to their fathers—yet, the edifice of male power remains' (Segal 1987: 211). The other proposal is that 'motherhood' be inserted into politics and citizenship in the form of maternal thinking. But 'motherhood', in another sense, has been incorporated into politics for a very long time.

Motherhood as a political status, as a major vehicle of women's incorporation into the political order, has shaped women's duty to the state and women's citizenship. I want to approach women's political duty and service from two directions: the structure of the welfare state and the question of the political obligations of citizenship. (Within the confines of the present essay, I cannot discuss the way in which much of women's political activity also reflects motherhood as a political status; for example, as participants in bread riots, as 'women's auxiliaries' in strikes or, more recently, as participants in the anti-nuclear movement or, like the Mothers of the Plaza de Mayo, taking action on behalf of the 'disappeared'.)

The basis of the 'social insurance' model of the Anglo-American welfare state is that individuals make a 'contribution' that then entitles them to the benefits, or what T.H. Marshal called the social rights of citizenship, of the welfare state (Marshall 1963). Paid employment becomes central to the welfare state because the 'contribution' is taken from the pay-packet of the worker.[4] Except in feminist discussions it is rarely noticed that it is men, as 'workers' and 'bread-winners' and recipients of the family wage, who have been regarded as those 'individuals' able to make the 'contribution' to the welfare state.

Women have not been (seen as) capable of making the same contribution as men and so have not had the same entitlements in the welfare state. This was made plain by William Beveridge in his report, which laid the foundations for the comprehensive British welfare reforms of the 1940s, when he wrote: 'the great majority of married women must be regarded as occupied on work which is vital though unpaid, without which their husbands could not do their paid work, and without which the nation could not continue' (cited in Dale and Foster 1986: 17). The tasks of a wife, and mother, were not the 'work' associated with equality and citizenship, and wives and husbands were treated differently under the National Insurance Act of 1946. That is not to say that women have been left out of the welfare state. Rather, they have not usually benefited as citizens. Over the past decade or more, feminist scholars have shown how women, now the major beneficiaries of the welfare state and the majority of the poor, still tend to receive their benefits not, like men, in their own right, but as dependents and subordinates of male citizens, the bread-winners.[5] Thus, the structure of the welfare state embodies (the patriarchal construction of) sexual difference.

But women also had a contribution to make that reflected their difference from men. The paradoxical contribution demanded from women was – welfare. This was not the public welfare of the 'welfare state', but the contribution of private, unpaid welfare in their homes. Women, as mothers, nurture the next generation of citizens, and, as wives and daughters, tend to the sick, the infirm and the aged. The welfare state has always depended upon women's contribution, but it remains unacknowledged and set apart from (political) citizenship. In the present period of 'privatization', women's private tasks assume an even greater importance.

The early development of the British welfare state also illustrates the importance of a different kind of contribution or service to the state that is vital for an understanding of the politics of motherhood. During the First World War, the British government paid 'separation allowances' to the wives of soldiers and sailors and it was at this point, Susan Pederson argues, that the '"logic" of social citizenship structured around maintaining the domestic rights of the male citizen became established' (Pederson 1990: 985). In effect, the welfare state replaced the husband as 'bread-winner' while he was absent making another kind of contribution. As one MP commented, the allowance was 'paid by the state as part of the wage of the soldier'; it was not the entitlement of his wife (Pederson 1990: 997). Benefits paid to men as entitlements due for service as citizens, whether as workers or soldiers, could not belong to wives. 'Women' and 'citizenship' are opposed, and women had their own 'different' contribution to render.

The primary form that wives' (women's) service has taken can be seen by looking at the respective contributions of women and men from another direction; by considering arguments about the political obligation and duty of the citizen. The ultimate test of the allegiance of the citizen and the ultimate duty of citizenship are to die for the state. As one political theorist wrote recently: 'the duty to give life, should it be necessary to do so, in order to sustain or generate a political order is one of the central duties of citizenship' (Dunn 1980: 251). Michael Walzer also discusses another duty of citizens, 'the obligation to live for the state', or the duty not to renounce citizenship through suicide, that requires citizens to endure the vicissitudes of everyday living. Walzer notes that, for eighteenth-century writers, the capacity to commit suicide was part of the right to life; 'the best proof of [men's] standing as free and rational creatures' (Walzer 1971: 176).

I do not want to discuss the question of suicide but to ask a question that remains unasked in the discussions of political obligation with which I am familiar; namely, is the duty of men and women to die and live for the state interpreted and performed in the same way? In standard arguments about the two duties, theorists of citizenship do not ask whether either of them applies to women. Both the duty to die for the state and the duty to live for the state are typically discussed with reference only to men. The duty to die for the state is taken for granted to mean the duty of the citizen to take up arms at the behest of the state and, as Hobbes put it, 'protect his Protection', even if he must forfeit his life in so doing (Hobbes 1968: 375). It is easy enough to see that bearing arms and dying on the battlefield for the state have been held to be beyond the reach of women. The 'jewel' in the arguments of the anti-suffragists was the insistence that women were unable and/or unwilling to use physical force and that their citizenship would, therefore, place the state in peril.[6] The argument still continues in the contemporary controversy over women and combat.

Few political theorists explicitly discuss the duty to live for the state, or the service owed to the state every day in the course of a lifetime, but discussions of citizenship in the welfare state make it plain that the major duty is to engage in paid employment – again, a duty of men. T.H. Marshall, for instance, argued that individuals have a general duty of service as citizens to promote the general welfare;

he wrote: 'of paramount importance is the duty to work', and not merely to have a job, but 'to put one's heart into [it] and work hard' (Marshall 1963: 123, 124). In Marshall's argument, the unpaid work of women which Beveridge mentioned, 'without which the nation could not continue', disappears without a trace. This is not the work of citizens, part of their political duty, but the work that women owe to the state because of their sex, which thus falls outside citizenship. None the less, women, like men, have a political duty to live for the state, not least because women can be called upon to die for the state during the course of their mundane, unrecognized duty. That women, too, have a duty to die for the state is not noticed by political theorists because the duty is fulfilled in the private realm, not in the public arena of the battlefield. Women's duty is suited to their ambiguous position in the state, exemplifying nature and (sexual) 'difference', not the conventional life of the public world of equal citizenship. Women's ultimate political duty is motherhood, to give birth for the state, and, if nature so decrees, to give their lives in creating new life, new citizens.

Michel Foucault has argued that in the modern era there has been a shift from sovereignty symbolized by the sword and the right of the sovereign to put his subjects to death, to a new form of rule and discipline concerned with the quantity and quality of life of the population (Foucault 1979; 1980). Foucault fails to ask the question, 'where does that population comes from?' He thus ignores the fact that the patriarchal meaning of sexual difference and the manner of women's incorporation into the political order are an integral part of the interest of modern state in the number and condition of the population. Many states, today and in the past, have been greatly exercised whether or not they have sufficient population to be 'great' and powerful, or to stand against other populations that are seen as a threat because of their size or ethnic composition. Whether or not women were performing their political duty has thus been a major concern of the state, and a wide array of measures have been deployed to ensure that their duty was fulfilled. An enthusiastic performance of their political duty could receive official reward in a manner similar to exemplary soldiers. In 1920, in France, where the size of the population has long been a source of anxiety to the state, particularly fecund women were acknowledged by a medal, with ribbons (Offen 1984: 669–70),

Earlier in the twentieth century, in both Australia and the United States, a decline in the white birth rate led to fears of 'race suicide'. The position of women and the political duty of motherhood were, therefore, at the centre of national policy concerns. Inquiries were held into the problem, and in Australia in 1904 the childless woman was condemned as 'selfish' and portrayed by the most shrill pro-natalists as 'a menace to social purity and national stability' (cited in Pringle 1973: 20). More recently, the Ceausescu regime in Romania enforced women's duty in the harshest fashion to try to attain a population of 30 million at the end of the twentieth century, banning contraception and abortion and policing women workers to ensure that all pregnancies were detected and brought to term. (The resulting large-scale abandonment of babies into squalid institutions by poor, overburdened mothers has, since the overthrow of the regime, received much publicity, unlike the policy itself.)

The state has been interested in the 'quality' and not merely the quantity of the population. If women have had the duty to give birth for the state, not all women have been seen as fit to be mothers. Middle-class white women, above all, as 'superior' genetic stock, have been seen as undermining the nation by limiting the extent of their service, or avoiding service altogether, by 'unnatural' means. Other women have been subject to measures to prevent them from fulfilling their duty; women from indigenous, migrant or black minority populations in western countries have been sterilized without their consent, and arguments surface regularly about the deleterious effects of differential birth rates of women classified according to IQ or class. As I was writing this essay, the *Philadelphia Inquirer* published a controversial editorial advocating incentives to encourage poor black women to use a new birth control implant, which could keep them from becoming pregnant for up to five years, and a judge in Visalia, California, ordered another black woman, who had been convicted of badly beating her children, to use the same device as condition of her probation (reported in Rosentiel 1990: A32).

The most horrific and graphic example of this aspect of the politics of motherhood was the policy in Nazi Germany. The Nazi regime is often seen as pro-natalist and as placing a high value on motherhood, and pictures of rosy, flaxen-haired mothers and children are familiar enough. But, as Gisela Bock's very important research has shown, Nazi 'racial hygiene' doctrine did not even regard all German women as fit mothers. From 1933 onwards, a public policy of forced sterilization and compulsory abortion was practised. The mentally and physically handicapped, in addition to the 'inferior' groups, the Gypsies, Jews, Slavs and so on, were the targets, and it was the extreme anti-natalism, not pro-natalism, which sets the Nazi regime apart from other western countries of the period (Bock 1992).

The service and sacrifice demanded of women as child-bearers and the service and sacrifice demanded of men as soldiers are often compared (even if they have never been brought together by political theorists). For example, President Theodore Roosevelt compared the 'cowardly' or 'selfish' woman who shirked her duty to become a mother with the man who 'fears to do his duty in battle when the country calls him', and declared them both to be equally contemptible (cited in Ehrenreich and English 1978: 171). From the feminist side, August Bebel stated that 'a woman who brings children into the world does the community at least as great a service as a man who defends his country'. He noted that the casualty rate among child-bearers was probably greater than among soldiers on the battlefield and commented that 'this is reason enough to entitle women to complete equality with men' (Bebel 1886: 149). Again, the English feminist Maude Royden declared during the First World War:

> The state wants children, and to give them is a service both dangerous and honourable. Like the soldier, the mother takes a risk and gives a devotion for which no money can pay; but, like the soldier, she should not, therefore, be made 'economically dependent'.
>
> (cited in Pederson 1989: 91)

No one, she insisted, held that a man 'must depend on his wife for maintenance because he is a soldier…You cannot, indeed, pay for all that motherhood means, but neither can you pay for a man to die. Yet soldiers are "endowed" by the State' (Royden 1917: 140).

Royden's reference to 'economic dependence' brings motherhood together with both dimensions of men's service to the state. British feminists saw the separation allowances being paid during the war in a very different light from the prevailing view that they were part of the soldier-worker's pay. Feminists argued that the wives' allowances should be seen as an entitlement, as a right of a citizen in return for her service to the state that she gave in the home; as Eleanor Rathbone stated, the payment should be treated as 'a statutory payment to a woman in respect of her [citizenship] functions as a wife and a mother' (cited in Pederson 1990: 1003). Rathbone was at the forefront of the wide movement in western countries that began in the early part of the twentieth century for state endowment for mothers. At her most radical she saw the endowment as a means of remedying the subordination of wives by helping to eliminate their economic dependence on the family wage of husbands. Rathbone contended that payment to mothers would 'once and for all, cut away the maintenance of children and the reproduction of the race from the question of wages' (cited in Cass 1983: 57). The way would then be open for women workers to be paid the same wages as their male counterparts.

Feminist comparisons of the risks run by mothers and soldiers, and arguments that an endowment for mothers should be payment for their service as citizens, ran up against Wollstonecraft's dilemma. Women's duty to give birth to the state is not a duty of citizens, and the casualties of motherhood are not included among those who have fallen in the service of their country. From this perspective, death in childbirth cannot be a sacrifice like that of a soldier, but must stand as a casualty of nature, as the antithesis of the human heroism of death under fire.[7]

Similarly, when family allowances (as the endowment for mothers came to be called) were finally instituted in Britain after the Second World War, the payment was made directly to mothers and so could be seen as a mark of recognition for their contribution – but as private persons, not as citizens. Moreover, family allowances were also widely viewed as a means of alleviating poverty among children and as a supplement to the family wage.

A feminist strategy that calls for the integration into citizenship of women's distinctive contribution, or compares women's service to that of men as workers or soldiers, rests on the assumption that 'women' and 'difference' need to be brought into the political order. The pertinent question is assumed to be whether sexual difference is politically relevant, or how 'difference' could be relevant. Thus, the vital question is overlooked of how to subvert and change the manner in which women have already been incorporated, and so to transform the relation between 'equality' and 'difference'. The task of political reconstruction remains daunting, but, at the end of the twentieth century, some significant changes – a few too recent to assess readily – have taken place in the context in which the politics of motherhood is played out.

Not only men but, at least in the United States, mothers are now soldiers. The American troops who recently waged war against Iraq included mothers among the women (about 6 per cent of the total force) who were deployed in non-combat positions. The comparison of the casualty rates of mothers and soldiers has also lost much of its strength now that the dangers of childbirth have been so greatly reduced for most women in western countries. For the very first time, the means are available for women to choose whether and when to perform their political duty, although a powerful movement now exists to enforce motherhood as an involuntary duty for women – rather in the way that men can be conscripted as soldiers – by banning contraception and abortion. In 1989, the US Supreme Court judged that it was constitutional for the States to prohibit the use of public facilities and employees for abortions; poor women were thus deprived of part of their social rights of citizenship. At the same time, there are indications that motherhood is beginning to be seen as a right and not only as a duty. Much of the publicity and rhetoric surrounding the new reproductive technology and so-called surrogate motherhood suggests that women have a right to be fertile or to expropriate the fertility of other (usually poor) women.[8] The welfare state, notwithstanding its patriarchal structure, has also changed the position of mothers. Welfare benefits enable a mother to choose to live, if not well in the Anglo-American system, at least independently of a man's economic patronage. (And artificial insemination – an old technique put to new uses – allows women to become mothers without engaging in sexual relations with men.)

Perhaps most obviously, more mothers than ever before are now workers, but women generally are still paid less than men so that their economic dependence remains, albeit less severe than in the past. Nor has the sexual division of labour in private life been greatly affected by women's participation in the public workplace, as the instructive example of Sweden reveals. National labour market policy and 'equality policy' since the 1960s have enabled and encouraged women to be worker-mothers, especially through the provision of generous income replacement payments for parents who care for very young children and public child-care facilities. Despite the numbers of young men to be seen pushing prams, very few fathers take parental leave, and the sexual segregation of the occupational structure is the greatest among the OECD countries. Even in a society with a remarkable degree of equality in many respects, the connection between male employment and citizenship (or, indeed, men bearing arms and citizenship) has not yet been broken (see e.g. Hernes 1987: ch. 7).

The meaning of 'equality' in Swedish 'equality policy' brings me back to my starting point: 'equality' and 'difference' are opposed, or, at best, some compensation is allowed for 'difference' (so women, for instance, have flexible working hours and maternity leave; child care is provided and shops are open in the evening). The large measure of formal equality now won by women still excludes 'difference' while leaving intact much of women's inclusion through 'difference'. Another major problem, however, is precisely that the terms of the argument have been framed as 'equality' and 'difference'. There are good reasons for this, as my historical examples have been designed to show. The examples should also illustrate that the heart of the matter is not sexual difference but women's subordination. 'Equality', like other central political categories, is a contested term; but whereas 'equality' in some of its possible meanings can encompass 'difference', no sense of 'equality' compatible with a genuinely democratic citizenship can accommodate subordination. By a 'genuinely democratic citizenship', I mean that both sexes are full citizens and that their citizenship is of equal worth to them as women and men. For that to be the case, the meaning of sexual difference has to cease to be the difference between freedom and subordination. The issue in the problem of 'difference' is women's freedom.

Some of the more fervent advocates of difference seem to imply that equality is not important. Yet one fundamental dimension of women's freedom is the freedom inherent in equal citizenship. It bears repeating that the rift in the 1920s over 'equality' and 'difference' was between women who had all fought for the equal citizenship of the suffrage. The equal political standing of citizenship is necessary for democracy and for women's autonomy. If the political meaning of sexual difference is to change, and women's citizenship is to be worth the same as men's, patriarchal social and sexual relations have to be transformed into free relations. This does not mean that all citizens must become (like) men or that all women must be treated in the same way. On the contrary, for citizenship to be of equal worth, the substance of equality must differ according to the diverse circumstances and capacities of citizens, men and women. Motherhood no longer fills women's lives, or takes women's lives, as it once did, nor is women's citizenship only a matter of motherhood, but motherhood and citizenship remain intimately linked. Only women can give physical life to new citizens, who, in their turn, give life to a democratic political order.

Acknowledgements

I am extremely grateful for the assistance of Keith D. Watenpaugh in revising this essay.

Notes

1   US District Court for the Northern District of Illinois, Eastern Division, *EEOC v. Sears, Roebuck & Co.*, 1986, Civil Action no. 79–C–4373. (An appeal in 1988 confirmed the judgement; the case covered the period 1973–80. The verdict, and the expert testimony of historians on opposite sides, has led to a prolonged and often acrimonious debate.)
2   Unlike the other contract theorists, Hobbes holds that men and women are free by nature. On Hobbes see Pateman 1989a.
3   I have discussed these matters in Pateman 1988.
4   The importance of paid employment for men in the development of the welfare state is discussed in Pateman 1989b.
5   For some empirical evidence see Pateman, 241–42.
6   The phrase is from Harrison 1978: 73.
7   The difficulty of reinterpreting the meaning of motherhood so that it appears to be public service and sacrifice like that of soldiers is nowhere better illustrated than in Beauvoir 1975, the famous feminist study. She argues that, in risking their lives as hunters

or warriors, men transcend a merely natural, animal existence. Women, cursed by being 'excluded from these warlike forays' (1975: 95), merely repeat or reproduce life rather than placing their lives in jeopardy for 'reasons that are more important than the life itself' (1975: 96). This is why young people laugh at a pregnant woman, 'who has become life's passive instrument' (1975: 513).

8   New international dimensions of the politics of motherhood have also developed that are far removed from the international co-operation between members of the women's movement in the past. Current problems have to be seen in a neo-colonialist context, in which oral contraceptives ('the pill') were tested on Third World women and a trade exists in the – sometimes kidnapped – babies of poor Third World women to the affluent west.

References

Bacchi, C.L. 1990. *Same Difference: Feminism and Sexual Difference.* Sydney: Allen & Unwin.

Beauvoir, S. de. 1975. *The Second Sex.* Ed. and trans. H.M. Parshley. Harmondsworth: Penguin.

Bebel, A. 1886. *Woman in the Past, Present and Future.* London: Reeves.

Bock, G. 1992. 'Equality and Difference in National Socialist Racism'. In G. Bock and S. James (eds) *Beyond Equality and Difference: Citizenship, Feminist Politics and Female Subjectivity.* London: Routledge, 82–101.

Cass, B. 1983. 'Redistribution to Children and to Mothers: A History of Child Endowment and Family Allowances'. In C. Baldock and B. Cass (eds) *Women, Social Welfare, and the State.* Sydney: Allen & Unwin.

Dale, J. and P. Foster. 1986. *Women and the Welfare State.* London: Routledge & Kegan Paul.

Dietz, M. 1985. 'Citizenship with a Feminist Face: The Problem with Maternal Thinking'. *Political Theory* 13(1): 19–37.

Dunn, J. 1980. *Political Obligation in its Historical Context.* Cambridge: Cambridge University Press.

Ehrenreich, B. and D. English. 1978. *For Her Own Good.* New York: Anchor Press.

Foucault, M. 1979. *Discipline and Punish.* Trans. A. Sheridan. New York: Vintage.

—— 1980. *The History of Sexuality,* vol. 1. Trans. R. Hurley. New York: Vintage.

Harrison, B. 1978. *Separate Spheres: The Opposition to Women's Suffrage.* London: Croom Helm.

Hernes, H.M. 1987. 'The Welfare State Citizenship of Scandinavian Women'. In *The Welfare State and Woman Power: Essays in State Feminism.* Oxford: Oxford University Press.

Hobbes, T. 1968. *Leviathan.* Ed. C.B. Macpherson. Harmondsworth: Penguin.

Kerber, L.K. 1980. *Women of the Republic: Intellect and Ideology in Revolutionary America.* New York: Norton.

Landes, J.B. 1988. *Women and the Public Sphere in the Age of the French Revolution.* Ithaca, NY: Cornell University Press.

Marshall, T.H. 1963. 'Citizenship and Social Class', in *Sociology at the Crossroads and Other Essays.* London: Heinemann.

Offen, K. 1984. 'Depopulation, Nationalism and Feminism in *fin-de-siècle* France'. *American Historical Review* 89(3): 648–76.

Pateman, C. 1988. *The Sexual Contract.* Cambridge: Polity Press, and Stanford, CA: Stanford University Press.

—— 1989a. '"God hath ordained to man a helper": Hobbes, Patriarchy and Conjugal Right'.

In C. Pateman, *The Disorder of Women: Democracy, Feminism, and Political Theory.* Cambridge: Polity Press, and Stanford, CA: Stanford University Press.

—— 1989b. 'The Patriarchal Welfare State'. In C. Pateman, *The Disorder of Women: Democracy, Feminism, and Political Theory.* Cambridge: Polity Press, and Stanford, CA: Stanford University Press.

Pederson, S. 1989. 'The Failure of Feminism in the Making of the British Welfare State'. *Radical History Review* 43: 86–110.

—— 1990. 'Gender, Welfare, and Citizenship in Britain during the Great War'. *American Historical Review* 95(4): 983–1006.

Pringle, R. 1973. 'Octavius Beale and the Ideology of the Birth-rate: The Royal Commissions of 1904 and 1905'. *Refractory Girl* 3.

Rosentiel, T.B. 1990. *LA Times.* 20 December.

Royden, A.M. 1917. 'The Future of the Woman's Movement'. In V. Gollancz (ed.) *The Making of Women: Oxford Essays in Feminism.* London: Allen & Unwin.

Ruddick, S. 1981. 'Maternal Thinking'. In J. Trebilcot (ed.) *Mothering: Essays in Feminist Theory.* Totowa, NJ: Rowman & Allanheld.

Scott, J.W. 1988. *Gender and the Politics of History.* New York: Columbia University Press.

Segal, L. 1987. *Is the Future Female?* London: Virago.

Smith, H. 1990. 'British Feminism in the 1920s', in H. Smith (ed.) *British Feminism in the Twentieth Century.* London: Edward Elgar.

Walzer, M. 1971. *Obligations: Essays on Disobedience. War and Citizenship.* New York: Simon & Schuster.

Wollstonecraft, M. 1975. *A Vindication of the Rights of Woman:* New York: Norton.

9

THREE QUESTIONS ABOUT WOMANHOOD SUFFRAGE (1994)

Voting and elections have been central to political science for half a century, but only recently, since feminist scholars began to draw attention to the neglect of women voters, have articles and books been appearing in any number that focus on women's participation in the electoral process. The work of feminist political scientists has not yet been influential enough, however, to change the long-standing neglect in the discipline of such fundamental questions as why it took women so much longer than men to win the vote in Britain and the United States (the two countries I shall discuss in this chapter), the political significance of the entry of women into national electorates, or why it has taken women so long to be elected in any numbers to national legislatures. The omission is curious, to say the least, in view of the importance of such issues for democratic theory and practice, and the size and duration of the womanhood suffrage movement. One historian has called the final stages of the suffrage campaign in the US 'the greatest independent political movement of modern times' (O'Neill 1969: 7).

There are other questions, too, that have received scant attention, for example, the reasons why women won the vote before 1910 in some peripheral countries – New Zealand, Australia, Finland and Norway – or why, in Britain and the US, it was the national suffrage that was strenuously contested. By 1900 women had been enfranchised not only in New Zealand, but in South Australia and Western Australia, in the Isle of Man, in the states of Wyoming, Colorado, Utah and Idaho, and had won the municipal franchise in Britain. Nor has there been much exploration of the importance of the belief that if women were enfranchised they would all vote for conservative parties, although the policies of the parties and manoeuvrings in parliament have been investigated (see Morgan 1972; 1975). But perhaps the lack of interest in votes for women is not so surprising; most research in political science is still guided by the assumption that relations between the sexes and the structure of relations in domestic life are irrelevant to the public world of politics. Yet the connection between private and public was central to the question of womanhood suffrage and to the intense opposition to votes for women. The hostility is not treated as a serious problem in itself, and consequently, three crucial questions remain unasked and unanswered: firstly, why did it take so long for women to get the vote? secondly, why did women themselves organise against their own enfranchisement? thirdly, why was the vote won in the end?

In New Zealand, women won the vote after a relatively short organised campaign beginning in 1885, and in Australia it took twenty years from the 1880s until women became citizens of the Commonwealth in 1902. Women in Britain and the US had to fight a much more prolonged battle. One of the resolutions at the first women's rights convention in the USA, held at Seneca Falls in 1848, read, 'it is the duty of the women of this country to secure to themselves their sacred right of the elective franchise', but American women were unable to fulfil that duty until 1920, although they began campaigning at the end of the Civil War. In Britain, the question of votes for women was first raised in the House of Commons in 1832; the organised campaign began in 1865 with the collection of signatures for a petition that John Stuart Mill, then an MP, presented to Parliament in 1866. Suffrage was not won for all women until 1928.

Vast multitudes of women from all walks of life participated in the suffrage movement. By 1915 the National American Woman Suffrage Association had nearly two million members, and in June 1911 the British suffrage societies could call on forty thousand participants in a seven-mile-long procession in London, who marched with banners and floats to the music of the 'March of the Women', composed by Ethel Smyth. Suffragists engaged in the full range of conventional political activities – though these were hardly conventional for women at the beginning, when it was still scandalous for a woman even to speak in public. The American suffrage leader, Carrie Chapman Catt, summarised fifty-two years of campaigning as follows; there were

> 56 campaigns of referenda to male voters; 480 campaigns to urge Legislatures to submit suffrage amendments to voters; 47 campaigns to induce State constitutional conventions to write woman suffrage into State constitutions; 277 campaigns to persuade State party conventions to include woman suffrage planks; 30 campaigns to urge presidential party conventions to adopt woman suffrage…and 19 campaigns with 19 successive Congresses to get the federal amendment submitted and ratified.
>
> (cited in Degler 1980: 360)

In addition, the militants, particularly the members of the Women's Social and Political Union (founded in 1905) engaged in some very unconventional activities, which included arson and hunger strikes in prison, an aspect of the campaign that Mrs Pankhurst called a 'civil war' by women (Pankhurst 1972). It is hard to believe that a political movement of similar variety, magnitude and duration that involved men would be treated so cursorily.

This is all the more surprising since voting is typically seen by political scientists as *the* political act of a citizen in a democracy; voting is now taken for granted. It is thus easy to forget that Aboriginal people were not brought into the Australian electorate until the 1960s (they were deliberately excluded in 1902), that it was not until the 1960s that black people in the US could freely exercise the franchise, that in Britain one person/one vote has existed only from 1948, or that women did not get the vote in Switzerland until 1971. A more general illustration of the lack of historical perspective can be found in Robert Dahl's famous description of the individual as *homo civicus*. Dahl writes that 'among his resources for influencing officials, *homo civicus* discovers the ballot' (Dahl 1961: 224). To write of an offhand 'discovery' of the ballot shows how far removed is the contemporary view of the franchise from the perception of the vote before it was won.

Both manhood and womanhood suffrage were bitterly contested, although students usually learn only that votes for men were opposed because it was believed that mob rule, class legislation and the expropriation of property would ensue. The reasons for the even deeper opposition to womanhood suffrage are left unexamined. On the other side, advocates of both manhood and womanhood suffrage had extravagant hopes of what the vote would achieve. Yet political science has virtually nothing to say about how such hopes and fears could disappear so completely and how universal suffrage has come to be treated in the discipline as a natural feature of the political landscape.[1]

The impression conveyed is that, while the achievement of universal suffrage was a long process, it took place by a gradual, logical extension of the franchise to all adults. On the contrary, by the time that the organised movement for womanhood suffrage got under way on both sides of the Atlantic, large numbers of men had been admitted to the electorate but women had been excluded, even when, as in the state of New Jersey, for example, the constitution initially enfranchised them. That this largely goes unnoticed is not surprising when important dates and pieces of legislation, such as the First Reform Act of 1832 in Britain, are cited without qualification as landmarks of the extension of the franchise and democracy. In fact, such milestones actually mark two developments: one, the widening of manhood franchise; two, the denial of votes to women. In Britain, women were first explicitly excluded from the electorate, defined as male persons, in 1832. John Stuart Mill failed in his attempt to amend the Second Reform Act in 1867 by replacing the word 'man' with 'person'. In 1870 the Fifteenth Amendment to the American Constitution enfranchised only former male slaves, not black women. These reforms made electoral democracy the preserve of men.

The suffragists' task was made even more difficult because supporters of progressive legislation where men were involved and who, on the face of it, should have been their allies, were often indifferent to or firmly opposed to votes for women. This meant that the suffragists were faced with some extremely difficult political choices. They either had to wait patiently until their demands ceased to be put at the bottom of political agendas, until opponents had a change of heart, or until male legislators began to take their case seriously. Or they had to take action and so lay themselves open to even further criticism. What were suffragists in the US to do when black men were enfranchised? The decision of Elizabeth Cady Stanton and Susan Anthony to oppose the Fifteenth Amendment split the American movement. In Britain, opinions differed sharply on the question of whether they should seek votes for women on the same terms as men – namely being householders (in the 1900s only about one third of the adult population could vote) – the position of most suffragists, or whether, as some suffragists argued in the 1870s and 1880s, they should begin by trying to gain votes for unmarried women.

Another alternative was to insist on universal suffrage, as did the new Labour Party in the first two decades of the twentieth century. On the face of it, this sounds democratic, but adult suffrage stood hardly any chance of being granted at the time. To support adult suffrage was thus an extremely useful tactic for opponents of votes for women, as John Stuart Mill had pointed out in 1870. He wrote to Sir Charles Dilke that universal and womanhood suffrage should be separated. 'To combine the two questions', he stated,

> would practically suspend the fight for women's equality, since universal suffrage is sure to be discussed almost solely as a working man's question… there is sure to be a compromise, by which the working men would be enfranchised without the women…and therefore with their selfish interest against our cause instead of with it.
>
> (Mill 1972: 1728)

The suffragists have often been accused of being racist and elitist, and attacks in the US on votes being given to uneducated, unwashed men, immigrant men and black men, while educated, cultivated, well-born women were denied the franchise, certainly fall well short of today's standards of political correctness and were hardly democratic. Yet it is easy to see why they argued in this fashion when they faced such unrelenting hostility from all sides even to the suggestion that *some* women should be enfranchised.

The resistance ran very deep, as reactions in Britain to the militant wing of the movement, the suffragettes, made very clear. Street sellers of the paper *Votes for Women* were subjected to obscene abuse and physical harassment, and, on the infamous Black Friday in November 1910, 300 suffragists on a peaceful march to Parliament Square were set upon by police and male onlookers for six hours, continually beaten and sexually assaulted. Nor has the hostility disappeared. The title of the final chapter of a biography of Christabel Pankhurst, published in 1977, is 'Bitch Power'.[2] The views and attitudes which lay at the heart of the opposition to votes for women have not yet died out, despite the major changes in the position of women since the early part of the century.

The existence of this tenacious resistance to womanhood suffrage is the reason why it took women so long to win the franchise. But merely to point to the extraordinary depth of opposition does not explain why such hostility existed or why women in the US and Britain had to struggle longer than men to be admitted to the national electorate.

Why did womanhood suffrage take so long?

An understanding of the hostility generated by the demand for votes for women requires attention to some much deeper-seated matters than the intricacies of parliamentary and party political manoeuvrings, the tactics of the militants (the suffragettes), or the opposition of interests such as the liquor trade. The short answer to my first question is that the franchise appeared to pose a radical challenge and threat not just to the state but to the powers and privileges of men as a sex. Indeed, Susan Kent argues that, in Britain, 'the threat posed by women's challenges to patriarchal order was seen to be even greater than that of the working classes' (Kent 1987: 30). This was the basis of the high hopes for the vote on the one side and the fears of the consequences if women were to use the ballot box on the other.

In his study of the British anti-suffragists, Brian Harrison comments that, apart from the vote, 'it is difficult to think of reforms for which late Victorian women energetically campaigned and which they were not granted' (Harrison 1978: 60). There was, however, one reform, or series of reforms, central to the struggle over the suffrage, that was not achieved; namely, reform of the law of coverture. Under coverture, in the middle of the nineteenth century a married woman had no independent legal and civil standing; she was deemed to be 'covered' or represented by her husband for public purposes. Coverture meant that, like many other aspects of women's position, the suffrage was, at bottom, 'the wife question' (which is why some suffragists were willing initially to limit their demands to votes for spinsters).[3] The law gave husbands despotic powers, and, in such a context, to demand reform of marriage law, to demand an end to men's monopoly of education and paid employment, including professional occupations, to demand that men should curb their sexual rapaciousness, and to link all this to the vote, was to make an extremely radical claim.

Womanhood suffrage, as Ellen DuBois has emphasised, 'exposed and challenged the assumption of male authority over women' (1978: 46). The vote promised women a public standing as individuals that was independent of their general subordination as women and, especially, as wives in the private sphere. The question of votes for women turned the separation of the public and private spheres into a political problem – and that is precisely the political problem that, as I have noted, political scientists ignore. Yet the separation of the two spheres explains why suffrage at a national level was so vehemently opposed. Many anti-suffragists did not object to women voting in local and municipal elections, and they often supported other reforms, such as property rights and access to education, that would improve women's social position.[4] Anti-suffragists were able to present such changes as an improvement in women's position in the private world, or as an extension of women's private tasks, that left the public arena to men.

The vote was, therefore, a potent symbol of all that was entailed in an equal social and political standing for women. But the vote was also demanded as a practical weapon of reform, so the threat posed by the suffrage to the patriarchal order seemed very real. The suffragists believed that, once they had the vote, the way would be open for major changes in the private realm as well as public life, although in Britain they also tried to reduce anxieties by drawing on the example of Australia and New Zealand to show that votes for women had not led to neglect of homes and families (Sawer and Simms 1993: 10–16). All those involved in the battle over womanhood suffrage were well aware of the significance of the vote for the division between private and public, for men's power, and the conventional understanding of what it meant to be a man or a woman. Both sides saw a connection between the sexual order, sexual identity and the political order.

Anti-suffragists wrote to the Illinois legislature in 1897, that 'we believe that men are ordained to govern in all forceful and material matters, because they are men' (cited in Degler 1980: 351). A member of the House of Commons stated in a debate on a suffrage bill in 1873, 'our object ought to be to enfranchise independent voters; but the female sex must in the nature of things remain in a position of dependence' (cited in Shanley 1989: 114). Such views reflect ideas about the political meaning of sexual difference that go back to the seventeenth century. The study of the historic texts is an important part of political theory, but most standard interpretations of the texts still overlook the fact that virtually every theory is formulated around men as political actors. Theoretical exclusion of women from political life in these texts facilitated and legitimised the deliberate exclusion of women from the suffrage. The famous theorists declared, almost to a man, that women naturally lack the liberty and independence needed for public life, and so must be governed or 'protected' by men. Womanhood itself is a disqualification for citizenship (Pateman 1988). This view of sexual difference as the political difference between freedom for men, and subordination or 'protection' for women, had become institutionalised by the mid nineteenth century in the denial of civil standing to wives and the exclusion of women from the public sphere.

The suffragists countered these ideas through three major lines of argument (often put forward simultaneously). Firstly, they insisted that the promise to women inherent in the universal language of individual freedom and equality, the rights of citizens and the consent of the governed, should be fulfilled. Women were prevented from participating in the public world not by nature but by men's monopoly of education, training, paid employment and the suffrage; women as a matter of justice should have full standing as citizens. Secondly, they argued that the suffrage was vital if women were to be able to carry out their work in the private sphere in a morally acceptable context; the vote was necessary to eliminate men's domestic tyranny and to strengthen women's position in private life. The suffragists agreed that men and women had their own tasks to perform, but they demanded some radical changes in marriage law and in the relation between the private and public spheres.

Thirdly, from at least the 1790s, the argument was made that women had a distinctive and valuable contribution to make. By the beginning of the twentieth century, suffragists were pointing to the increasing legislative concern with social welfare, and arguing that women, who had charge of the welfare of their families and who had long been encouraged to devote themselves to charitable work and philanthropy, had special knowledge and skills to bring to the political arena. Women, Jane Addams argued in the US, should take part in public affairs to build up 'that code of legislation which is alone sufficient to protect the home from the dangers incident to modern life' (Kraditor 1981: 69). Moreover, many suffragists, middle and working class, linked the vote to women's economic independence – even Christabel Pankhurst in her much derided polemic about the suffrage and venereal disease (Pankhurst 1987: 227). In the 1900s, tens of thousands of women workers and trade unionists in the cotton towns of Lancashire formed their own suffrage associations. They saw the vote as a way to improve their working conditions and their position as workers in male-dominated workplaces; but they were also wives, and their husbands feared for their comforts. One of these suffragists remarked that 'no cause can be won between dinner and tea…domestic unhappiness, the price many of us paid for our opinions and our activities, was a very bitter thing' (Liddington and Norris 1978: 217).

The suffragists were also directly at odds with their opponents over another aspect of women's natures. The suffragists emphasised the consent of the governed, and many also claimed that womanhood suffrage would usher in a new era of peace. The anti-suffragists, in contrast, placed great stress on force as the basis of the state, and they saw the suffrage as a threat to stability and national order. Women's natures, they argued, made them dangerous to the state. In Britain, anti-suffragists argued that 'government rests ultimately on force', and that 'women could not undertake the physical responsibilities of enforcing any law, which, by their votes, they might cause to be enacted' (cited in Kent 1987: 181). In the US, the electorate was seen as a 'militia on inactive duty' (cited in Kraditor 1981: 29). Women, it was claimed, could not be part of this militia, since they were, by nature, unable and/ or unwilling to use the force necessary to impose the will of the majority. Nor could they maintain an imperial government; 'imagine', one British anti-suffragist proclaimed, 'the women of England governing India' (cited in Harrison 1978: 75).

In both the suffragist and the anti-suffragist camps, many saw the battle over the suffrage as a war between the sexes. For instance, the British anti-suffragist Frederic Harrison proclaimed in 1909 that 'equal electoral rights could not fail to inflame a standing war between the sexes', and he believed that the 'inevitable result of female franchise would be…a weakening of men's respect for women'. If women got the vote, the anti suffragists claimed, all restraints would be weakened and physical strength would rule; 'once let loose the wild beast, which the law holds in chains and who', asked one anti-suffrage paper, 'are likely to fall the quickest and easiest prey?' (cited in Kent 1987: 57, 181). The suffragists' political activities invaded the public space monopolised by men, who responded not only by opposing the suffrage, but by reasserting their masculinity, often, as on Black Friday, in violent ways. The obscene remarks made to street sellers of *Votes for Women,* the fruit, stones and other missiles thrown at suffrage speakers, attacks on suffrage offices and the sexual assaults, provided more evidence for the suffragists of the need for a radical change in men's sexual morality. They argued that the law and social opinion gave men virtual *carte blanche* to use force against women. In his speech in 1867 supporting the suffrage, John Stuart Mill raised the problem of the brutal treatment and murder of wives. For suffragists, the vote, and the equal political standing that it would bring, was the means through which men could be brought to give women genuine respect and genuine protection.

One difficulty faced by the suffragists was that they were often attacked not for their political aims but as women. There was a brisk trade in postcards portraying the suffragists as muscular and plain, with captions such as 'It's not a vote you want – it's a bloke!' (Young 1988: 283, 287). The militant suffragettes, in particular, were portrayed as unsexed women and as madwomen. The best-known example of this genre is Sir Almroth Wright's *The Unexpurgated Case Against Womanhood Suffrage,* published in 1913. He stated that 'there is mixed up with the women's movement much mental disorder'. The book reveals a deep-seated fear of women's sexuality; the state, he believes, would be 'well rid' of spinsters – that is, women not under the control of husbands – and he comments that the hope that men and women could work side by side could not be fulfilled, because 'even in animals… male and female cannot safely be worked side by side, except where they are incomplete' (Wright 1913: 79, 181, 170).

The reason for the length of the struggle for womanhood suffrage was, then, that it was not merely participation in the government of the state that was seen to be at issue, but the patriarchal structure of relations between the sexes and conceptions of masculinity and femininity. However, if this explanation illuminates the reasons why men were so opposed to the enfranchisement of women, it does little to explain why women themselves, in large numbers, opposed the suffrage.

Why did women organise against their own enfranchisement?

No other group, to the best of my knowledge, has so actively opposed equal rights for themselves. Indeed, women not only campaigned against the suffrage but in the 1970s organised again in opposition to the Equal Rights Amendment (ERA) in the US. The reasons for the opposition are complex; some of the first opponents of the ERA in the 1920s (it was first introduced into Congress in 1923) had been suffragist leaders who continued to press for other social changes to benefit women, just as some anti-suffragists supported other reforms. Large numbers of women enlisted in the anti-suffrage cause, although they seem to have come from different parts of the social spectrum in Britain and the US.

In Britain, women active in the National League for Opposing Women's Suffrage (founded in 1908) were overwhelmingly upper-class, many titled; 'two types of woman embodied the anti-suffragist idea…the political hostess and the female philanthropist' (Harrison 1978: 81). By virtue of their class, these women had political influence behind the scenes and access to male leaders, such as the imperialist Lords Curzon and Cromer, who led the anti-suffrage movement. No doubt they feared that their private manipulations would be upset if women became legitimate public actors. The anti-suffrage groups in the US, in contrast, were mainly led by women, and the organisations were much less socially exclusive, involving 'the active opposition of thousands of women'; the New York State organisation may have had 20,000 members in the 1890s (Degler 1980: 349–50). In the 1970s, women, such as Phyllis Schlafly of the Stop ERA organisation (founded in 1973), were again prominent leaders against the ERA; activist women were more likely to be housewives and to be more conservative in their politics and religion than supporters of the ERA.

The historian Carl Degler has explored the reasons why American women opposed the suffrage, and his conclusion is that 'many women perceived in the suffrage a threat to the family, a threat so severe that the vote did not seem worth the possible cost'. One American anti-suffragist asked 'is there any escape from the conviction that the industrial and political independence of women would be the wreck of our present domestic institutions?' (Degler 1980: 350, 353–54). But the question still remains of why the anti-suffrage women believed that the vote would have this consequence.

It is, of course, difficult, now that elections have become the benchmark of democracy, to imagine all the spectres conjured up by the prospect of women voting. Still, there is a remarkable continuity between the arguments used by the anti-suffragists and many of those used by opponents of the ERA, and in the symbolic importance attached to both reforms. The anti-suffragists and the suffragists were bitterly divided over the issue of 'protection' of women, protection that the anti-suffragists believed was secured through the separation of the public and private spheres. The anti-suffragists insisted that women's protection would be eroded, posing a grave danger to the family, once the separation was breached by the vote. Women would then be forced to compete with men and become ever more vulnerable to men's greater strength and social power; as one British anti-suffragist proclaimed, 'clamours for equality' by women meant that 'man's protecting instinct will dwindle and die' (cited in Kent 1987: 179). A bleak view of men's characters is implicit in these arguments.

Nor was the independence symbolised by the vote welcomed by all women; for many, it seemed to place their future in jeopardy. The ideal of separate spheres and the protection given by a husband held out the promise of economic subsistence and a defined social place as a wife to women from all respectable classes. Although women's economic opportunities had improved by the end of the nineteenth century, they were still very limited, and middle-class husbands could offer their wives a more comfortable existence than spinsters could provide for themselves. Working-class women also feared the likely outcome if, as anti-suffragists forecast, they were forced into economic competition with men.[5]

These same fears surfaced again in the 1970s in the opposition to the ERA; the ghosts of the anti-suffragists seemed to be walking abroad.[6] The question of 'protection' arose in a number of different ways, including the issue of the armed forces and combat, but the emphasis placed on the threat that the ERA was held to pose to the family and the insistence that men and women should occupy separate spheres is particularly striking. Opponents of the ERA argued that equal rights for women meant that husbands would no longer perform their duties as breadwinners and wives would lose their claim to subsistence from their husbands. A picture was painted of men abandoning their families or refusing marriage altogether, and women being left as prey for rapacious men, if legislators supported the ERA (Mansbridge 1986: ch. 6; Mathews and DeHart 1990: ch. 6; Mayo and Frye 1986). The ERA symbolised a range of threatening forces. Many women apparently feared that they would be forced to abandon their femininity and cease to be 'women', in the sense in which they understood that term, if the ERA was ratified, just as the suffrage was once feared as a measure that would 'unsex' women (Mathews and DeHart 1990: 159).

The fact of, and the character of, the opposition to the ERA raises a major question, the third of the questions with which I am concerned here; namely, why were women enfranchised in the end? After all, resistance to women's equal rights on the part of both women and men has persisted in considerable strength and on much the same grounds from the 1860s for over a century. The ERA has still not been ratified, and in 1992 in Iowa a state ERA was defeated by 52 per cent to 48 per cent, a majority of men voting 'no'.

Why did women win the vote?

The conventional way of approaching my third question, if, indeed, it is even raised as a real problem, focuses on two points. Firstly, the most popular answer to the question is trotted out. Women got the vote, so it is said, because of the impact of the war, or, more specifically, as a reward for their work during World War I (see e.g. Garner 1984: ch. 7; Turner 1986: 60). This is not a very convincing answer. For example, it does not explain why, in Britain, only women over 30 were enfranchised in 1918 when younger women had done most of the war work. More strongly, Sandra Holton has recently argued that, in light of the change in the political climate by 1914, 'it might even be said that the war postponed the vote' (Holton 1986: 130). A more plausible argument along these lines is that women's determined efforts, which continued during the war, were a major reason why the US, Britain, and also Canada and Nordic countries, enfranchised women before or at the end of the war; all these countries had 'highly organised labour or feminist movements demanding the vote for women', whereas, for instance, France and Italy did not (Katzenstein 1984: 11).

Secondly, various facilitating factors are canvassed; in the case of Britain, reference is made, for instance, to the war-time coalition government, the commitment of the Labour Party by 1914 to a wider franchise that included women, a lessening of opposition in the House of Lords and the need for a new electoral register after the war. In the US after 1910, a major reason for the passage of the Nineteenth Amendment was Carrie Chapman Catt's brilliant 'winning plan'. The suffragists turned their attention to a Federal Amendment and to gaining suffrage in the states so that pressure could be brought on Congressmen at federal level by women voters (McDonagh 1992). By 1916 the President and the two parties had endorsed the suffrage.

One difficulty with both these arguments is that, while they help explain many of the final mechanisms through which the vote was won, they do not explain why the hostility to women's rights continued. This is also true of Carl Degler's answer to the question. He argues that American women got the vote because of 'a decline in the fear that the suffrage threatened the family' (Degler 1980: 357). If this is the case, it seems very odd that fifty years later the ERA was again seen to threaten the family. Moreover, none of these answers helps explain why there has been such distrust of women's involvement in other aspects of electoral politics. Women still form only a very small portion of the members of Congress or of the House of Commons; in Australia it took four decades from the time that women became eligible to stand for election in 1902 for a woman to be elected to the Federal Parliament. No woman has ever run for the office of US President for either of the two main parties, and, although Margaret Thatcher became the first British woman prime minister in 1979, British Cabinets continue to be almost exclusively male territory. All this points to another answer to my third question; that it was not views about women or the family that had undergone a radical change by the end of the Great War but views about the vote.

Political scientists, as I emphasised earlier, now take the vote completely for granted. They display little curiosity about the enormous change from the perception of universal suffrage as a threat to the social and political order to a recent argument that the vote is an insurance against the collapse of the democratic system (Downs 1957). More generally, voting is now seen as *the* means of providing legitimacy to governments. At the same time, however, the consensus of opinion is that womanhood suffrage had little or no political impact. Expectations about the vote by suffragists and their opponents cannot be taken seriously; predictions of a political transformation and the hopes and fears on both sides were manifestly over-inflated. One writer states that winning the suffrage was 'a sad and hollow victory, an anti-climax to a long campaign' (Garner 1984: 103); another writes that women's 'final victory led to no noticeable political change at all' (Shklar 1991: 60).[7]

One possible answer to the question of why women were given the vote is suggested by the political theorist C.B. Macpherson (1977: 64–69). He argues that the democratic franchise was 'tamed' through the development of the party system. Typically, however, he looks only at manhood suffrage and class. Macpherson argues that when the franchise and elected office was confined to the (male) propertied class, elected representatives had to be responsive to their electors. With a broader franchise, and the development of national parties that encompassed a wide array of different interests and groups, representatives had to look to a broad national, rather than class, interest. At the same time, elected office became the preserve of candidates endorsed by parties, and representatives had to back their party leaders in legislatures or risk loss of their seats, so that the result was minimal accountability to the wider party membership or the electorate. Using this line of argument in the case of women, it seems that the fear of an electorate that included women had abated considerably by the end of World War I. Universal suffrage had become necessary to produce legitimate governments, but, thanks to the party system, governments and legislatures were well insulated from voters. But this argument does not explain the persistence of hostility to women's rights. It is necessary to turn to an aspect of the development of parties and government ignored by Macpherson, and most other political scientists; that is, the relationship between womanhood suffrage, party politics and patriarchal power.

One obvious point is that parties and governments were, and, to a significant extent remain, men's clubs. In the US, for instance, from the 1820s onward, but particularly in the late nineteenth century, men were strong partisans of the two parties, and a large majority not only voted but took part in the rallies, parades and many other fraternal social activities, often referred to in military terms, that were organised around the parties and electoral campaigning. Women were spectators of these events; their participation was large confined to dressing up to represent such figures as Liberty (Baker 1984: 627–29; see also Ryan 1990). Elections also confirmed the masculine character of parties and politics; 'elections [were] held in saloons, barber shops, and other places largely associated with men', and 'participation in electoral politics…define[d] manhood' (Baker 1984: 629, 638). In the early twentieth century, electoral participation and allegiance to parties declined, and men's political activities were no longer closely tied to local fraternal communities, instead they moved to wider economic, national and other interests – a development that was part of the taming of the franchise.

But even when women were enfranchised, men still dominated party politics. Just as women's demands for the vote – or ratification of the ERA – had to wait upon the favour of male party members and legislators, so the fate of policies and legislation of concern to women, and especially feminists, was in men's hands. Men were not going to rush to change party platforms or enact legislation to diminish their power over women because women had the vote. It also needs to be emphasised that women were incorporated as auxiliaries into political parties long before they became voters. In Britain, for example, the very successful Primrose League of the Tory Party was founded in 1884, and the Liberals set up the Women's Liberal Federation in 1886. Women were then required to put allegiance to the party first, above any other interests they might have.

C.B. Macpherson also mentions that 'imperial expansion' allowed governments in the late nineteenth and early twentieth century 'to afford handouts to their electorates'. In other words, this was the period when the first welfare state measures were introduced. Macpherson sees this development as blunting working–class pressure for reform, thus also helping to 'tame' the franchise, but what he fails to notice is that these early reforms and the manner in which the welfare state was consolidated reinforced men's position as breadwinners and heads of households. The welfare state, as feminist scholars have now amply demonstrated, has a patriarchal structure (Pateman 1989). Possession of the vote and policies that improved women's lives went hand in hand with the maintenance of large areas of men's power and continued hostility to women's participation in the public realm.

To amend Macpherson's argument in this way is, however, to present only one side of the picture. The opponents of womanhood suffrage were correct in one respect; once women gained public standing as voters, a practical statement had been made that traditional arguments for women's exclusion from electoral politics, and for their government by men, were now illegitimate. The vote and other elements of civil and political equality won by women in the half century since 1920 have highlighted the continuing power and privilege of men as a sex, and it is hardly surprising that since the revival of the women's movement in the late 1960s an attack has been mounted against these private and public bastions, with greater or lesser success depending on the issue. Moreover, the franchise might have been tamed, but the achievement of womanhood suffrage was not completely inconsequential. There have been manifold changes. Women's votes have helped to obtain legal and policy changes from 1920 to 1990 that would have been almost unthinkable to women in the mid-nineteenth century. Women were strong advocates of the consolidation of the welfare state in Britain and welfare measures in the US, which have assisted women's economic independence. Women also worked for changes in marriage law, for access to education, to the labour market, for support for mothers and their children, and all the other measures that have transformed women's position. The difficulty lies in determining exactly how important *voting* is in this transformation compared to other forms of political activity – women, like other citizens, have never confined themselves to voting alone – and compared to long-term social and economic change. Once again, this question, difficult though it is to investigate has received very little attention.

More questions

A large amount of material is now available about suffrage in Britain and the US, thanks to historians, but there are important political questions about which we know very little, not only about votes for women in these two countries, but around the world. There is, for instance, the question that I mentioned at the beginning of this essay: why did women win the vote so much earlier in peripheral regions and countries? Was it, as is sometimes suggested, that women formed a small enough proportion of the population that they did not seem threatening? Or was it that they were seen as a civilising influence in frontier areas? Or were quite different factors important? Comparisons between the countries where women, won the suffrage around the turn of the century also raise much broader questions about the common features, if any, in the global struggle for the suffrage. We know remarkably little about how women won the vote around the world. How important are local circumstances and local political configurations, or struggles for national self-determination? How important are cultural differences, or differences in political regimes? Nor is much attention paid to the fact that there are still some countries – Kuwait, for example – where women are disenfranchised.

Little interest has been displayed, as I have indicated, in the question of the political significance and consequences of womanhood suffrage. What differences has it made, for example, to women or to national politics, that in New Zealand women have been voting for a century and in Switzerland only since 1971 (and in the canton of Appenzell only since 1989)? Does women's absence from participation in elections make a difference to their position in society, in relations between the sexes, to women's political activities or to public policies or institutions? What difference does it make to women's rights if women are voters? How important is it that women can vote in transitions from authoritarian to democratic regimes? It is not easy to investigate or answer such questions, but it is important for democratic theory and practice that the attempt at least is made to confront them.

The fact of women's long exclusion from national electorates (even in Europe, in Belgium, France and Italy, women were not enfranchised until the 1940s) has not been seen by most students of politics as of any special relevance for democracy. Nor have women as citizens been seen as influenced by the fact that, in Britain and the United States, women were enfranchised while still subordinate in marriage, and were voting while being incorporated into the welfare state as men's dependants rather than as citizens with their own entitlements. More generally, lack of interest in the deep seated and vehement hostility to votes for women, and the continuing difficulties women face in entering legislative and other public bodies, means that possible insights have not been forthcoming into the mechanisms underlying hostility towards other groups and categories of the population.

The question of votes for women is all too often seen as a rather boring and insignificant matter. On the contrary, it is a fascinating and complex subject, and one that can teach us a great deal about political development and the structure of institutions. There is still an enormous amount of work to be done, and I regret that my own discipline has contributed so little; political scientists are still resistant to the necessary reconsideration of the standard conception of their subject matter. But feminist scholars are growing in number, so perhaps by the time of the 125th anniversary of womanhood suffrage we shall know a lot more about the politics of votes for women.

Notes

1   How could it come about, for example, that two investigators could exclude voting from their scale of conventional political participation because, they write, voting 'occurs only rarely, is highly biased by strong mechanisms of social control and social desirability enhanced by the rain-dance ritual of campaigning, and does not involve the voter in major informational or other costs'? (Barnes and Kaase 1979: 86).

2   Mitchell states that the 'provocativeness of the maiden warriors' on Black Friday gave the men 'a splendid excuse' for their actions, and claims that the assaults were 'in some cases' what the suffragists 'really wanted'. His hysterical tone in many places seems, judging from the final chapter, to be as much a result of his fear of the revival of the women's movement in the 1970s as his obvious dislike of Christabel Pankhurst and the militants. He goes so far as to claim that her main contribution was 'the "terrorist" touch, the taste of blood', and to compare what he sees as the 'blind obedience' of the suffragettes to members of the Manson family (Mitchell 1977: 160, 321, 371).

3   The law was confused about the effect of coverture on local politics. In 1872 the Court of Queen's Bench ruled that married women were disqualified by the law of coverture from exercising the municipal franchise, but the effect on school boards, for example, was not clear (Shanley 1989: 111). The last vestiges of coverture in Britain have only just

been eliminated; for example, the law finally recognised that a husband could rape his wife in 1991.

4 For example, 'An Appeal Against Female Suffrage', reprinted in Hollis 1979.

5 The lack of interest in the suffrage by the tens of thousands of women involved in the Chartist movement in Britain in the 1840s, who acted on behalf of their menfolk, is instructive here. In the first draft of the Charter women's suffrage was included, but it was quickly dropped, on the grounds that its adoption 'might retard the suffrage of men' (Thompson 1976: 132). By 1841 a Chartist speaker was repeating the claim that 'men, as fathers, husbands, and brothers' would look after women's interests (cited in Taylor 1983: 271).

6 In the 1920s the issue of 'protection' arose in a different way. By 1923, when the ERA was first introduced into Congress, legislation protecting women workers and mothers and children had been enacted. The opponents of the ERA feared that the legislation would be jeopardised by equal rights. Their fears were reinforced when the Supreme Court held that minimum wage laws were not required for women because they were protected under the Nineteenth Amendment.

7 See also the comments about historians in Baker 1984: 643.

References

Baker, P. 1984. 'The Domestication of Politics: Women and American Political Society, 1780–1920'. *American Historical Review* 89: 620–47.

Barnes, S.H. and M. Kaase. 1979. *Political Action: Mass Participation in Five Western Democracies.* Beverly Hills, CA: Sage.

Degler, C.N. 1980. *At Odds: Women and the Family in America From the Revolution to the Present.* New York: Oxford University Press.

Downs, A. 1957. *An Economic Theory of Democracy.* New York: HarperCollins.

DuBois, E. 1978. *Feminism and Suffrage: The Emergence of an Independent Women's Movement in America, 1848–1869.* Ithaca, NY: Cornell University Press.

Garner, L. 1984. *Stepping Stones to Women's Liberty: Feminist Ideas in the Women's Suffrage Movement, 1900–988.* London: Heinemann Educational Books.

Harrison, B. 1978. *Separate Spheres: The Opposition to Women's Suffrage in Britain.* New York: Holmes & Meier.

Hollis, P. 1979. *Women in Public: The Women's Movement, 1850–1900.* London: Allen & Unwin.

Holton, S.S. 1986. *Feminism and Democracy: Women's Suffrage and Reform Politics in Britain, 1900–1918.* Cambridge: Cambridge University Press.

Katzenstein, M.F. 1984. 'Feminism and the Meaning of the Vote'. *Signs* 10(1): 4–26.

Kent, S.K. 1987. *Sex and Suffrage in Britain, 1860–1914.* Princeton, NJ: Princeton University Press.

Kraditor, A.S. 1981. *The Ideas of the Woman Suffrage Movement: 1890–1920.* New York: Norton.

Liddington, J. and J. Norris. 1978. *One Hand Tied Behind Us: The Rise of the Women's Suffrage Movement.* London: Virago.

Macpherson, C.B. 1977. *The Life and Times of Liberal Democracy.* New York: Oxford University Press.

Mansbridge, J. 1986. *Why We Lost the ERA.* Chicago: University of Chicago Press.

Mathews, D.G. and J. DeHart. 1990. *Sex, Gender and the Politics of ERA: A State and Nation.* New York: Oxford University Press.

Mayo, E. and J.K. Frye. 1986. 'ERA: Postmortem of a Failure in Political Communication'. In J. Hoff-Wilson (ed.) *Rights of Passage: The Past and Future of the ERA.* Bloomington, IN: Indiana University Press.

McDonagh, E.L. 1992. 'Materialist Praxis and the Woman Suffrage in the American States: The Historical and Contemporary Significance of the Nineteenth Amendment', unpublished paper.

Mill, J.S. 1972. *The Collected Works of John Stuart Mill,* vol. XVII. In F.E. Mineka and D.N. Lindley (eds). Toronto: University of Toronto Press.

Mitchell, D. 1977. *Queen Christabel.* London: MacDonald & Jane.

Morgan, D. 1972. *Suffragists and Democrats: The Politics of Woman Suffrage in America.* East Lansing, MI: Michigan State University Press.

— 1975. *Suffragists and Liberals: The Politics of Woman Suffrage in England.* Totowa, NJ: Rowman & Littlefield.

O'Neill, W.L. 1969. *The Woman Movement: Feminism in the United States and England.* London: Allen & Unwin.

Pankhurst, C. 1987. 'The Great Scourge'. Repr. in Jane Marcus (ed.) *Suffrage and the Pankhursts.* London: Routledge & Kegan Paul.

Pankhurst, E. 1972. 'When Civil War is Waged by Women'. In Miriam Schneir (ed.) *Feminism: The Essential Historical Writings.* New York: Random House.

Pateman, C. 1988. *The Sexual Contract.* Cambridge: Polity.

— 1989. 'The Patriarchal Welfare State'. In C. Pateman, *The Disorder of Women: Democracy, Feminism, and Political Theory.* Cambridge: Polity Press, and Stanford, CA: Stanford University Press.

Sawer, M. and M. Simms. 1993. A *Woman's Place: Women and Politics in Australia,* 2nd edn. Sydney: Allen & Unwin.

Shanley, M.L. 1989. *Feminism, Marriage and the Law* in *Victorian England, 1850–1895.* Princeton, NJ: Princeton University Press.

Taylor, B. 1983. *Eve and the New Jerusalem: Socialism and Feminism in the Nineteenth Century.* London: Virago.

Thompson, D. 1976. 'Women and Nineteenth Century Radical Politics: A Lost Dimension'. In Juliet Mitchell and Ann Oakley (eds) *The Rights and Wrongs of Women.* Harmondsworth: Penguin Books.

Turner, B.S. 1986. *Citzenship and Capitalism.* London: Allen & Unwin.

Wright, A.E. 1913. *The Unexpurgated Case against Womanhood Suffrage.* New York: Paul B. Hoeben.

Young, A. 1988. '"Wild Women": The Censure of the Suffragette Movement'. *International Journal of the Sociology of Law* 16: 279–93.

PART III

Political theory of welfare

10

THE LEGACY OF T.H. MARSHALL (1996)[1]

There has been a remarkable revival of interest in citizenship in the 1990s, a topic now debated across the political spectrum, and this has prompted renewed attention to T.H. Marshall's classic essay, "Citizenship and Social Class." There are now few discussions that do not make at least a passing reference to his name, and there are at least three books concerned with his arguments (Barbalet 1988; Turner 1986; Bulmer and Rees 1996). It seems very fitting, therefore, in a lecture named in honor of a great Norwegian sociologist, to take this opportunity to reflect on the legacy of an eminent British sociologist, particularly as encapsulated in "Citizenship and Social Class."

The focus of the work of the two sociologists (who were contemporaries) was very different, but there are points of common concern. For example, Vilhelm Aubert's collection of essays *In Search of Law* (1983: 163, 171), includes a discussion of human rights, and, in some brief remarks, he treats both welfare legislation and the right of citizens to participate in government and social life as matters of human rights. To put citizenship into the context of human rights provides a different perspective from that found in Marshall's work, and I shall come back to human rights later.

If asked about the most important legacy of Thomas Humphrey Marshall (1893–1981), most commentators would undoubtedly refer to his tripartite classification of citizenship into the three elements of civil, political and social rights. He developed the classification in lectures presented at Cambridge University in 1949, which were first published as *Citizenship and Social Class* in 1950, and then reissued in 1963 in the volume *Sociology at the Crossroads*. At that time, sociology was still a small discipline in Britain, but Marshall's essay quickly influenced such major figures as Reinhardt Bendix, Ralf Dahrendorf, Seymour Martin Lipset and Talcott Parsons, although political scientists displayed relatively little interest.

Marshall argued that the three elements of citizenship had developed in England over 250 years, each one emerging, with some overlap, in different centuries: civil rights in the eighteenth, political rights in the nineteenth, and social rights in the twentieth century. The civil element contains the rights required for individual freedom, such as freedom of speech, the right to own property and includes the right to justice. The political element contains the rights surrounding the electoral and other political processes. It is the social element, that, perhaps I hardly need to say, arouses most controversy.

Marshall's "social rights" is a very broad category that includes not only "the right to a modicum of economic welfare and security," but all that is necessary for citizens "to share to the full in the social heritage and to live the life of a civilized being according to the standards prevailing in the society. The institutions most closely connected with it are the educational system and the social services" (1963: 74). Social rights, for Marshall, indicated the advent of an "enriched" citizenship, in which real income and monetary income had begun to diverge. Market worth was no longer the only thing that counted: "Equality of status is more important than equality of income" (1963: 107).

A good deal of the recent discussion of Marshall's essay focuses on this classification, and critics have asked, for instance, whether his chronology of the development of the elements of citizenship is acceptable, or whether the tripartite division into civil, political and social rights is adequate. I also have some questions to ask about Marshall's classification. Later I shall look at his equivocation about social rights, which anticipates an important strand in the current debate about citizenship, centered round the question whether social rights are "rights" in the same sense as the civil and political components of citizenship.

First, however, I want to explore some other relatively neglected aspects of his legacy. There are some curious omissions and mistakes in his essay that, despite all the attention being paid to his work, have either not been sufficiently explored or are barely noticed at all. Marshall established much of the prevailing framework within which citizenship is being discussed. To a large degree, his commentators, even when critical, remain within the framework, so that an examination of Marshall's arguments throws light onto the limits of much current discussion of citizenship. His work also illustrates the limitations of a good deal of argument about democratization.

Anthony Giddens (1996: 65–66) has recently commented that Marshall "did not use the term 'democracy' all that often." Nevertheless, he argues, Marshall's essay "can be understood as a theory of democratization." In *Citizenship and Social Class*, Marshall has very little to say about democracy (he refers to "democratic citizenship" in the last paragraph). In a later essay, "Value Problems of Welfare-Capitalism," originally published in 1972, Marshall added a term to the phrase in his title and wrote of "democratic-welfare-capitalism," because, he stated, "democracy deserves to have a position as a third party of independent status, not just to be taken for granted" (Marshall 1981: 104). The essay was reprinted in 1981 with an "After-thought," and a subtitle, "The 'Hyphenated Society'," but Marshall did not pursue at any length the implications of ceasing to take democracy for granted. By 1972 he was drawing on economic theories of democracy; he refers to Schumpeter, and to Arrow's social choice theory. He treats democracy as majority rule and elections as expressions of voters' "egotism" (Marshall 1981: 108). In the "Afterthought," he states that welfare is concerned with "what minorities need" (Marshall 1981: 126). This raises important questions about the relationship between Marshall's three rights of citizenship and democracy.

Citizenship is frequently discussed by other scholars in terms of membership rather than democracy. One book on Marshall opens with the statement that citizenship "defines those who are, and are not, members of a common society" (Barbalet 1988: 1). Marshall states that citizenship "is a status bestowed on those who are full members of a community. All who possess the status are equal with respect to the rights and duties with which the status is endowed" (1963: 87). He also writes that it requires "a direct sense of community membership based on loyalty to a civilization which is a common possession. It is a loyalty of free men endowed with rights and protected by a common law" (1963: 96).

But membership and citizenship are not the same, and nor does citizenship necessarily define membership. The relationship between the two requires at least the following distinctions: a) those subject to law but who are neither members nor citizens (e.g. slaves in the Old South); b) those who are members in some sense, but are not citizens (e.g. women before enfranchisement, or non-naturalized permanent residents); c) those who have gained the formal elements of citizenship but who are not full members (e.g. women virtually everywhere, or African-Americans in the USA). These distinctions also illustrate that citizenship and democracy are not synonymous. Until the latter part of this century, citizenship rights were the privilege of only a part of the population in most Western countries. It is only in recent decades that the whole adult population in most countries have won even that emblem of citizenship, the suffrage (and women are still excluded in, e.g. Kuwait).

Moreover, it is, to say the least, very misleading to define citizenship in terms of a "community" or "common society" in the late twentieth century. Citizenship is not a status or (as I prefer, following Judith Shklar (1991) a standing) in a society, but standing in a state. Of course, standing in, and membership in, the society or societies encompassed within any state is closely connected to citizenship within the state, but the connections are complex. Marshall has nothing to say about the British state and citizenship. He is interested in a different subject; the integration of the (male) working class as members of a common "civilization" and "social heritage."

Until quite recently, there was a widespread consensus that class was *the* major social problem, and that democratization was a matter of a process that Marshall called "class abatement." Much of the discussion of Marshall has focused on such matters as his view of, or neglect of, class struggle, and whether he presents a rather complacent, evolutionary view of class abatement. But, with increasing frequency, attention is now drawn to the inadequacy of an exclusive focus on class at a time when the restructuring of capitalism has led to the very rapid decline of the working class as Marshall knew it, and ethnic diversity has increased. It is also pointed out that citizenship has been integral to the consolidation of the nation state, that Marshall had a parochial focus on England, and that his chronology is not necessarily applicable elsewhere. The most recent discussions are likely to refer to, if not usually to explore, Marshall's neglect of women. (For example, Andrews 1991; Barbalet 1988; Bottomore 1992; Bulmer and Rees 1996; Giddens 1982; Held 1989; Mann 1987; Turner 1986; van Steenbergen 1994; Vogel and Moran 1991).

Yet, despite the increasing volume and range of criticism, his commentators typically fail to appreciate the peculiar narrowness of Marshall's interest in citizenship, which runs in one direction only. He analyzes the three elements of citizenship and their impact on class, but he assumes that, in 1949 with the development of social rights, citizenship is enjoyed in the same way by all citizens. He fails to ask whether rights are of equal worth to all citizens, or, to make the point in another way, whether citizenship means the same for all individuals. This failure helps explain why he said so little about democracy. He asked about the social integration, and the material and cultural condition, of the – male – working class. He did not consider whether there were other citizens who might be described as second class.[2]

Moreover, neither Marshall, nor his contemporary critics, question whether in Britain in 1949 "citizenship" was the appropriate category to use. The relevance of what might seem a strange comment becomes clear if Marshall is put into the context of his time. Perhaps if, like Aubert, he had been interested in the sociology of law, Marshall might have asked this question.

One of the editors of *Citizenship Today*[3] remarks that "if any intellectual figure of the period can be said to embody the spirit of the 'post-war settlement' it is Marshall" (Bulmer and Rees 1996: 22). But to assess Marshall's legacy, his work has to be set in a broader context than that of the "settlement." I want to do this by considering the significance of five legal and other developments in 1948, the year before Marshall's lectures, when, I assume, he was thinking about the issues discussed in his lectures. I want to begin, first, with the British Nationality Act, and, second, the arrival at a British port of the *Empire Windrush*, a ship carrying 500 immigrants from the West Indies.

Despite all the discussion of Marshall, the 1948 Nationality Act is rarely mentioned. For example, Anthony Rees (Bulmer and Rees 1996: 17) notes that, in the Ireland Act of 1949, full citizenship rights were given to "settlers from a country that had voluntarily left the Commonwealth and had not offered reciprocal arrangements." In another article on Marshall, Rees (1995: 345) comments that in 1949 "membership of the polity could be largely be taken for granted," and he refers again to the Ireland Act as an example of the "relaxed attitude" of the time. But the 1948 Act is an even more significant example. In the closing chapter of *Citizenship Today*, the editors remark in passing that "almost all post-war immigrants from the New Commonwealth have enjoyed full citizenship rights from the moment they reached [British] shores" (Bulmer and Rees 1996: 278). The passengers on the *Empire Windrush* enjoyed these rights, and the reason was that they were *British subjects*.

Curiously, Marshall ignores the legal category of British subject, and so fails to mention that, in 1949, the "citizens" who are the subject of his essay had barely achieved legal existence. Now, it is true that, in a social and political sense, Marshall's three rights of citizenship had been developing in England, and had been campaigned and fought for, since the seventeenth century. But it is also true that "citizenship" during the same three centuries, legally, politically and socially, was part of the imperial expansion of Britain. Marshall's own understanding of his subject matter is clear enough. He states that (1963: 75) "the citizenship whose history I wish to trace is, by definition, national" – and the nation in question is England. Marshall gives a sketch of the emergence of the national institutions of the courts, parliament and the Poor Law. He refers to the development of "national consciousness" from the eighteenth century onward, including jingoistic patriotism, linked to a sense of a common social heritage. However, he does not connect the nation and jingoism to the Empire or reflect on the relation of the citizen to the British subject.

There is a two-fold repression of empire in Marshall's essay; in his unselfconscious assimilation of the peripheries of the United Kingdom under "England," and in his silence about the 1948 Act and the British subject. In his definition of citizenship that I quoted earlier, Marshall referred to protection by a "common law." But he failed to investigate the importance of "common law" in another legal sense. The common law tradition of England played a central role in shaping citizenship, and its legacy can still be seen in some of the most pressing problems today.

Marshall gave his lectures and published his essay at a point when the legal distinction between British subjects and citizens of the United Kingdom had not yet been clearly delineated. The remarkable point about the Nationality Act of 1948 was that it reaffirmed the old common law doctrine of *jus soli*, on which the status of British subject was based. The doctrine, which took authoritative legal form after 1608, and was codified in the British Nationality Act of 1914, meant that birth within the British Empire, under the jurisdiction of the British Crown, created British subjects.[4] The 1948 Act introduced "citizenship" into the law for the first time by creating a category of citizenship of the United Kingdom and Colonies, or Commonwealth citizens.[5] As one legal commentary notes, after 1948 the status of British subject involved "the possession of the nationality of one or more of nine countries: the United Kingdom and Colonies, and the eight Commonwealth Countries" (Parry 1951: 67).[6]

By 1949 the heyday of the British Empire had passed and there was a signpost to the decolonization to come. The Indian subcontinent, "the jewel" of the Empire, had gained independence in 1947 as India and Pakistan. The position of the white Dominions was also changing. Just prior to the 1948 Act, a Commonwealth Conference had agreed that each Dominion could enact its own citizenship laws (Canada had instituted its own citizenship in 1946). These new citizens would continue to share the status of British subjects, but each Dominion could now decide what that status meant within its jurisdiction.[7]

The West Indian laborers who landed in Britain in 1948 had the same legal status as the British working class, and, in a sense, shared membership in the Empire, yet their relationship to Marshall's English "civilization" and "social heritage" was very different. Ironically, not only has Marshall nothing to say about the making of

British citizens out of the British subject, he conveys nothing of the international and imperial context of British capitalism. From the outset, capitalism and class were bound up with the development of the modern international system of states, through discovery, conquest, settlement, and trade, including the slave trade, and the transport of labor across the world. In 1949, class abatement had a long way to go. The upper and lower classes in Britain were still distinguished by language and dress, as well as other social and cultural markers. Nevertheless, the working class shared a heritage of color, imperial superiority and Marshall's "jingoistic patriotism" with their national and social betters. If they felt a bond of a shared heritage and civilization with other members of the Empire, it was likely to be with the settlers in such white Dominions as Australia or Canada.

The full significance of the arrival of the *Empire Windrush* is only apparent with hindsight. Nevertheless, to claim that "Marshall could not anticipate...new inequalities and disparities which do not follow the logic of class divisions. Immigration is a case in point..." (Halfmann 1997: 266), is to ignore not only the Empire and the British subject (together with the black residents of Britain) but the circumstances of the 1940s.[8] A policy decision during the Second World War might have brought such matters to Marshall's attention. From 1942, after the USA joined in the war against the Axis powers, American troops were stationed in Britain, and the American army was then racially segregated. The British government had to decide whether segregation should continue to be upheld on British soil. This was an issue of more than local importance, since the British army included troops from throughout the Empire, and the allied forces, it was widely proclaimed, were fighting for democracy. The response of the British government was to aid and abet segregation, even for recreational purposes (Rich 1990: 150–55).[9]

It is worth stressing these historical details because the British case is so instructive about current problems of citizenship, now being discussed under the heading of multiculturalism. Imperial chickens have, so to speak, come home to roost across Europe and North America. And the manner in which the British subject was turned into the British citizen foreshadowed the restrictions now being erected against any further roosting. The legacies of the common law rapidly began to be dismantled from the 1960s onward, initially through the use of immigration restrictions, and the question of who could and should share in the English social heritage and civilization became central to the making of UK citizenship.[10] By the mid-1980s, a status that included peoples of varied culture and heritage from around the world had been cast into history, and many British passport holders found themselves with worthless documents. Paradoxically, however, the "British citizen" in the strict sense had a very brief existence. In 1973 Britain joined the EEC (as it then was) and the issue of European citizenship and freedom of movement soon arose.

Such a sweeping change in British law could be made with relative ease because *jus soli* had always been joined with another principle, *jus sanguinis*, under which status was determined through descent (or blood-line). Both doctrines had been codified in the 1914 Nationality Act, which specified two forms of birth into the status of British subject. The second (as stated in Part I, 1 (b) of the Act) was that "any person born out of his Majesty's dominions whose father was, at the time of that person's birth, a British subject" was also a British subject. *Jus sanguinis* was central to the provisions of the 1981 British Nationality Act, under which unrestricted entry into and "right of abode in the United Kingdom" from outside the EU became confined to "patrials," a category determined by descent. In 1981 the explicitly patriarchal character of *jus sanguinis* was abolished, and mothers gained the capacity to pass their citizenship to their children born overseas.

This improvement in the political standing of British mothers brings me back to Marshall and to a notable mistake in *Citizenship and Social Class.* Consider the significance of two other developments in 1948, the third and fourth on my list. Third, under the 1948 Nationality Act, women who married alien men ceased to lose their status as British subjects; and, fourth, in 1948 women were finally admitted to full membership of Cambridge University – where, the following year, Marshall presented his lecture.[11]

I noted earlier that Marshall defines citizenship as a status of "free men." In discussing the early Factory Acts in the nineteenth century, he also referred to "the adult male – the citizen *par excellence*" (1963: 84), and he talks unselfconsciously of boys and men throughout his essay. This is not merely the language of his day, but arises from the fact that he is completely oblivious to another part of English common law, the doctrine of coverture, central to the construction of citizenship. And this led to a mistake about civil rights that is typically overlooked by commentators. Marshall erroneously states that, by the nineteenth century, civil rights had a "democratic, or universal, character" (1963: 79), and that "citizenship in the form of civil rights was universal" (1963: 80). He also notes (1963: 79) that the status of married women was "in some important respects peculiar," but apparently the peculiarity was not sufficient to make him pause before he made his statements about civil rights. In fact, civil rights were far from universal in the nineteenth century.

Under coverture, in the mid-nineteenth century married women had no independent civil or political standing; they disappeared under the "cover" of their husbands and had no rights over their persons, property or children. And since they were "covered," they must take the nationality of their husbands. Feminists, for good reasons, compared marriage to that peculiar institution, slavery, and the women's movement spent a great deal of effort to gain reform of the law governing marriage, and to win civil as well as political rights (on coverture, see Pateman 1988). In discussing the Factory Acts, Marshall (1963: 84), referred to the exclusion of adult male workers from the protections of the Acts. The protection, he noted, was provided as an *alternative* to citizenship, and the adult man was excluded from this legislation, "out of respect for his status as a citizen, on the ground that enforced protective measures curtailed the civil right to conclude a free contract of employment." On the other hand, the Factory Acts applied to adult women. Women, Marshall claimed, "were protected because they were not citizens." But, significantly, Marshall got this the wrong way round. Rather, it was because women were seen as incapable of protecting themselves and had to be protected ("covered") by their husbands, that they lacked civil rights.

Commentators who note that Marshall ignored women's citizenship usually do not see a connection between his silence about half the population and their history, and his argument about the process of class abatement. Yet his view of the impact of citizenship upon capitalism was that it would create a society of gentlemen.

Marshall was born into the privileged circumstances and high culture of the Bloomsbury circle, destined for a future that combined "private cultivation and public duty" (Halsey 1984: 1). He has been described as "a gentleman in the authentic sense" (Bulmer and Rees 1996: xi), albeit that "the meaning of that persona,…is now largely lost" (Halsey 1984: 5). Thomas Humphrey Marshall's Cambridge lectures were named in honor of the economist Alfred Marshall, who also talked of the progress of the working classes. The economist had referred to steady development until every man was a gentleman by occupation, was independent, and had manly respect for himself and others. T.H. Marshall began his own argument at this point. His gloss on Alfred Marshall was that each man should enjoy the standard of life seen as appropriate to a gentleman, which meant that they should be full members of society and citizens. Thus he called for the replacement of "the word 'gentleman' by the word 'civilized'" (1963: 72).

The effect of Marshall's change of words is the same as the very popular current practice of replacing "he" by "she and he." The problem of the masculine character of the citizen is left intact beneath an empty change of words; no effort has been made to understand why the term gentleman (or he) was used in the first place. In post-war England, Marshall believed, any man could become civilized, or a gentleman and citizen. He failed to acknowledge, however, that no lady can ever become a gentleman.

The term "civilization" embodies all the problems of far-flung British subjects and whether they could share in the social heritage of the English nation (especially once they landed on British shores) – but it also embodies problems about women's citizenship. "Civilization" is typically seen as a masculine creation and a masculine heritage – one reason why the gentlemen of Cambridge University fought so long to exclude women from taking a degree. That Marshall's citizenship has little if any recognized place for women is clear from his discussion of the duties of citizens. This part of his essay is much less well known than his classification of rights, although it is very revealing in a number of respects.

Marshall wrote (1963: 85) that "[t]he duty to improve and civilize oneself is therefore a social duty…because the social health of a society depends upon the civilization of its members." But, once again, he was writing with men in mind. For example, in discussing the duty to improve, i.e. educate oneself in a broad sense, he makes no mention of the difficulties women had faced in gaining entry to educational institutions, or to widely held convictions at the time about the need for a different form of education for men and women.

Towards the end of *Citizenship and Social Class*, Marshall lists some other duties of citizens. Among these is the duty to perform military service, but in post-war Britain young women were excluded from conscription. Another duty is to pay taxes and national insurance contributions, yet this, too, applied largely to male citizens. In Britain in 1949, wives were not taxpayers in their own right. Until 1990 the Inland Revenue adhered to the doctrine of coverture and treated wives' income as if it belonged to their husbands. Nor were married women workers expected to contribute to the system of social insurance payments. The National Insurance Act (1946) encouraged them to opt out of the contributions that entitled them to such benefits as old age pensions in their own right, in favor of eligibility through their husbands' contributions (the majority of them opted out).

These, however, are specific duties. Marshall argued that the duty to work, i.e., to be employed, was the only clear example of a general duty of citizens. He also noted (1963: 122–23) that to give "such service as one can to promote the welfare of the community" is a very vague requirement. Once again, Marshall gave no recognition to women's service; he implicitly took it for granted that male citizens were the "workers" and breadwinners. Unlike William Beveridge (who had appointed Marshall as tutor in social work at the London School of Economics in 1925) in his famous *Report on Social Insurance and Allied Services* (1942) that set the foundation of post-war social rights, Marshall saw no service of significance in housework and caring for children and other adults.

Beveridge (§§107–17) treated housewives as part of a team with their husbands; "each of [the] partners is equally essential." In a passage much quoted by feminists in recent years, Beyeridge wrote that "the great majority of married women must be regarded as occupied on work which is vital though unpaid, without which their husbands could not do their paid work, and without which the nation could not continue." In particular, mothers "have vital work to do in ensuring the adequate continuance of the British race and of British ideals in the world." Marshall, in contrast, in an address given in 1945 (published as *Work and Wealth*, 1963: 219), while stating that "support of a family is a form of service," was referring only to the male breadwinner. Despite Beveridge's view of wives as part of a team, it might be suggested that Marshall leaves the more realistic legacy on this point. Women's service as housewives and as mothers has never counted as part of citizenship. In the 1990s, with the rise of workfare, the notion that it might count is more remote than ever. Attempts are being made in the USA to enforce Marshall's duty to work – a duty, that, he strongly emphasized, was voluntary – even in the case of young, single mothers with small children.

The limitations of Marshall's essay as a theory of democratization are particularly obvious in the case of women and wives. Marshall never sees that there are questions to be asked about the sense in which they were members as well as citizens, and whether their citizenship has the same value as men's contribution and standing. The consequence of the process of social integration or class abatement was the creation of a largely masculine "democracy," and this is a legacy which most of Marshall's commentators prefer quickly to pass over.

I now want to turn to another, much discussed, aspect of Marshall's argument. He identified social rights as the major mechanism through which class abatement, or limitation of the operation of the capitalist market, was taking place. In *Citizenship and Social Class* he asked how two "opposing principles," as he called them, the equality of citizenship and the class inequality of capitalism, "could grow and flourish side by side in the same soil?" At times, according to Marshall, the opposing forces of citizenship and class were allies instead of antagonists, but in the twentieth century, "citizenship and the capitalist system have been at war" (1963: 87). Citizenship, notably the element of social rights, had begun to make a substantive impact on social inequality and capitalism.

Marshall's argument was, however, more complicated than this dramatic statement about the war between citizenship and capitalism implies. Citizenship does not merely modify or abate the class system, but, he argued, creates a new system of class divisions and new inequalities. He gives the example of the Education Act of 1944. All children were to be assured of an education, but allocation by merit into different types of schools (secondary modern, grammar and technical) meant that they would be distributed across occupations, and hence, across classes, as a result. Anticipating John Rawls, Marshall argued that, even so, there was a significant difference between the new social divisions and the old class system, with its hereditary privileges; the new inequalities could be seen to have a legitimate basis, and so in were in accord with social justice.

So what, exactly, was Marshall's argument about social rights? Even in *Citizenship and Social Class*, his argument can be interpreted in two ways; I shall call these the strong or democratic and the weak versions. In general, social rights were the key to class abatement because they broke the nexus between location in the market (i.e. the labor market) and standing as a citizen. Thus Marshall writes of "a progressive divorce between real and money income" (1963: 125), and of a "universal right to real income which is not proportionate to the market value of the claimant" (1963: 100). That is to say, social rights were "at war" with capitalism in the sense that, as he put it in 1972 "the central function of welfare…is to supersede the market by taking goods and services out of it, or in some way to control and modify its operations.…" The aim of social rights was, therefore, to produce "a general reduction of risk and insecurity, an equalization between the more and less fortunate at all levels" (Marshall 1981: 107). As citizens, everyone should enjoy the "same general amenities" (1963: 123) and have access to, and be able to participate in, social life and the common heritage.

I shall now turn to the strong argument that can be derived from *Citizenship and Social Class*. Marshall, of course was writing at a point when the great post-war social reforms – the "settlement" referred to earlier – had only just been introduced in Britain. It was a period of optimism about the future, and there was a widely shared expectation that the social misery and inequalities of the pre-war era would be abolished once and for all. One way of encapsulating this outlook is that the Poor Law and the Poor Law mentality, with the specter of the workhouse that had haunted the working classes for a century, would be abolished once and for all. Under the Poor Law until 1918, relief could be obtained only if civil and political rights were forfeited. Marshall wrote (1963: 83) the "significance of [the] final removal [of disenfranchisement] has, perhaps, not been fully appreciated." That is to say, it meant that the maintenance of a certain material standard through public provision should be seen as a right of a citizen, not as something that diminishes citizenship. Or, more emphatically, the abolition of the Poor Law means that all citizens are *entitled* to a standard of life and amenities sufficient for membership and participation in the social heritage.

On this reading, citizenship is upheld and maintained through social rights as unconditional entitlements. Marshall stated that social rights "imply…the subordination of market price to social justice, replacement of the free bargain by the declaration of rights" (1963: 115). He discussed this in terms of the "invasion" of contract by status, but this is misleading terminology. The status, or equal standing, of twentieth century citizenship is quite different from the old, hierarchical "status" in Sir Henry Maine's (1917 [1861]) original formulation of movement "from status to contract." Still, Marshall's point is quite clear. Citizenship is incompatible with an untrammelled capitalist market and the coercive discipline (the "incentive to work") and loss of standing of the Poor Law.

His most significant statement of the strong interpretation of social rights occurs in a discussion of trades unions and collective bargaining. He wrote, in a little noticed passage, that "to have to bargain for a living wage in a society which accepts the living wage as a social right is as absurd as to have to haggle for a vote in a society which accepts the vote as a political right" (1963: 116). Marshall took it for granted that a "living wage" was a family wage, the earnings of a male breadwinner. A *democratic* interpretation of his argument is that each citizen should have an entitlement to a standard of life, and education and access to social and cultural amenities, that enables them to participate fully (or as fully as they wish) in all aspects of social and political life. In short, social rights are entitlements in exactly the same sense as the suffrage is an entitlement of citizenship.

But the strong interpretation is only one reading of Marshall's argument on social rights. The problem is that there is also (to borrow the title of Anthony Rees' (1995) article) "the other T.H. Marshall" – another Marshall whose weak argument points in a direction taken by many governments in the last twenty years. In the 1990s a strong view of social rights is widely regarded as completely unrealistic and hopelessly outdated.

With hindsight, the post-war settlement in Britain looks far less consensual from the outset than is often supposed, and the outcome, in W.G. Runciman's words (1996: 52), "looks more like an expression of the ideals of 1918–22 [Lloyd George's time] than of 1945–51." Indeed, Runciman draws attention to the similarity between the aspirations of manual workers in the earlier period and today. In the 1920s, they wanted decent pay, working conditions and housing, and protection against poverty arising from unemployment, sickness and old age, "but they were as tenacious in defence of differentials in earnings, and as vehement in their disapproval of 'scroungers', as non-manual workers" – and as large a minority of them were Conservatives as were socialists (Runciman 1996: 54). If we now turn to "the other Marshall", we find echoes of this outlook.

In another part of his discussion of trades unions in *Citizenship and Social Class*, he characterized social rights as follows; "social rights imply an absolute right to a certain standard of civilization which *is conditional* only on the discharge of the general duties of citizenship" (my emphasis) (1963:98).This is a curious formulation. A right cannot be both an "absolute" right, or an entitlement, and conditional upon performance of duties. Moreover, Marshall had one duty in particular in mind – the duty to work, or to be employed. Marshall (1963: 124) saw the duty to work as a recent creation that was "attached to the status of citizenship." This was because, with the abolition of the Poor Law, (male) citizens could no longer be compelled into employment through market disciplines. He wrote, "if the obligations of contract are brushed aside by an appeal to the rights of citizenship, then the duties of citizenship must be accepted as well" (1963: 118). Social rights thus become conditional upon employment.[12]

In his later writings, there is little to be found of Marshall's strong version of social rights. For example, in 1969 in a discussion of power (which, he said, stemmed from his earlier interest in rights) he argued that "social rights – the rights to welfare in the broadest sense of the term – …are not designed for the exercise of power at all. They reflect…the strong individualist element in mass society, but it refers to individuals as consumers not actors" (Marshall 1981: 141). Social rights are thus severed from citizenship. The place of a consumer depends on private resources, not political rights.

Anthony Rees (1995) provides examples of the weak version of social rights in Marshall's later work. He notes Marshall's shock at the actions of the unions in 1979 ("the winter of discontent"), and how, in publications in 1981, he shared some of the popular sentiment about "scroungers." But even in 1949 in *Citizenship and Social Class*, Marshall had already begun to worry about unofficial strikes, and to fear that rank and file trade unionists were not inspired to the same extent as their leaders "by a lively sense of responsibility towards the welfare of the community" (1963: 117). By 1981, he was wondering whether the term "welfare state" should still be used when it was too vague to serve as a unifying principle of the social order, and so much of the "spirit and practice" of the 1940s had vanished (Marshall 1981: 98). What was appropriate was "welfare" as part of "the hyphenated society" – but, as I noted earlier, this he now saw as an issue of "minorities." Welfare, he believed, had lost its status. Marshall mentions the failure to prevent poverty as one reason for this, but he comes back again to strikes, and "abuses" of the system (Marshall 1981: 129, 132–33).[13]

Rees (1995: 358, 360) comments about Marshall's later work that, "in these formulations the rights of citizens seem to disappear utterly," and concludes that, "in the end," Marshall seems "to have lost faith in the concept" of citizenship. This conclusion goes too far; Marshall surely did not lose faith in civil and political rights.These rights are needed for the economic view of democracy that, as I noted earlier, he seemed to have adopted by the 1970s. But "the other Marshall" antici-pates a very common view in the 1990s – one that goes back a long way – that social rights are not, properly speaking, rights. Barbalet (1988: 67–72), for example – in a book that sticks very closely to Marshall's perspective – claims that social rights are merely means to other rights. They are substantive and concerned "with social and economic disabilities," so cannot be universal, and they depend on the fiscal health of the state. He states that "they are wholly unlike…the legal and political components of citizenship…social rights can never be more than secondary rights of citizenship."[14]

There is another important point that requires emphasis about Marshall's view of social rights. In *Citizenship and Social Class* he assumed that social rights, like the citizen's duty to work, were predicated on full employment for male workers, a policy basic to the post-war "settlement." Consider these words of Beveridge in 1945:

> The necessity of preventing after this war a return to the mass unemployment between the two wars is formally admitted by all. The possibility of doing so, if we are prepared to will the means as well as the end, is not open to reasonable doubt.
>
> (Beveridge 1945: 249)

In the late 1990s, there are reasons to have such doubts. High levels of unemployment have existed for a long time, and, in Britain, some of the conditions have reappeared that Marshall thought were gone for good. Social inequalities have been deepening for two decades.

At the close of *Citizenship and Social Class* (1963: 127), Marshall referred to a comment of Lionel Robbins' about the difficulties of combining egalitarian real incomes with inegalitarian money incomes. Marshall's response was that the difficulty was not a result of muddled thinking but a conflict of principles – that is, the two principles with which his essay is concerned. The compromise between them in the late 1940s was "not dictated by logic." He concluded: "It may be that some of the conflicts within our social system are becoming too sharp for the compromise to achieve its purpose much longer." The compromise perhaps lasted rather longer than Marshall feared, but it had broken down by the late 1970s. Marshall's balance between the market and "welfare" then began to be tipped heavily towards the market. The increase in inequality has been driven by the political victory of an economic doctrine based on nineteenth century dogmas, complete with an updated Poor Law.

The paradox in the 1990s is that democracy is more popular than ever before, but the conditions under which all citizens can enjoy the standing of full members of the polity are under serious threat. There has been a marked increase in insecurity for very many citizens. The jobs for the male breadwinners who constituted Marshall's working class have declined dramatically, and, as the global restructuring of capitalism continues, many of those jobs are being replaced by low wage and part-time or casual employment. Britain has been described (Hutton 1995: 13) as a 30–30–40 society: 40% of adults of working age in secure positions (their number has been shrinking for 20 years); 30% in structurally insecure positions; and 30% either unemployed or economically inactive. These developments have, of course, been taking place as public provision has been decreased. A graphic illustration of the shift from the late 1940s is the contrast between Marshall's statement that "public policy has unequivocally given the citizen a legitimate expectation of a home fit for a family to live in" (1963: 109), and the spectacle of homeless citizens begging in the streets, and living under pieces of plastic or in cardboard boxes.

Britain is not, of course, the only country where these processes are at work, but Britain, along with the USA and New Zealand, are, so to speak, the primary social laboratories among the rich countries. These are global trends; inequality is increasing, as nineteenth century dogmas have also underpinned international economic policies. The gap between the richest and poorest countries has widened over the past twenty years, countless women and children, in particular, have been impoverished, and some African countries are now worse off than they were in the 1960s.

Consideration of democracy and citizenship in the 1990s cannot be confined within state borders, and this brings me to the fifth on my list of developments in 1948; namely, the proclamation of the United Nations Universal Declaration of Human Rights. Human rights are being taken more seriously today than ever before, but there is a long way to go before they are linked firmly enough to democratization. The major problem with citizenship has been, and remains, its exclusionary character. Within states, there are many problems about the citizenship of women, and many other peoples and categories of inhabitants, and internationally citizenship has always been tied to inclusion in particular states. Human rights are crucial because, in principle at least, they give standing to individuals irrespective of their citizenship or lack of citizenship, and so help open the way for democratization and membership to become less state-centered.

It is not often noticed that the limits of Marshall's essay run parallel, in two respects, to the limits of the theory and practice of human rights. First, from 1789 and the Declaration of the Rights of Man and the Citizen, human rights have been interpreted literally – as the rights of men. In the past few years, feminist legal scholars and activists have mounted a vigorous attack against this interpretation. Some success, in principle at least, was achieved at the World Conference on Human Rights in 1993, especially on the problem of violence against women, and a few countries have begun to amend their regulations about political asylum.

Second, the critics of Marshall's social rights are repeating claims made for at least thirty years about the relation between the two UN Covenants, one on Civil and Political Rights, and the other on Economic, Social and Cultural Rights. The argument that economic and social rights do not have the same status as proper "human rights" was made, for example, in 1967 by Maurice Cranston (1967) in a well-known paper. The division of human rights into the two Covenants, like Marshall's tripartite classification of rights, invites doubt about the status of social rights. The division, and Marshall's classification, need replacing by a conception of *democratic rights*. That is, rights that help constitute full standing and full membership, and are of equal worth to all citizens.

If Marshall lost faith in the idea of citizenship, and if he did so because he came to believe that social rights were at best secondary rights, then he lost faith for the wrong reason. The objection that it is "contradictory" to have universal rights (or duties) that also take into account particular circumstances (Barbalet 1988: 70) is not convincing if democratization is taken seriously. Both claims rely on a simplistic notion of universalism, and on the belief that the goal of public provision is to rescue the "minorities" with "social and economic disabilities," the casualties of the capitalist market, rather than creating democratic standing. In fact the combination of universal policies and particularism is quite familiar. The taxation system and criminal justice system, for example, take account of individual incomes or individual circumstances (O'Neill 1989), and, in the 1990s, we expect people in wheelchairs or with other handicaps to be able to have access to buildings along with the able bodied.

This is not to deny that the creation of democratic rights involves some extremely difficult policy decisions, but that is a different matter. The difficulties are compounded because democratization can no longer be centered on Marshall's "working class," the white, male breadwinners; women and a multiplicity of ethnic groups and indigenous peoples are now on the political stage. The policies are also difficult because, at a time when it is an open question whether full employment (for all citizens, not just white males) is any longer a feasible goal, the connection between citizenship and employment is being strengthened. Thus the idea that employment is the only significant duty or contribution of a citizen is being reinforced. The problems are multiplied because neither the exclusionary character of citizenship nor the political unit of the nation state can any longer be presupposed.

But let me conclude with a positive part of Marshall's legacy. I have seen no discussions of his comparison between the right to the suffrage and the right to a living wage – or, as I would translate this in the 1990s, the right to a mode of life entailed by democratic standing. The suffrage is now, almost universally, seen as an entitlement (a necessary part of "free and fair" elections), so it provides an apt standard for other democratic, human rights. In one of his later writings Marshall stated that education "is a process by which citizens are made" (1981: 90), but that is true for democratic rights as a whole. They are the stuff out of which citizens are made; citizens with the standing, resources – educational, material and cultural – and capacities, to participate fully in social and political life. If democratization worth the name is to characterize the coming decades, then democratic rights need to be taken a great deal more seriously than in the twentieth century.

Notes

1 This chapter is the text of the Vilhelm Aubert Memorial Lecture, which I had the honor to deliver at the University of Oslo in the fall of 1996. I have made a few minor additions and stylistic improvements.
2 Marshall (1963: 86–87) states that his interest is in the impact of citizenship on social inequality, and he will discuss class in light of this "special interest." In fact, as I discuss below, he has little interest in "social inequality" apart from the position of the male working class.
3 The twelve chapters in the book were originally presented as the T.H. Marshall Memorial Lectures at the University of Southampton between 1983 and 1995.

4 Part I 1 (i) of the 1914 British Nationality and Status of Aliens Act stated that: "The following persons shall be deemed to be natural-born British subjects:- (a) Any person born within his Majesty's dominions and allegiance". (There were certain conditions attached, but these are not relevant to my present argument).

5 A number of other categories were also created (see Bevan 1986: 113; and Parry 1951). British nationality law continues to generate numerous, complex categories.

6 The 1948 Act also separated those acquiring British nationality by virtue of birth (or naturalization) in the UK from those acquiring it elsewhere.

7 Provision was also made for British subjects who did not take the citizenship of their country of residence, say, upon independence, to become UK citizens (Bevan 1986: 113).

8 Immigration was already becoming an issue. In 1947, for instance, some Labour MPs called for immigration restrictions (Fielding 1998: 91). It seems that the passengers on the *Empire Windrush* and other immigrants from the West Indies were not expected to remain very long. In 1948 the Colonial Secretary said that they "have British passports and they must be allowed to land. There's nothing to worry about because they won't last one winter in England" (quoted in *The Times*, 2 May 1998: 19, in a commemoration of the fiftieth anniversary of the ship's arrival).

9 There were some 170,000 American troops, and about 10% were black. On relations between the black American servicemen and white British women see Enloe (1990: 68–71). Rich also notes that the British government imported some workers from the West Indies (as "Bevin Boys") to assist in war production (on this and the position of African students as well as black residents of Britain, see Rich 1990: ch. 7).

10 Some forty years before Marshall's lectures, the problems inherent in talking about British citizenship had been canvassed by prominent legal, political, academic and religious authorities in *United Empire*, the journal of the Royal Colonial Institute. Their opinions diverged markedly about whether the term citizenship had any meaning at all, or what it might mean beyond a synonym for British subject. They were also divided about the capacities of those outside of Britain for exercising citizenship rather than being governed as subjects of the Crown (Sargant 1912).

11 In 1998 it was announced that the women who graduated before 1948, over 900, were to receive their degrees with proper ceremony.

12 For a recent interpretation of Marshall that takes this view see Mead 1997. He writes (1997: 197, 211) that "a policy of enforcing work and other civilities is the truest to Marshall's idea," and that "if work [i.e. paid employment] is taken to be an obligation of citizenship…one cannot exempt the poor from it if one wants to justify provision for them on the basis of citizenship."

13 In 1972 Marshall (1981c: 115) briefly mentioned "the 'women's lib' movement" and the demand for free contraceptives and free abortion on request. He commented that, if contraceptives were available, "the case for free abortion in all cases is not self-evident." He added that such measures "may also increase the possibilities for 'scrounging' on public funds."

14 Zolo (1993: 264) agrees that there is a strong case to be made that social rights "are not rights at all."

References

Andrews, G. (ed.) 1991. *Citizenship*. London: Lawrence & Wishart.

Aubert, V. 1983. *In Search of Law: Sociological Approaches to Law*. Oxford: Martin Robertson.

Barbalet, J.M. 1988. *Citizenship: Rights, Struggle and Class Inequality*. Milton Keynes: Open University Press.

Bevan, V. 1986. *The Development of British Immigration Law*. Beckenham: Croom Helm.

Beveridge, W.H. 1942. *Report on Social Insurance and Allied Services*. HMSO. CMND 6404. New York: Macmillan & Co.

—— 1945. *Full Employment in a Free Society*. New York: Norton.

Bottomore, T. 1992. 'Citizenship and Social Class, Forty Years On'. In Marshall, T.H. and T. Bottomore (eds) *Citizenship and Social Class*. London: Pluto Press.

Bulmer, M. and A.M. Rees. (eds) 1996. *Citizenship Today: The Contemporary Relevance of T.H. Marshall*. London: UCL Press.

Cranston, M. 1967. 'Human Rights, Real and Supposed'. In D.D. Raphael (ed.) *Political Theory and the Rights of Man*. Bloomington, IN: Indiana University Press.

Enloe, C. 1990. *Bananas, Beaches and Bases: Making Feminist Sense of International Politics*. Berkeley, CA: University of California Press.

Fielding, D. 1998. 'Brotherhood and the Brothers: Responses to "Coloured" Immigration in the British Labour Party, c. 1951–65'. *Journal of Political Ideologies* 3(1): 79–97.

Giddens, A. 1982. *Profiles and Critiques in Social Theory*. Berkeley, CA: University of California Press.

—— 1996. 'T.H. Marshall, the State and Democracy'. In Bulmer and Rees 1996: 65–80.

Halfmann, J. 1997. 'Immigration and Citizenship in Germany'. *Political Studies* 45: 260–74.

Halsey, A.H. 1984. 'T.H. Marshall: Past and Present'. *Sociology* 18: 1–18.

Held, D. 1989. *Political Theory and the Modern State: Essays on State, Power and Democracy*. Cambridge: Polity Press.

Hutton, W. 1995. 'High-risk Strategy is not Paying Off'. *Guardian Weekly*. 12 November: 13.

Maine, Sir H.S. 1917 [1861]. *Ancient Law*. London: J.M. Dent.

Mann, M. 1987. 'Ruling Class Strategies and Citizenship'. *Sociology* 21: 339–54.

Marshall, T.H. 1963. *Sociology at the Crossroads and other Essays*. London: Heinemann.

—— 1981. *The Right to Welfare and Other Essays*. London: Heinemann.

O'Neill, O. 1989. 'Friends of difference'. *London Review of Books*. 14 September.

Parry, C. 1951. *British Nationality including citizenship of the United Kingdom and Colonies and the Status of Aliens*. London: Stevens.

Pateman, C. 1988. *The Sexual Contract*. Cambridge: Polity Press, and Stanford, CA: Stanford University Press.

Rees, A. 1995. 'The Other T.H. Marshall'. *Journal of Social Policy* 24: 341–62.

Rich, P.B. 1990. *Race and Empire in British Politics*. Cambridge: Cambridge University Press.

Runciman, W.G. 1996. 'Why Social Inequalities are Generated by Social Rights'. In Bulmer and Rees 1996: 49–64.

Sargant, E.B. 1912. *British Citizenship*. London: Longmans, Green.

Shklar, J.N. 1991. *American citizenship: The quest for Inclusion*. Cambridge, MA: Harvard University Press.

Turner, B.S. 1986. *Citizenship and Capitalism: The Debate over Reformism*. London: Allen & Unwin.

van Steenbergen, B. (ed.) 1994. *The Condition of Citizenship*. London and Thousand Oaks: Sage.

Vogel, U. and M. Moran (eds). 1991. *The Frontiers of Citizenship*. New York: St. Martin's.

Zolo, D. (1993. 'Democratic Citizenship in a Post-communist Era'. In D. Held (ed.) *Prospects for Democracy*. Cambridge: Polity.

11

FREEDOM AND DEMOCRATIZATION

Why basic income is to be
preferred to basic capital (2003)

Basic income and basic capital[1]

Despite the popularity of democracy in the 1990s, relatively little attention has been paid in recent academic debates to the democratic significance of a basic income. The focus is usually on such questions as social justice, relief of poverty, equality of opportunity, promotion of flexible labour markets, and individual freedom. I am not suggesting that these questions are unimportant or unrelated to democracy. Rather, this approach reflects the extent to which recent political philosophy tends to put democracy in a separate compartment or merely takes for granted a democratic background in order to analyse social justice and other questions. Two other aspects of contemporary scholarship on stakeholding also work in the same direction. First, the insights available from three decades of feminist scholarship have been neglected, even though they bear directly on some central questions about basic income, basic capital, and democracy. Argument is often contained within some narrow parameters set by controversies about, for example, liberalism and communitarianism. Second, the theoretical framework adopted is frequently drawn from neo-classical economics.

In this chapter, more precisely, I am concerned with democratization. That is, with the creation of a more democratic society in which all citizens, women and men alike, have full standing and enjoy democratic rights and individual freedom. I shall argue that, if democratization is taken seriously, a basic income is to be preferred to basic capital (often called a stake). My idea of a 'basic income' is that a government pays a regular sum over an adult lifetime to each individual citizen. By 'basic capital' or a 'stake' I mean a one-off capital grant from a government to all citizens at, say, age 21. In both cases the payment is unconditional.[2]

Basic income and basic capital have come to be seen as two different ways of giving individuals a 'stake in society' so that they can feel that they belong and have a reason to be a responsible member of their community. For democracy to function well individuals need to be stakeholders, but if their standing and freedom as citizens are also at issue, then a stake in the form of basic capital is insufficient, and a basic income is required. Although I am going to argue for a basic income, I am not dismissing basic capital. A stake would be an advance over present arrangements in the Anglo-American countries, and, in the current political climate, may well be more easily accepted than a basic income by both the public and politicians.

Philippe Van Parijs's *Real Freedom for All* (1995) and Bruce Ackerman and Anne Alstott's *The Stakeholder Society* (1999) have become central to the debate about basic income and basic capital respectively, and I shall take these arguments as my points of reference. In many ways they are two very different books. Van Parijs presents a 'real libertarian' argument and discusses recent arguments in analytical political philosophy, while Ackerman and Alstott draw on republican political theory and write for a more general audience.

Apart from their influence, the other reason that I am concerned with *Real Freedom for All* and *The Stakeholder Society* is that in both books the aim of stakeholding is individual freedom. Ackerman and Alstott see a stake as 'making freedom's promise universal and concrete' (1999: 44), and Van Parijs is concerned with *real* individual freedom. They also agree that 'freedom' means opportunity for individuals. To frame the debate around whether basic income or a stake would best promote freedom as individual opportunity pushes aside the question of the adequacy of such a view of freedom for democratization.

Neither the idea of a basic income nor of a basic capital grant, in itself, stipulates a level at which the income or grant should be set. Ackerman and Alstott argue for a stake of $80,000, and Van Parijs argues that a basic income should be set at the highest sustainable level. My assumption is that, if a basic income is to be relevant to democratization, it should be adequate to provide what I shall call a modest but decent standard of life. This is a level sufficient to allow individuals a degree of control over their lives and to participate to the extent that they wish in the cultural, economic, social, and political life of their polity.

My argument will be that, from the perspective of democratization, a basic income should be seen as a fundamental or democratic right, like universal suffrage. This is because a basic income would help remove impediments to freedom, help citizens enjoy and exercise citizenship, and help provide the security required if citizenship is to be of equal worth to everyone. My understanding of individual freedom is as self-government or autonomy. I see this as a political form of freedom in contrast to an economic form of freedom as individual opportunity. The latter is necessary in a democracy, but is insufficient for democratization, the political process through which all citizens obtain full standing, and become first-class – democratic – citizens.

As a democratic right a basic income has the potential to assist democratization because, unlike basic capital, it can help break the longstanding link between income, marriage, employment, and citizenship. Both basic income and a stake would enlarge individual opportunities, but the opportunities provided by a basic income would be much wider. A major difference between the two forms of stakeholding is that a basic income would give citizens the freedom not to be employed. A basic income opens up two possibilities important for democratization. First, it would encourage citizens to reflect on the place of the institution of employment in a democracy; second, it has the potential to foster institutional change and uncouple standard of life and citizenship from employment.

In much discussion of basic income and basic capital the implications for women's citizenship and women's freedom is ignored. Contrary to my own view, some feminists have criticized proposals for a basic income and I discuss their criticisms below. In 1919, Bertram Pickard, who was much more aware than contemporary scholars that a state bonus (a forerunner of a basic income) was important for women, wrote that the state bonus 'must be deemed the monetary equivalent of the right to land, of the right to life and liberty' (1919: 21). My conception of the democratic significance of a basic income is in the spirit of Pickard's statement.

At first sight, it might seem that there is little to choose between basic income and basic capital as means for strengthening citizenship. Ackerman and Alstott (1999: 88, 197) state that stakeholding is 'a citizenship program', and that a stake 'serves as a mark of citizenship'. The ideal of free and equal citizenship is, they suggest, 'the master key to stakeholding' (Ackerman and Alstott, 1999: 33). Moreover, the republican tradition within which Ackerman and Alstott situate themselves emphasizes the connection between property and citizenship.

Earlier versions of republican political argument were not democratic. Only property-holders were deemed capable of exercising the rights of citizens; the propertyless were excluded from citizenship. Ackerman and Alstott universalize property-holding in the form of basic capital, but depart from republican argument by reversing the direction of the link between property and citizenship. They present a capital grant as 'creating a public foundation for private life' (1999: 186). This is a depoliticization of republican theory in which property was a private foundation for political life, for active citizenship. The sense in which Ackerman and Alstott see stakeholding as a citizenship programme is that it underwrites economic citizenship. They compare 'one citizen one vote' as the mark of political citizenship to 'one citizen one stake' as the emblem of economic citizenship. But the comparison of basic income with universal suffrage is much more apt. The standing of 'citizen' and the right to vote continue for an individual's whole adult life. Basic capital is a one-off payment at the beginning of adulthood, whereas a basic income is paid regularly throughout life. It thus provides the security necessary to participate in social and political life and to exercise citizenship; heroic efforts are not required. Universal suffrage is the emblem of equal citizenship, and a basic income is the emblem of full standing as a citizen, of citizenship that is of equal worth.

The comparison between a basic income and universal suffrage was first suggested to me by a little-noticed passage in T.H. Marshall's *Citizenship and Social Class* (1963: 116): 'to have to bargain for a living wage in a society which accepts the living wage as a social right is as absurd as to have to haggle for a vote in a society which accepts the vote as a political right'. However, there are two problems with Marshall's argument.

First, as indicated by his reference to a living wage, he linked standard of life to employment, by which he meant male employment (an issue I shall return to shortly). Second, Ackerman and Alstott's separation of citizenship into economic and political components echoes Marshall's famous categorization of social, civil, and political rights of citizens. The problem is that dividing up citizenship in such ways causes needless difficulties in thinking about democratization. Attention gets diverted into endless wrangles about which category is primary (is it economic or political citizenship?), or which rights properly can be seen as 'rights' (do social rights count?). The issue of what constitutes the democratic rights required for autonomy and full standing for all citizens is then glossed over.[3]

By a democratic right I have in mind a fundamental right in Henry Shue's (1996) sense of a right that is essential if other rights are to be enjoyed. A basic income as a democratic right can be compared to the suffrage, another fundamental right. Universal suffrage underpins an orderly change of government through free and fair elections, and so enhances citizens' security, and enables each citizen to share in collective self-government. A basic income provides the security required to maintain full standing as a citizen, and enables each citizen to exercise individual self-government. I shall first say something about security and then turn to freedom as self-government.

Ackerman and Alstott reject basic income as an illegitimate, paternalistic constraint on freedom, but Van Parijs, although presenting a libertarian argument, introduces a 'mild' paternalism. The issue of paternalism arises in connection with the question of whether payment of income to individuals in a single lump sum at one point in time (basic capital), or as a series of regular payments during their lifetime (basic income) best promotes individual freedom. The choice between the payment methods is more than a matter of administrative convenience, since, from the perspective of individual opportunity, basic income can be seen as an unjustified restriction on freedom.

The most obvious reason for preferring the regular instalments of a basic income is that a lump-sum capital grant could very easily and quickly be squandered or lost, even if individuals avoided Las Vegas or prolonged spending or drug sprees. Many responsible individuals could lose their basic capital: small businesses, for instance, have high rates of failure despite the best efforts of their owners, and stock markets crash. In Ackerman and Alstott's words a stake provides a launching pad – but an individual's trajectory could be very short indeed (1999: 215).

In his discussion of payment method, Van Parijs remarks that if the problem of individuals throwing away their stake is that the consequent poverty leads to theft, and puts at risk human dignity and worth, then income paid at regular intervals is 'the obvious choice'. Further justification is required if 'the rationale is phrased in terms of real freedom' (1995: 46). To be sure, more argument is necessary, but there is no need, as this comment suggests, sharply to separate an argument about freedom from an argument about poverty, dignity and worth, not, at least, if freedom as self-government is at issue. Dignity is not the same as freedom, but a basic income is necessary to maintain the dignity and autonomy, and to uphold the standing, of all citizens, not just those near destitution; regular payments provide the security required for the enjoyment of citizenship of equal worth.[4]

In contrast, Ackerman and Alstott see the risk of losing a stake as part of freedom. Basic capital does not offer paternalistic protection. Adults know that their actions have long-term consequences, even if many outcomes are unexpected, so they should not be prevented from deciding for themselves what to do with a lump-sum payment. Each 'competent citizen should be deemed responsible for shaping the larger contours of his existence – for better or for worse. To treat him otherwise is to treat him as an eternal child' (1999: 213). Thus, they reject the alternative suggested by Le Grand and Nissan (2003). The latter propose that their £10,000 capital stake should be administered by trustees who will scrutinize requests for payment and allow it to be paid only for a number of approved uses, such as education, starting a business, or a down payment on a home. Ackerman and Alstott see such limitations on payment of the capital sum as unacceptable 'freedom-within-boundaries' (1999: 215).

Nonetheless, Ackerman and Alstott introduce an element of paternalism into their argument in two ways. They propose that basic capital should be paid to each individual in four instalments. Individuals can then learn from any mistakes they may make at first. In answer to the problem of individuals rapidly squandering their basic capital, Ackerman and Alstott propose a combination of a capital grant with retirement pensions that are paid unconditionally to all citizens (which makes their scheme more complicated than a stake or basic income alone). This ensures that if young citizens lose their stakes they will not be destitute in their old age.

In *Real Freedom for All,* Van Parijs's real libertarianism turns out to be fairly weak and involves some significant departures from the logic of libertarianism, including the introduction of paternalism. A typical libertarian would take a position similar to that of Ackerman and Alstott. Indeed, Van Parijs duly notes that individual freedom (opportunity) would be increased if individuals received their income as a single lumpsum payment and could do with it as they wished. But he argues for basic income as follows: he assumes that individuals 'in their right minds' at any point in their lives wish to protect their freedom in later years against unwise actions when younger. Thus 'a mildly paternalistic concern for people's real freedom throughout their lives…makes it sensible to hand out the basic income in the form of a (non-mortgageable) regular stream' (1995: 47).[5] This is not a very convincing argument from a libertarian standpoint, nor is it very compelling as an argument for basic income if democratization is a concern.

Ackerman and Alstott are concerned about paternalism because the opportunities opened to individuals by basic capital are opportunities to use their energies and abilities to become economically successful. This is also the view of Le Grand and Nissan (2003) who state plainly that the point of a capital grant is that it provides 'a springboard to accumulate wealth'. The problem with which Ackerman and Alstott begin is that of young individuals' unequal economic starting points. Some begin their adult journey with a handicap because of their parents' lack of economic resources. A capital stake gives each young citizen his or her fair share. It ensures that he faces a 'level playing field when he enters the marketplace as an adult', and provides resources to meet the challenges of competitive markets (1999: 22). Whether or not individuals make the most of these opportunities is up to them. As Ackerman and Alstott state, they 'are interested in opportunities, not outcomes' (1999: 24).

Equipped with their basic capital grant, young citizens, Ackerman and Alstott declare, will be able to 'inaugurate a new age of freedom' (1999: 217). However, the 'massive increase in effective freedom', and the 'promise [of] more real freedom for all' is an opportunity, no more (1999: 35, 76). A universal stake would make a big difference to the lives of many citizens, not least, as they point out, to members of minority groups and to women, but stakeholding is not a 'cradle-to-grave safety net' (1999: 119). It relies on youthful energy and enterprise, unlike a basic income; a 'basic income cushions failure; stakeholding is a launching pad for success' (1999: 215).

Paternalism looms large when freedom is seen as individual opportunity because basic income inevitably seems like a constraint on freedom. But if one begins from another conception of freedom, and from the perspective of democratization, then the problem is different. Assisting young people to make a start in their adult lives is all to the good, but basic capital is insufficient to answer the problem of how the necessary security can be furnished to enable citizens, at any time in their lives, to enjoy individual autonomy, and participate when they wish in the life of their society. The problem is not paternalism, but concerns the necessary social and political change to create a robust democracy for all citizens, whether successful or not. A basic income offers part of an answer to this problem.

Equality of opportunity is, of course, part of democracy, but individual freedom as self-government is the core requirement. To see why this is the case, it is necessary to consider very briefly why freedom is a central principle of democracy. Modern (that is, universal) democracy could not have developed without the assumption that individuals were born free, or were naturally free, and were equal to each other. It follows from the assumption of universal freedom and equality that all individuals are self-governing or autonomous – a political form of individual freedom. It also follows that the only justification for government of one individual by another (or one group by another) is agreement (consent). If individuals are to maintain their autonomy they cannot be mere subjects who are governed, they must become citizens with rights that allow them to govern themselves collectively and individually.

In *Real Freedom*, Van Parijs rejects any necessary connection between individual freedom and democracy. On this question he follows standard libertarian doctrine, and assumes that democracy is merely incidental to freedom. He distinguishes a free society – one that can determine its own fate and exercises collective sovereignty – from a society in which the members are also individually sovereign, and considers two possible answers to the question of what constitutes individual freedom or sovereignty.

The first is that individuals have equal power in making collective decisions. Such individuals live in a 'maximally democratic society', one that 'subjects everything to collective decision making'. A 'thoroughly democratic form of collectivism' involves 'public ownership of both people and capital' (1995: 8). Not surprisingly, he rejects this nightmarish view of democracy. He also rejects a second conception of individual sovereignty, closely related to the first: that is, individual sovereignty as active participation in collective endeavours. Both these views of individual freedom are inadequate, he argues, because they posit a necessary, rather than instrumental, relationship between individual freedom and political life. They make the 'individual's relationship to…political life…a matter of definition' (1995: 17). Any connection between democracy and a maximally free society is contingent, a possible empirical condition for individual freedom.

Van Parijs identifies democracy with collective decision-making, and sets it at odds with individual freedom. But to see maximal democratic decision-making as radically collectivist is to beg a great number of questions about the meaning of 'democracy'. My references to collective self-government have nothing to do with 'collectivism' as public ownership; they refer to citizens' participation in the government of a political system. At a minimum this requires a democratic electoral procedure – 'free and fair elections' – based on universal suffrage, with its associated civil and political liberties. Individual freedom of opportunity is one of the liberties, and some citizen participation is required to keep the electoral system in operation.

Indeed, Van Parijs seems to have this conception in mind when setting out his three conditions for real freedom, that is, a society in which all the members have maximum freedom. One condition is that security in the form of a structure of rights is necessary. He says little about these rights, but his argument requires the rights necessary for formal freedom, a market economy, and the protection of private property. He occasionally refers, without elaboration, to a basic income as a right (for example, 1995: 37).

Democratic theorists have paid more attention to collective self-government than to individual self-government or autonomy. But individual freedom is not exhausted by participation in the government of the state (collective self-government). Another dimension of 'government' drops out of sight when individual freedom is interpreted as the availability of economic opportunities that individuals can pursue untrammelled by (governmental) paternalism, that is, government as the exercise of authority by one individual, or category of individuals, over another in any area of social life. Where government is unwarranted, enjoyment of self-government is denied or limited.

Individual autonomy depends not only on collective self-government and the extent of available economic opportunities, but also on the structure of institutions within which individuals interact with one another. Individual freedom as self-government requires that individuals interact within authority structures that enhance their autonomy, and that they have the standing, and are able (have the opportunities and means), to enjoy and safeguard their freedom. When the two dimensions of self-government are prised apart, questions never arise about individual freedom within familiar institutions, such as marriage. Yet feminist-political theorists have criticized the curtailment of wives' self-government for three centuries, and, at-least since the 1790s, have analysed the structural connection between marriage, women's livelihood and citizenship. But democratic theorists still do not give their arguments the attention they deserve, nor are they taken nearly seriously enough in the debate about basic income and basic capital.

Women and free riding

A basic income has the potential to open up avenues of institutional change necessary for democratization. For this to take place citizens must begin to consider the structural interrelationships between their institutions, and a basic income could encourage this reflection. An appreciation of the fashion in which the major social institutions of marriage, employment, and citizenship, developed together and mutually reinforced each other is absent from too many discussions of basic income and basic capital. Without such an appreciation, the democratic significance of basic income never gets onto the agenda.

As feminist scholars have been demonstrating for many years now, the social insurance system of Anglo-American countries was constructed on the assumption that wives not only were their husbands' economic dependents, but also they were lesser citizens whose benefits depended on their private status and husbands' contributions, not their own citizenship. Ackerman and Alstott acknowledge this in their proposal for unconditional retirement pensions. The addition of retirement pensions to a stake allows them to write of a transition from worker (that is, male worker) citizenship to universal economic citizenship. Their proposed unconditional payment to older citizens breaks the link, forged in the New Deal in the United States, between men's employment histories and retirement pensions. As they note, the pension would be particularly significant for older women whose benefits still largely derive from their husbands' employment.

To make this point another way, it is only paid employment that has been seen as 'work' (as the phrase 'going out to work' indicates), and as involving the tasks that are the mark of a productive citizen and contributor to society and the polity. Other contributions, notably all the work required to reproduce and maintain a healthy population, and care for the sick and infirm – the caring tasks, many of which are contributed without payment in the private household, and are undertaken by women – have been seen as irrelevant to citizenship. Despite reforms to the social insurance system, the institutional connections and beliefs about 'work', masculinity, and femininity, are still powerful social forces.

Few participants in discussions of basic income have noticed, as has Van Parijs, that free riding exists 'on a massive scale' in household interactions (1995: 143). Free riders are individuals, or a section of the population, who continually take advantage of the efforts of others with no contribution on their part. Discussions of a basic income are full of apprehension about free riding, but who are the free riders in the household?[6] Barry notes that full-time housewives can be seen as free riders (1996: 245).[7] Yet housewives are working, as feminist scholars have emphasized for a very long time, by undertaking many vital tasks in the home, not least the necessary caring work. The majority of wives are now in some form of paid employment, but their labour force participation is different from that of men. This reflects the legacy of a wage-system that enshrined the belief that husbands (men) not wives (women) are 'breadwinners'. Many more women than men work part-time, and women earn less than men. The private and public sexual division of labour, that is to say, continues to be structured so that men monopolize full-time, higher-paying, and more prestigious paid employment, and wives do a disproportionate share of unpaid work in the home. Given the structure of institutions and social beliefs, this appears as a 'rational' arrangement. The mutual reinforcement of marriage and employment explains why husbands can take advantage of the unpaid work of wives, and avoid doing their fair share of the caring work. That is why there is massive free riding in the household – by husbands.

The conditions under which the institution of employment and the Anglo-American social insurance system was constructed have now crumbled. 'Old economy' male breadwinner jobs are being swept away in global economic restructuring. New jobs have been created but many are low paid, lacking benefits, and temporary. Downsizing and economic insecurity are widespread. Views about femininity, masculinity, and marriage are changing, too. We are still in the midst of these changes and the eventual outcome is uncertain, but at present we are living in circumstances in which it has become possible to rethink the connections between income and paid employment, between marriage, employment and citizenship, between the private and public division of labour, between caring work and other work, and reconsider the meaning of 'work'. This is crucial if proper account is to be taken of women's freedom, which has received rather short shrift in discussions of a basic income.

In 1792, Mary Wollstonecraft (1993) argued that rights, citizenship, and full standing for women required, among other radical changes, economic independence for both married and single women. A basic income would, for the first time, provide women with life-long (modest) economic independence and security, a major reason why it is central to democratization. Thus feminists might be expected to support the introduction of a basic income, or, more generally, stakeholding (see Parker 1993; Alstott 2001; McKay and Van Every 2000).

Yet some feminists are critical of the idea of a basic income because they fear it would reinforce the existing sexual division of labour, the current pattern of free riding in the household, and women's lesser citizenship. They argue that provision of an income without having to engage in paid employment would, in light of women's position in the labour market combined with lingering beliefs about the proper tasks of women and men, give women an incentive to undertake more unpaid work in the household. Conversely, men would have a greater incentive to free ride by avoiding the necessary work of caring for others. That is to say, a basic income would reinforce existing limitations on women's freedom.[8]

Ackerman and Alstott address this issue. They argue that, in the longer run, basic capital can help diminish 'pervasive cultural vulnerabilities' (1999: 60). They reject the claim that a stake might reinforce such vulnerabilities by encouraging women to use their basic capital to subsidize their unpaid work, leaving them little better off as competitors in the market. Women's judgement, they argue, must be respected. In the short run, since it is women who are expected to combine paid employment and unpaid work in the home, basic capital will allow them to make a rational accommodation to this unfair arrangement. Over the longer term, a stake will enable 'enterprising women' to challenge tradition and 'make their own way in the world' (1999: 208).

No doubt enterprising women would improve their position if they had a capital stake – many already do – and a stake would help change women's bargaining position and view of themselves. But although cultural assumptions, views, and vulnerabilities are major obstacles to change, institutional structures are involved as well. A stake, in the long run, is much less likely than an income, which offers modest economic independence for life and makes employment truly voluntary, to change both cultural views and institutions. A basic income would also change women's standing as citizens since employment would be dethroned from its position as the only work that really counts. A basic income would not only encourage citizens to think about the implications of current arrangements, but would give men the opportunity to do their fair share of the unpaid work of caring for others.

One crucial difference between a stake and a basic income is that the new opportunities made available by a basic income (set at the requisite level) would not be confined to the competitive market. On the one hand, a basic income acts as a subsidy that allows individuals to take low-paid jobs. On the other, it gives citizens the freedom not to be employed and uncouples standard of life from the institution of employment. Both basic capital and basic income would enable individuals to make the kinds of choices discussed by Ackerman and Alstott in their 'profiles in freedom' (1999: ch. 4). Stakeholding would make it possible for anyone (at any point in their life, not merely while they are young, if they had a basic income) to go back to school, or to retrain to move to a new occupation, or to open a business.

But a basic income would do more than this. If it allowed citizens to live at a modest but decent standard, they could 'take time off', for example, to do voluntary work, develop their political capacities and skills, learn to surf, to write or paint, devote themselves to family life – or undertake caring work – or just have a period of self-reassessment or contemplation. By loosening the tie between marriage, income, and employment, a basic income can assist, in a way that basic capital for young people cannot, in removing impediments to freedom. It would allow individuals more easily to refuse to enter or to leave relationships that violate individual self-government, or that involve unsafe, unhealthy, or demeaning conditions.

The freedom to take a break from, or not to engage in, paid employment is a freedom that runs counter to the direction of recent public policy and much political rhetoric. Some commentators even claim that the capacities and skills necessary for citizenship can be developed only through employment. A widespread assumption underlying the reforms based on 'workfare' is that, ideally, the whole adult population should be in paid employment – including the mothers of young children, which is a major historical shift. Whether, in light of current technological change and productivity increases, such a policy of universal employment is feasible is an open question, especially if it is employment at a living wage ('full employment' in the past referred to male employment). The effect of such policies and rhetoric is to draw even tighter the long-standing link between employment and citizenship, at the very time when change makes possible a reassessment of the connection.

It is also worth noting that a reinforcement of male free riding is a likely outcome of universal employment. Advocates of workfare tend to remain silent about how the necessary caring work would be undertaken if all adults were employed. Either the tacit assumption seems to be that employment patterns would remain sexually differentiated, and women would continue to do most of the unpaid caring work. Or it is assumed that care would be provided through the market. But there seems little evidence that all citizens would have sufficient means to be able to purchase the necessary services, or that care of sufficient quality and quantity would be profitable enough to be made available.

To move the discussion of basic income forward, two changes are needed. First, democratization and women's freedom must be brought into the argument. Proposals for stakeholding are about social change, and the direction of social and political change depends, among other things, on the reasons why it is advocated and the claims made about what it is expected to achieve. If the beneficial consequences for women are not a prominent part of the debate, and if the reasons for supporting a basic income do not emphasize its democratic potential, then the outcome is unlikely to strengthen democracy or women's freedom. So it is vital for a case to be made in terms of democratization, which, if it is not to reproduce the long history of 'democracy' as a masculine preserve, necessarily includes women's standing and freedom.

Ackerman and Alstott argue that a stake encourages individuals, in a way that a basic income cannot, to reflect upon what they want to do with their lives, and appraise their situation. 'Civic reflection' and attention to 'the fate of the nation' become possible when economic anxieties are lifted (1999: 185). A 'purer form of patriotism' will arise out of the 'simple gratitude to the nation' that citizens will feel as they think about their capital grant and the debt that they owe to their country for the economic citizenship that comes with basic capital (1999: 186, also 43–44). Patriotism and gratitude, however, have only a tenuous connection to individual freedom.

Provision of a one-off capital grant will no doubt encourage individuals to consider what courses of action are open to them, and might even foster reflection on the debt they owe to their country. But it seems implausible that it would help open up reflection on the political implications of the structural connections between marriage, employment, and citizenship. A one-off payment, argued for in terms of economic citizenship and economic success, does not provide a context that gives encouragement to think about broader connections between social institutions and democratization. In contrast, a basic income, which provided a modest standard of living independently of employment, would offer an incentive for citizens to think in wider terms about the institutions within which they live. It has the potential to assist in an institutional and cultural democratic transformation.

It is impossible to predict what the outcome of a stake or a basic income might be. All human activities have unintended and unforeseen consequences. The fears of feminist critics of a basic income could be borne out, and the possibility is certainly increased if feminist scholars and feminist insights, together with democratization, remain outside the debates about a basic income.

The second requirement is that theoretical arguments about basic income acknowledge the relationship between individuals' freedom and the structure of institutions. Many unnecessary problems arise when political theorists borrow from neo-classical economic theory. An abstractly individualistic theoretical framework is imported that works against an appreciation of the democratizing potential of basic income. Van Parijs's conception of freedom illustrates how the separation of individuals from institutions robs real freedom of the limits required for a plausible account of basic income.

I referred earlier to Van Parijs's (1995) three conditions for real freedom. The first was the security of a structure of rights, and the second is that 'each person has the greatest possible opportunity to do whatever she might want to do' (Van Parijs, 1995: 25).[9] This is maximum freedom or real freedom for all (subject only to the limitations of security of rights and self-ownership).[10] He states that he decided against a definition of freedom in terms of what individuals actually want to do because focusing on 'might want' avoids the problem of want manipulation.[11] He argues that really to be free means not just that the formal right exists to do whatever individuals might want to do, but that they have the means to do so (another claim drawn from anti-libertarian sources). A basic income provides the requisite means. Whether or not Van Parijs's claim that a basic income should be set at the highest sustainable level involves a bigger or smaller amount than my assumption of a sum sufficient to sustain a modest but decent standard of life is an empirical question. However, I doubt that a level sufficient to underwrite his real freedom is possible, since real freedom has no limits.

Van Parijs states that real freedom is not merely the freedom to consume but to be able to choose among different ways of life. A real libertarian is not concerned with maintaining a living standard or obtaining what he wants. There must be opportunities to do what one might want to do. Van Parijs gives two brief examples: if a person lives in a commune, the assumption is 'innocuously enough' that they might, one day, want to live alone; if you live in the country, you might want to live in the city (1995: 38). But I might want to build and live in a replica of the White House in the Malibu hills, I might want to ride to an orbiting space station, I might want to…What I might want to do at some stage of my life is unlimited.

Van Parijs's argument rests on concepts, drawn from economic theory, such as preference satisfaction, rents, opportunity costs, and endowments. Despite Van Parijs's caveat about consumption, his 'individual' closely resembles the consumer of neo-classical economics. This individual has desires that know no limits, since what he might want to do is determined by his subjective preferences (measured through market prices), and individuals can have preferences or tastes for anything whatsoever.[12] Van Parijs's 'individuals' are, in effect, mere vessels for preferences, severed from social relationships.

Consider his analysis of free riding in the household. He recognizes that it occurs on a large scale, but he reduces the problem to a comparison of two sets of preferences or tastes. Free riding, Van Parijs states, occurs when benefits enjoyed by both partners in a household are produced by only one of them, the partner who happens to care most about the particular benefit. His example is that the partner who most strongly prefers tidiness will make sure that the home is tidy. But 'tidiness' is part of the more general work of housekeeping, and there is abundant empirical evidence that shows that it is the female partner who is most likely to do the housework, including tidying up. The empirical data do not show this pattern just by chance – female partners do not by some quirk happen to prefer tidiness more strongly than their male partners. Rather, as feminist scholarship has demonstrated at length, this persistent pattern of behaviour is the result of the interlocking structure of two institutions, marriage and employment, and social beliefs about what it means to be a wife or husband.

The institution of marriage has vanished in Van Parijs's analysis of free riding in the household and there are merely two individuals, indistinguishable except for their different tastes for tidy surroundings. Thus he can recognize that free riding exists, but not that it is a problem about men (husbands) and caring work. He has nothing to say about the structure of relations between the sexes and a whole area of debate is, therefore, removed from discussion of basic income.

Yet, in the end, either individuals and institutions have to be brought back together, or some other connection between them must be postulated. The connection that Van Parijs (1995: 230) makes in his closing pages is through 'solidaristic patriotism'. He argues that the 'political feasibility' of justice is, in part, a matter of the design of institutions that 'approximate one-man-one-vote [*sic*] democracy on a world scale' (1995: 228–29). Solidaristic patriotism is needed to foster a commitment to a conception of justice and 'pride in the collective project in which [individuals] are…involved' (Van Parijs 1995: 230). He even toys with the idea of compulsory public service to maintain social cohesion. This is hardly a move one would expect from a libertarian, but it is indicative of the problems generated by the abstractly individualist approach of economic theory. These familiar problems have been extensively explored by theorists such as Hegel, Durkheim, and Parsons. Yet political theory deriving from the concepts and assumptions of economic theory is written as if their arguments did not exist, and as if Hobbes had not given us his great lesson in the political consequences of atomistic individualism in *Leviathan*.

Van Parijs states that compulsory public service is the indirect and instrumental way that real libertarians can restrict freedom and take account of some 'anti-individualist' concerns of communitarians (1995: 231). But basic capital and basic income are about the enlargement of individual freedom, not compulsion; the resort to compulsion is an artefact of a theoretical starting point. And why should communitarians be the reference point, especially if the concern is individual freedom (see also Ackerman and Alstott 1999: 43–44, 186)? Have other contributors to political theory nothing to say of relevance to individual freedom?

Basic income as a citizenship right

I now want to return to the comparison between universal suffrage and a basic income, which raises a problem that I have not seen discussed. Universal suffrage means that the vote is no longer a privilege but a democratic right. Thus, virtually everyone must be able easily to meet qualifications for enfranchisement; hence the importance of age, or in the case of candidates for naturalization, length of residence, and being of sound mind.[13] Similarly, if a basic income is to be a democratic right, all citizens must be able to qualify: there can be no conditions.

Apprehension about free riding has led to many proposals for conditions for the payment of a basic income, such as Atkinson's (1996) 'participation income' (see Anderson 2001; Galston 2001; Phelps 2001). Both Ackerman and Alstott and Van Parijs introduce conditions. The former restrict full stakeholding to individuals who have a high school diploma, and make loss of part of basic capital a penalty for certain crimes. Van Parijs suggests that under certain conditions, usually found in poor countries, a work test is appropriate. Ackerman and Alstott could respond that their criteria resemble those for the suffrage: virtually everyone could meet them. Van Parijs believes the relevant circumstances are unlikely to obtain in rich countries such as the United States or Britain.

Once conditions are introduced, however generously interpreted, a basic income becomes a privilege not a right. The problem then arises of the status of those who fail to, or refuse to, meet the conditions. Are they to become second-class citizens? This problem has been glossed over in current debates, but once democratization is at the centre of argument the question of conditional citizenship becomes harder to avoid. It is unconditional – democratic – citizenship that is at the heart of the case for both basic income and basic capital. Ackerman and Alstott argue that, in the end, the justification of a stake 'rests on each American's claim to respect as a free and equal citizen' (1999: 209). Both basic capital and basic income have symbolic as well as material significance by helping to remove the temptation for some citizens to see others as less worthy of respect, and so as lesser citizens, because of their lack of economic resources.

They also argue that individuals (and their success) depend on a complex web of cooperation by others, and that stakeholding recognizes this social fact. Here Ackerman and Alstott are drawing on the tradition of argument that all citizens have a right to a fair share in the collective patrimony because the wealth and resources of a society are built by the cooperative endeavours of preceding and present generations. In the twenty-first century surely it is time that all citizens in a democracy should enjoy a share of the patrimony in the form of the security and freedom of a guaranteed basic income.

Notes

1 I have been interested in basic income for some years, but have only now begun to write about it. I wish to thank Manchester University for a Hallsworth Fellowship that gave me three months to read in 1997, and especially David Purdy for sharing his manuscript and for our conversations. Thanks also to Jürgen de Wispelaere, and participants at two seminars at the Research School of Social Sciences, ANU in the fall of 2000.

2 For ease of exposition I shall refer to 'citizens', leaving open the question of permanent residents. I shall also leave children aside, together with some other issues that are outside the scope of this chapter.

3 On Marshall, see also Pateman (1996). The problems are exacerbated by the existence of two UN Covenants, one dealing with civil and political rights, and the other with economic, social and cultural rights. Moreover, as feminist legal scholars have pointed out, standard interpretations of 'human rights' have endlessly reproduced the separation between public (political) and private, a separation that also characterizes most discussions of a basic income.

4 For an argument that destitution in the form of homelessness is a denial of individual freedom, see Waldron (1993).

5 Van Parijs and Ackerman and Alstott treat the question of method of payment as a problem about personal identity, in the sense of whether one is the same person at 60 as at 20. If the self is a series of discrete entities over time, then the later self cannot blame the earlier for youthful folly. The problem of personal identity is interesting, but of little concern in discussions of a stake and a basic income, which are about citizenship and social and political change, not individual identity. The latter issue assumes a central place in individualist theoretical frameworks (extreme individualism in Van Parijs's case).

6 I make some general comments on the free-rider objection in Pateman (2001).

7 McKay and Van Every (2000: 281) remark that critics of the free-rider objection argue in 'masculinist terms which ignore the implicit relegation of family carers to this category'.

8 Like Robeyns (2001) I have frequently encountered this objection when I have talked about a basic income, but less often seen it in academic discussions (see also the comments in Walter 1989: 123–25).

9 The third condition is self-ownership, which I will not pursue in this chapter. Van Parijs (1995: 9) states that the idea of self-ownership cannot be attacked on grounds of freedom. For such a criticism see Pateman (2002).

10 Strictly, real freedom involves leximin opportunity, but this is not relevant to my argument. Leximin means that the person with least opportunities has no fewer opportunities than does the person with least opportunities under any other arrangement. If there is such an alternative feasible arrangement, the calculation is made for the person with the second-least opportunities.

11 He also extends real freedom beyond coercion to include obstacles that have not been produced by anyone: 'Even stating that I am not free to travel faster than light is only slightly odd, if at all' (1995: 23). For some other comments on his conception of freedom see Barry (1996: 250–55).

12 The problem then arises of why, if tastes vary, income should not vary also. In discussing undominated diversity, Van Parijs rescues his assumption that a basic income will be paid at a uniform level by introducing the restriction that preferences must be genuine, and available to and understood by others. However, this presupposes the network of social relationships that is absent from his examples, which highlight such bizarre cases as individuals who prefer to be blind rather than sighted, crippled rather than able bodied.

13 The debacle in Florida in the 2000 Presidential election drew attention to the 14 states that continue to strip former felons of the franchise for life (around one and a half million people).

References

Ackerman, B. and A. Alstott. 1999. *The Stakeholder Society*. New Haven: Yale University Press.

Alstott, A. 2001. 'Good for Women'. In P. Van Parijs, J. Cohen and J. Rogers (eds) *What's Wrong with a Free Lunch?* Boston: Beacon Press.

Anderson, E. 2001. 'Optional Freedoms'. In P. Van Parijs, J. Cohen and J. Rogers (eds) *What's Wrong with a Free Lunch?* Boston: Beacon Press.

Barry, B. 1996. 'Real Freedom and Basic Income'. *Journal of Political Philosophy* 4: 242–76, reprinted in A. Reeves and A. Williams (eds) 2002. *Real Libertarianism Reassessed*. London: Macmillan.

Galston, W.A. 2001. 'What About Reciprocity? In P. Van Parijs, J. Cohen and J. Rogers (eds) *What's Wrong with a Free Lunch?* Boston: Beacon Press.

Le Grand, J. and D. Nissan (eds). 2003. 'A Capital Idea: Helping the Young Help Themselves'. In K. Dowding, J. De Wispelaere and S. White (eds) *The Ethics of Stakeholding*. London and New York: Palgrave.

Marshall, T.H. 1963. 'Citizenship and Social Class'. In *Sociology at the Crossroads and Other Essays*. London: Heinemann.

McKay, A. and J. Van Every. 2000. 'Gender, Family, and Income Maintenance: A Feminist Case for Citizens Basic Income'. *Social Politics* 7: 266–84.

Parker, H. 1993. *A Citizen's Income and Women*. BIRG Discussion Paper No. 2. London: Citizens' Income Study Centre.

Phelps, E.S. 2001. 'Subsidize Wages'. In P. Van Parijs, J. Cohen and J. Rogers (eds) *What's Wrong with a Free Lunch?* Boston: Beacon Press.

Pickard, B. 1919. *A Reasonable Revolution*. London: Allen & Unwin.

Shue, H. 1996. *Basic Rights: Subsistence, Affluence and U.S. Foreign Policy*. 2nd edn. Princeton, NJ: Princeton University Press.

Van Parijs, P. 1995. *Real Freedom for All: What (If Anything) Can Justify Capitalism?* Oxford: Clarendon Press.

Wollstonecraft, M. 1993. 'A Vindication of the Rights of Woman'. In J. Todd (ed.), *Political Writings*. Toronto: University of Toronto Press.

12

ANOTHER WAY FORWARD

Welfare, social reproduction, and
a basic income (2005)[1]

> Workfare has nothing to do with economics. It is about citizenship, and
> whether able-bodied adults who do not earn anything actively can be
> regarded as full citizens.
>
> —Judith Shklar, *American Citizenship* (1991: 98)

> Like capital, an individual moves faster when unencumbered.
>
> —Teresa Brennan, *Globalization and Its Terrors* (2003: 87)

In the United States, as many commentators have noted, welfare had an extremely
narrow meaning. In the 1980s and 1990s it came to refer not merely to residual,
means-tested programs but to one such program in particular, Aid to Families with
Dependent Children (AFDC), which provided benefits to single mothers with
children. Welfare is separated from social insurance, which in other countries is
treated as part of welfare, and divorced from other claims on the public purse that
provide assistance to private individuals, whether tax allowances for mortgages or
subsidies to private business. The Personal Responsibility and Work Opportunity
Reconciliation Act of 1996 (PRWORA) abolished AFDC and replaced it with
Temporary Assistance for Needy Families (TANF).

"Welfare" was replaced by workfare.[2] Recipients of assistance are now expected
to find employment and time limits have been set on how long they can receive
benefits.[3] It was generally agreed that the 1996 legislation was necessary to resolve
a crisis about "welfare." Although preceded by attempts to introduce workfare,
notably the Family Support Act of 1988, TANF marked a historic shift. Until
1996, "welfare" had provided support for single mothers to care for children at
home, but workfare implies that all able-bodied adults should be in the labor force,
even mothers with small children. The implication of the legislation is thus that
universal employment is now required.

The United States is not alone in introducing workfare – for example, Britain has taken a similar course – but is unusual in the focus on single mothers (for some details of British policy see, for example, King 1999: 246–55).[4] More generally, the United States stands apart from other rich countries in the extent of reliance on the labor market and other private sources to provide for the welfare of citizens. Employment is important in all welfare systems in the sense that wages are subject to a special tax, misleadingly seen as insurance, to help fund programs, but social insurance in the United States is remarkably limited compared to Western European countries. Older citizens enjoy Social Security (retirement pensions) and Medicare (medical insurance) – two very popular programs, unlike "welfare" – but there is no national health insurance even for children, and about 44 million people are currently uninsured. Medical insurance is largely provided through employment, with availability and coverage depending on employers' discretion. Most comparable countries also provide parents with assistance with the cost of child rearing, but the United States lacks a universal child endowment.

A crucial question in understanding and discussing any reform is the reason why it was implemented. PRWORA was designed to solve a problem about "welfare" that arose, it was argued, because too many citizens (in this case, single mothers) had been reduced to dependency by receiving their subsistence from welfare rather than from employment. The attributes of a citizen and the respect due to citizens can be gained, it was claimed, only through employment. Supporters of workfare also assume that employment is the social contribution owed by citizens.

At one level of my argument I discuss a number of issues about single mothers. Feminist scholars have criticized claims about dependency, the neglect of motherhood and women's caring work as a contribution to citizenship, and the identification of employment with "work." Part of my discussion will be along similar lines. These criticisms, however, depend on the deeper level of my argument: that the connection between employment and democratic citizenship, taken for granted by supporters of workfare, can be questioned and that, rather than solving anything, PRWORA exacerbates a major problem about social reproduction that has been growing since the late 1970s.

Social reproduction refers to a great deal more than motherhood, although motherhood is central to political life and public policy, whether or not this is explicitly acknowledged. It is about welfare in a very broad sense, about the maintenance and future of the public or common weal and the care of citizens. New generations must be produced and reared if a society is to reproduce itself, so women have to have babies, but if a society is not merely to continue but to flourish, and flourish as a democracy, social reproduction extends far beyond parenting. Each new generation has to be kept healthy, educated in appropriate ways, and exposed to cultural life. Just as important, however, existing generations, which include the parents of the new generation, must also be cared for: their welfare and development is critical to a flourishing society and democracy. Social reproduction is not something that can be undertaken by mothers or fathers alone, or through purely individual endeavors, but requires public provision. To be concerned with democratization, that is, with the creation of a more democratic society in which citizenship is of equal worth to all so that every citizen enjoys full standing, necessarily involves an interest in welfare and the requirements for social reproduction.

The controversy over "welfare" and PRWORA has focused on only one group of citizens, single mothers, and the narrow meaning of "welfare" diverts attention from the implications of current public policy for social reproduction. Democratic social reproduction requires public resources if time is to be available for parenting, if citizens are to be educated and cared for, if they are to develop and take part in social and political life and enjoy a dignified old age, and if the welfare of all citizens is to be treated as of equal worth. The problem is that social reproduction has been undercut by the direction of public policy for the past quarter century. Workfare and universal employment not only diminish the time available to citizens to be parents, but more generally, domestic and international economic policy emphasizes the market and privatization. Allocating public resources to the task of social reproduction, to the welfare and care of citizens, runs counter to the demands of prevailing (global) neo-liberal ideology and economic doctrines (Brennan 2003).

Another way of formulating this level of the problem, following but adapting T.H. Marshall, is that it is a contemporary manifestation of the conflict between two different logics – democracy and the Poor Law. Since the 1970s the balance of the conflict between the two logics has shifted toward the Poor Law. In his famous essay "Citizenship and Social Class," Marshall stated that in the twentieth century "citizenship and the capitalist system have been at war" (1963: 87). The conflict existed because citizenship, or more specifically what Marshall called social rights – all that is necessary "to share to the full in the social heritage and to live the life of a civilized being according to the standards prevailing in the society" – placed limits upon and regulated the market, and placed some goods outside of it altogether (1963: 74).[5] My argument is narrower: it is not about capitalism or the market but one market, the labor market. Lawrence Mead noted in 1992 that in the contemporary United States "the equivalent [of the Poor Law] would be to abolish AFDC or transform it into workfare" (255).[6] That has been achieved through TANF.

The logic of the Poor Law is part of the making and expansion of labor markets and the creation of the institution of employment. Able-bodied poor adults unwilling to participate in this institution are designated as undeserving and then receive public assistance only in exchange for employment (workfare). But to deem an individual as undeserving and so open to the coercion of workfare is to mark her out as lacking certain capacities and thus she is unlikely to be accorded the respect due to a fellow citizen.[7]

The logic of democracy is universalist and part of the making of citizenship. Citizenship is not necessarily democratic. Historically it has been a privilege reserved for only part of the population (the males, the propertied, those with white skins). When citizenship ceases to be a privilege and becomes universal, a matter of rights, it becomes democratic and in most countries today one universal element, the suffrage, is present.[8] Democracy is commonly given a minimal meaning as the institutional infrastructure required for free and fair elections. Universal suffrage is necessary but is set apart from other rights, especially those involved in the welfare of citizens. A more robust interpretation, which I follow here, takes universal suffrage, an entitlement of citizens, as the model for other rights necessary for democratic social reproduction and full citizenship.

I also offer an alternative policy and challenge some claims about workfare, free riding, and reciprocity. To solve the problem of social reproduction and the welfare of citizens it is necessary to move back to the universalism of democracy. I argue that an unconditional basic income for all citizens is a step in this direction.

TANF, employment, and citizenship

The two "attributes of an American citizen," Judith Shklar states, are "voting and earning" (Shklar 1991: 3). The connection between voting and being a citizen is fairly straightforward, but it is not so obvious why earning, being employed, is so closely connected with citizenship. To be sure, there are some general ideas, notably individual freedom and equality, that are necessary to both labor markets and democracies, and historically the establishment of civil and political rights (for white males at least) and the consolidation of employment have been associated. But the interpretation and deployment of these ideas and rights has been very different in the case of citizenship from that of employment.

The premise that individuals are "born free and equal" lies at the heart of arguments for democracy, and such individuals are necessarily self-governing; if self-government is to be maintained they must become citizens with rights. The right to vote, and other associated civil and political rights required for free and fair elections, upholds and expresses collective self-government. The influential minimalist view of democracy stops at that point and treats the citizen as another face of the consumer, spending votes rather than dollars.[9] However, although participation in the market depends on dollars, standing as a democratic citizen is not determined by an individual's income, wealth, or other particular attributes. Consumers look only to their own advantage or interest, but citizens often do more than this and are concerned with justice, equality or the public good. Martin Gilens, for example, argues that empirical data shows that when American citizens think about welfare they ask which policy is best overall and not just for themselves (Gilens 1999).

The minimalist view sees democracy in terms of the suffrage and collective self-government, but an alternative conception looks further to individual self-government (individual freedom or autonomy). To participate fully as citizens – that is, to participate in social and political life beyond periodically casting a ballot – individuals need a certain level of resources. Poor material circumstances can also lead to denial of respect by fellow citizens. To maintain and enjoy individual autonomy reqires that individuals interact with one another within authority structures that enhance rather than diminish their self-government (see also Pateman 1970; 2002), But in contemporary democracy the scope of citizens' autonomy is circumscribed and confined to a narrowly conceived political arena. A sharp line has been drawn between government and the undemocratic structure of authority in workplaces.

Proponents of "welfare" reform see employment as the key to citizenship but ignore lack of democracy in the workplace. Yet employment was once regarded with suspicion in the United States because it was seen as antithetical to self-government and therefore as a threat to free citizenship. In the past, in both political theory and practice, categories of the population deemed dependent and subordinate (such as wives) were excluded from citizenship. For a time in the United States, during the nineteenth century, the employed were seen as dependent (see Shklar 1991: ch. 2; Sandel 1996: ch. 6). Workers were instructed what to do by a boss, depended on the wages he paid, and could lose their jobs at will if their employer no longer wanted them. They lacked the independence demanded of citizens. More recently, political theorists of starkly different political persuasions, such as Friedrich von Hayek and G.D.H. Cole, have seen the employed as undermining freedom because they are trained in subordination and so do not develop the characters required of free citizens. The employed, Hayek wrote, are "in many respects…alien and often inimical to much that constitutes the driving force of a free society" (1960: 119).

Virtually nothing remains today (despite the vogue for Hayek's theories in the 1980s and 1990s) of the suspicion of employment. On the contrary, advocates of "welfare" reform see employment as the mark of independence and necessary for full citizenship. Mead, for example, has argued in the name of citizenship that nonworkers (that is, employable individuals who are neither employed or seeking employment) in receipt of "welfare" must be compelled to find employment, even if the wages are very low: "Low-wage work apparently must be mandated, just as a draft has sometimes been necessary to staff the military. Authority achieves compliance more efficiently than benefits, at least from society's viewpoint" (1986: 84).

The argument that employment, even coerced employment, is necessary for citizenship is not as convincing as proponents suggest. I have not, for example, come across any discussion of why and how participation, including coerced participation, in an undemocratic workplace creates the qualities needed for democratic citizenship. Joel Schwartz argues that, in the same spirit as nineteenth-century moral reformers, PRWORA promotes virtue and good behavior. Such virtues as thrift, frugality, punctuality, civility, or reliability may be required for employment, but further argument is needed to show that precisely the same set of virtues are central to democratic citizenship.[10]

The identification of independence with employment reflects adherence to the logic of the Poor Law rather than a demonstration of how self-government is promoted in workplaces. The British Poor Law was about the making of a national labor market, not about democratic citizenship. The major concern of the *Poor Law Report* of 1834, with its conception of the deserving and undeserving poor and doctrine of less eligibility, was the problem of the able-bodied male head of a household who received outdoor relief (Dean 1991: ch. 9). The report declared that "the great source of abuse is the outdoor relief afforded to the able-bodied on their own account, or on that of their families" (cited in Dean 1991: 159). These men were undeserving because they were potentially independent. Their condition, as the *Poor Law Report* stated, had been brought about by their own failings: it "originated in indolence, improvidence, or vice, and might have been averted by ordinary care and industry" (cited in King 1999: 228).

The solution was to put able-bodied men to work—just as Locke had recommended in 1697, declaring that "the true and proper relief of the poor…consists in finding work for them, and taking care they do not live like drones upon the labour of others" (1997 [1697]: 189). Men able to enter the labor market and earn a wage, even if not enough to raise them above poverty, must be compelled to do so. The "incentive" to enter employment was that relief would be given only under the less eligible conditions of the workhouse, so that employment would always be seen as the preferable alternative. Relief was, therefore, reserved for the deserving indigent individual (a pauper) who was "a person unable to labour, or unable to obtain, in return for labour, the means of subsistence" (cited in Dean 1991: 176).[11]

The marginal status of the "dependents" who entered the workhouse was underlined by depriving them of the standing of full citizens. Until 1918 in Britain, the condition of receiving relief in workhouses was forfeiture of political rights. The Poor Law, the abolition of outdoor relief, and loss of citizenship rights were carried to the United States: "as late as 1934, fourteen states' constitutions removed relief recipients' right to vote or hold public office" (King 1999: 266).

The Poor Law was about men, who were assumed to be heads of families. By the 1840s in Britain the idea that wives, properly, were their husbands' economic dependents had gained a firm foothold, and employment for the male breadwinner was established as the only respectable way for all those outside the aristocratic or pauper classes to find a livelihood. Widows were seen as deserving and were assisted, and it appears that women with children were viewed more generously than men. The implication of the Poor Law for single mothers is less clear, but they constituted only around 5 percent of the pauper population (Dean 1991: 167–71). PRWORA, in an historic shift, brought women (single mothers) within the logic of the Poor Law. Single mothers were the only remaining major category of able-bodied adults explicitly exempt from participation in the labor market. Some married women still remain outside the paid labor force but most wives were employed by 1996, and the social expectation that wives should remain at home has lost most of its force (I shall return to these points). The implication of arguments about employment and citizenship is that all able-bodied adults should be employed. Receipt of "welfare" no longer entails being stripped of rights in a formal sense, but workfare involves diminution of freedom and standing; recipients are deemed undeserving, seen as free riders who are legitimately open to coercion, and conditions are imposed on their citizenship.

Supporters of TANF would respond that this is the wrong way to look at the reform. Employment is central to citizenship for two reasons. First, when they leave welfare for employment former recipients cease to be dependent and thus become more free, not less; even if they are still below the poverty line they become independent. Second, they also appear more deserving to other citizens because they have ceased to be free riders (getting something for nothing).

The first part of this response relies on the peculiar meaning of dependence in the debates about "welfare" and the fact that only one category of beneficiaries of the public purse have been labeled as dependents. Dependence is a social relationship – and more often than not a euphemism for a relationship of superiority and subordination – but in the controversies in the 1980s and 1990s "dependence" referred not to a social relationship but to characteristics of individuals.[12] In the tradition of the Poor Law, the need for "welfare" is held to be the consequence of individual flaws of character. The assumption underlying TANF is that the individual attributes signifying dependence are present if a citizen is reluctant to seek work, that is, employment. The reluctance is treated as a form of individual pathology, yet there are a variety of reasons why someone may wish not to enter employment. Nonwork stemming from problems such as drug abuse or individual incapacity[13] is very different from a refusal to accept a job with below poverty wages or poor conditions, or a desire to be a full-time mother to a small child.

It is not obvious that single mothers caring for their children are dependent merely because they gain their subsistence from public provision. They may remain on the rolls (many cycle on and off) not because of the small payment but from "the lack of anything else (such as education, training in high-tech skills, or child care)." Their confidence, too, can be eroded by the general hostility toward recipients combined with the conditions under which "welfare" is given, including "endless waiting, unhelpful and even exploitative caseworkers who refuse to provide advice or guidance, and the contempt that many in social services barely hide for their 'clients'" (Hirschmann 2003: 153).[14] Single mothers on "welfare" can be seen as endeavoring to be independent, or as independent as a small benefit would allow. "Welfare" offers women freedom from dependence on men's wages, and enables them, if necessary, to leave an abusive or unsatisfactory relationship with a man.

PRWORA contains provisions to encourage marriage, but the assumption that marriage encourages independence can be questioned; another view is that this provision reflects unease about too much independence for women. Women usually earn less than men, and since the earnings of husbands tend to be seen as the primary earnings, wives are still perceived as partially dependent. Marriage can actually add to women's burdens because it is far from guaranteed that husbands will contribute their fair share of daily caring work.[15]

"Welfare" reform is also seen as a means of decreasing the incidence of births to women on their own. Murray, for example, states that the "main reason for scrapping welfare is to reduce the number of babies born to single mothers" (Murray 1994: 29). However, evidence from experiments in the 1990s is inconclusive about the effects of welfare reform on the birth rate. Rates of births out of wedlock began to decline in the 1990s, but this began before PRWORA, and the contribution, if any, of the legislation to the decline is unclear.[16]

Motherhood, whether single or married, illustrates graphically that dependence is an inescapable feature of human relationships. All infants depend completely on mothers and other adults, we all become dependent on others during serious illness, and many adults become dependent to a greater or lesser extent in their old age.

Husbands still largely depend on their wives to take care of their daily needs and their children so that they can appear, ready for the day, at the workplace door. We all rely on the complex webs of interdependence or reciprocity that constitute social life. This interdependence is reflected in the arguments of the early modern theorists of an original contract who make mutual aid and forbearance, which is the web of social life, the primary law of nature.

This brings me to the second reason why supporters of "welfare" reform see employment as central to citizenship. The assumption is that "welfare" creates a category of citizens who weaken the web of interdependence and undermine reciprocity (I will return to reciprocity). Citizens who are not employed are free riders; they are nonworkers who fail to do their duty and make the necessary social contribution. Mead argues that if these citizens are to do their social duty "they must be made *less* free in certain senses rather than more" (1986: 4).

Like the language of dependence, the language of nonwork is also odd. To put single mothers into the category of nonworkers is possible only because "work" has become identified with employment. This narrow meaning of work was reinforced by the structure of the Social Security system set up in 1935 and the reforms in Britain in the 1940s. "Going out to work," that is, engaging in paid employment, was what counted for citizenship. Single mothers and other able-bodied individuals outside of the labor force can thus be seen as avoiding the duties of citizens – because they are not employed.[17]

But this raises a very basic question: what counts, or should count, as a contribution of a citizen or toward standing as a citizen? This is not an easy question to answer, as T.H. Marshall's discussion reveals. He notes that the requirement to give "such service as one can to promote the welfare of the community" is vague (1963: 123).[18] Moreover, it is not clear in which direction, so to speak, one should begin to look to give it more content.

Citizenship as a formal political status is a vertical relationship between an individual and the state. Thus Marshall noted that two specific duties were the performance of military service and payment of taxes.[19] Similarly, in a list of social obligations, Mead includes law–abidingness (1986: 243; and see William Galston's (2005) comments on required performance and obeying the law). With the introduction of TANF, the state mandates that in return for subsistence a certain duty must be performed. But citizenship can also be seen as a horizontal relationship between citizens; that is to say, it becomes part of the social web of interdependence. This view makes it much harder to distinguish activities that fulfill specific duties of citizens from those that contribute to general social well-being, to democratic social reproduction (see Pateman 1985). Much of the discussion of "welfare" suggests that the dereliction involved in dependency is failure to perform a duty owed to fellow citizens. Universal employment seems to fit more easily into the horizontal view; are not individuals outside of the labor force, it can be asked, "harming others by failing to fulfill their obligations to their fellow citizens?" (Gutmann and Thompson 1996: 278). Marshall concluded that the only clear general duty of citizens is the duty to work, that is, to be employed (he confined this duty to male breadwinners).

But why should employment be given special status as the contribution of citizens? The institution of employment is one way of organizing the production of goods and services required for the welfare of citizens, and in that sense to be in paid employment is to make a social contribution. However, the institution of employment lies at the center of the capitalist system of production, a form of undemocratic organization that has as its aim not a social contribution but private profit. As Schumpeter clearly saw, if a social function was performed, if a social contribution was made, that was merely a happy by-product of profit-seeking. In his comparison of economic competition and the electoral competition for political office he wrote that "the social function [of the latter] is fulfilled, as it were, incidentally – in the same sense as production is incidental to the making of profits" (Schumpeter 1943: 282). The connection of employment to citizenship is at best indirect.

A more direct argument is that employment is the basis of social respect and thus equal standing. Citizens have a duty to participate and thus a duty "to develop their capacities to do so. One of these capacities is the acquisition of the social respect that work [that is, employment] brings" (Gutmann and Thompson 1996: 203).[20] But, again, capacities developed through employment are fostered within an undemocratic structure. How then do they contribute to democratic citizenship? Moreover, this argument begs the question of why employment should be so crucial for social respect. Why should other contributions not bring respect?

There are many ways of contributing to social life and duties other than employment are involved in the network of mutual aid and forbearance. The reproduction, education, and care of the population – social reproduction – is a basic social necessity and crucial for citizenship. Citizens, young and old, must be cared for, their welfare must be addressed, and thus there is much work to be done in addition to the work central to the Poor Law. Many aspects of the welfare state in the European sense can be seen as a public solution to the problem of caring for citizens. Yet public provision has always rested heavily on the private, unpaid welfare provided by wives, mothers and daughters. Much of the work of care has been seen as women's work – husbands, and men in general, typically are free riders in these tasks.

Universal employment and cuts in public provision have created a major problem of democratic social reproduction. From the Poor Law until the 1970s the problem was not so urgent. Wives were available for the much of the caring work and the development of Western welfare states, as Marshall emphasizes, shifted the political balance away from the Poor Law toward citizenship. Today, economic policies of structural adjustment and privatization have swung the balance back again to the Poor Law and most women, including mothers, are now in the paid workforce.[21] TANF both reflects this new context and exacerbates it, and symbolizes the distance from earlier arrangements.

International trade and the extraction of resources by imperial powers from around the globe existed, of course, at the time of the Poor Law, but the scope and rapidity of expansion, extraction and production has increased and now includes the construction of (integrated) labor markets around the world (that is, global "work"). The problem is that reproducing and providing for the welfare of the population cannot be speeded up in the same way. Social reproduction requires time and human and other resources. Yet "welfare" reform demands that all able-bodied adults be employed at the same time that public provision is reduced. The costs of, and time needed for, the replenishment, education and care of the population have become a drag on profit-making in the new economic order: "Time spent on human reproduction is time spent away from the speedy pursuit of profit across space" (Brennan 2003).[22]

Motherhood and welfare

The recent controversies over "welfare" give little indication that marriage, motherhood and fatherhood have been at the heart of the development of welfare. The standard view, which goes back at least to Hegel, is that the major aim of public provision is to remedy damage to male workers from the operation of the labor market. Assistance is given to those who cannot find employment, who are sick, injured or retired. Welfare rescues workers from poverty and so from becoming "undeserved exile[s] from society" (Moon 1988: 29). From the time of the Poor Law, however, the wage was much more than a payment to an individual that enabled him to continue to participate in the institution of employment. It was a family wage that in principle (the practice was often very different) was sufficient to enable a man, as a husband and father, to maintain his wife and children without his wife entering paid employment.

"The laws of marriage," Nancy Cott has written, "sculpt the body politic" (2000: 5).[23] For most of the twentieth century, the institutions of marriage, employment, and citizenship were firmly locked together. Married women's political standing was still shaped by coverture,[24] by their private status as wives and their tasks as mothers. As wives, they had a legal entitlement to support from their husbands and so most, it was assumed, would not "work." But, as feminist scholars pointed out from the 1970s onward, this was connected to lesser citizenship. In the Social Security Act (1935), wives were treated primarily as the economic dependents of their husbands whose tasks were to be fulfilled – unpaid – at home. Male breadwinners made a contribution through their wages to social insurance, and were, therefore, full citizens entitled to benefits. Their wives typically received benefits as the dependents of citizens, not as citizens in their own right.[25]

European countries, too, usually structured social insurance systems around the male breadwinner, but the United States stood apart in having no national measure to support child-rearing. Europe and the Antipodes established universal support for children, and in Britain and Australia the allowance was paid directly to the mother, who was much more likely than her husband to spend it on the children. Debate over these measures did not pass entirely unnoticed in the United States, but child endowment was never on the political agenda.[26]

On the one hand, the lesser citizenship of married women was part of the structure of social insurance. On the other hand, the earlier arrangements looked to social reproduction in the assumption that wives would not be employed but would bear and rear children. There was thus at least an implicit recognition that mothers were performing significant work, albeit that it was not seen as a relevant contribution for social insurance. This was made explicit by William Beveridge in his report, which laid the foundation for the major reforms in Britain in the 1940s. He wrote that "the great majority of married women must be regarded as occupied on work which is vital though unpaid, without which their husbands could not do their paid work, and without which the nation could not continue." Husband and wife are "a team, each of whose partners is equally essential." In particular, mothers "have vital work to do in ensuring the adequate continuance of the British race and of British ideals in the world" (1942: §§107, 117).

As Christopher Beem emphasizes, the conceptual framework was then still available through which mothers could be seen as making a civic contribution. He calls this framework republican motherhood, but the label is misleading. Feminist historians have devised the term to refer to the eighteenth-century argument that women's task was to bear and rear the next generation of citizens even though women were at the same time regarded as naturally unfit for, and so excluded from, citizenship. By the 1940s, husbands and wives may, for Beveridge, have been a team in which both members were doing important work, but only the husband's employment was the work that counted as part of full citizenship. In contrast, the feminist argument, as Beem notes, was that women should be included as full citizens and that motherhood should count as contributing to, or even as part of, their citizenship.[27] One aspect of the current problem of social reproduction (on which I shall comment shortly) is that women have won all the formal rights of citizens but motherhood in the United States is seen as a private undertaking.

Some of the earliest welfare measures in both Europe and the United States were concerned with motherhood. In 1883, for example, Germany introduced very modest and optional benefits for maternity leave, and maternity benefits were introduced in Britain 1911, in Italy in 1910, and in France and the Netherlands in 1913. In the United States there was concern about single mothers from the 1880s; public support began early in the twentieth century and was reasonably popular until the 1960s.

The first Mothers' Aid legislation to assist women raising young children on their own was passed in 1911, and by 1920 forty states had enacted similar measures (see Gordon 1994: chs. 3 and 4; Skocpol 1992: chs. 6, 8, and 9). The recipients of mothers' pensions were not, significantly, the welfare mothers who came to haunt the popular political imagination of the late twentieth century. They were predominantly widows (80 percent of recipients by 1931); only fifty-five unmarried mothers were granted pensions nationwide. The great majority was white: only 3 percent of recipients were African American and only 1 percent members of other minority groups (Skocpol 1992: 471; Nelson 1990: 39). Funding for the pro gram was never adequate, many mothers were not assisted, and the payments were meager (see Gordon 1994: 189).[28] Single mothers who received aid were therefore likely to be in paid employment: a study in 1923 of urban areas found that over half were employed and that their children were more likely than those of other mothers to be in the labor force (Skocpol 1992: 476; Nelson 1990: 142).

The white widow left alone with her children to struggle to manage was seen as eminently deserving. Indeed, the women's organizations that had campaigned for mothers' pensions supported tests of moral fitness, which were common for other programs at the time, and mothers were monitored to ensure that they maintained eligibility. Thus the mothers' pension programs were much closer to charitable poor relief (though many charities had opposed them) and to the spirit of the Poor Law than to the workers' compensation schemes established in forty-two states by 1920.[29]

The Mothers' Aid model was brought to Washington and into the Social Security Act in the form of Aid to Dependent Children (ADC) through a network of women activists who worked largely through the Children's Bureau, set up in 1912 and staffed by women, which drafted the proposal for ADC (see Gordon 1994: chs. 6, 9, and 10; Skocpol 1992: ch. 9; and Michel 1993). They brought with them the social work perspective, moralistic criteria and monitoring practices of the state programs. ADC was thus set apart from the social insurance side of the 1935 legislation, foreshadowed by the workers' compensation schemes. From the beginning, ADC resembled "welfare."

Southern politicians determined to maintain very low wages for their workforce opposed the 1935 legislation in Congress. Agricultural, domestic, educational and hospital workers were not covered, thus excluding most black, Latino, and women workers, and vagrancy laws were also used to compel black individuals into employment. Under ADC, like mothers' pension programs, African American and other minority women were largely excluded from assistance, and nonwhite women were considered "employable mothers" (see Kerber 1998).[30] Moreover, the work of single mothers caring for their young children was already being devalued as a contribution of citizens; "mothers' monthly entitlement was only half that of other categorical recipients of public assistance" (Mink 1990: 112).

ADC was relabeled as AFDC in 1962, but by then the popularity of the program had begun its rapid decline (Teles 1996: 43–45).[31] From the end of the 1970s, government support for many forms of public provision declined as neoliberalism ascended politically.[32] The public, however, were more discriminating, and though not as supportive of welfare as Europeans, are by no means opposed to it. Americans "not only support most of the welfare-state programs that currently exist, but they also think that in most areas the government is not doing enough to help its citizens" (Gilens 1999: 27; see also Teles 1996: ch. 3). Public hostility was focused on "welfare," on AFDC and single mothers. Other programs for the poor, such as Food Stamps and Medicaid, did not suffer the same level of opprobrium and Social Security remained extremely popular.

A number of factors contributed to the opposition to AFDC. By the 1970s the number of beneficiaries of the program had greatly expanded and their composition had changed. From 1939 many (white) widows were included under the survivors provisions of Social Security, and the remaining mothers were the most impoverished – "divorced, or not married, or widows of men without histories of wage earning in occupations covered by social insurance" (Skocpol 1992: 536).[33] Many more mothers from minority sections of the population were receiving AFDC by the 1960s. The increase in nonwhite beneficiaries was important for two reasons. First, Gilens's evidence shows that many white Americans overestimate by a wide margin the percentage of African Americans both in the population and among "welfare" recipients. Second, the hostility to "welfare" arose from the perception of moral failure on the part of the mothers in AFDC. "Welfare" recipients are seen as unwilling to help themselves, and, above all, to be unwilling to seek employment; blacks, in particular, are perceived as lazy. Thus welfare mothers became emblematic of the undeserving poor.[34]

The other major element in the rise of antagonism toward welfare was the change in the position of women. The proportion of married women in the paid labor force increased rapidly, especially from the 1960s: 70 percent of households in 1940 had only one breadwinner; by 1980, 28 percent did (Orloff 2001: 150). Some wives have always, due to economic necessity, had to be employed, but changing conceptions of masculinity and femininity meant that "going out to work" became respectable. Women were also able to gain educational qualifications, and many were keen to enter the paid labor force at a time when the rise of service industries had increased the availability of women's employment. More recent structural economic change has taken a different, global form; old economy jobs for male breadwinners are being swept away, and the new jobs are often casual or with no benefits and low wages, even as the spread of downsizing and economic insecurity mean that for many families there is now little choice whether both spouses will be in the labor force.

By 1996 the situation of single mothers who received "welfare" to look after their children full-time at home was thus at odds with that of most other mothers, who were in the paid work force. This, Orloff argues, explains why there was little opposition to PRWORA among women's organizations (2001: 151–53). Welfare reform made the circumstances of all mothers more similar. As Mead (2005) reports, the result of the introduction of TANF was that the numbers of recipients of welfare dropped by 62 percent from 1994 to 2001, and many more single mothers are now employed.

In addition, by 1996, thanks to the success of the women's movement in bringing about legal reforms, coverture had finally ended (that is, wives were no longer official economic dependents of their husbands), women had achieved formal civil and political equality, and discrimination was squarely on the public agenda. But in the individualistic political culture of the United States, in contrast to other Western countries, such equality is widely seen as incompatible with support for women as mothers. Maternity leave (which depends primarily on arrangements of employers), for example, had to be treated as a disability, like a man's loss of an arm in a piece of machinery, to rescue it from legal rejection as special treatment for a privileged group. The result is that mothers in the United States are employed "with less public support such as child allowances, child care, or paid leaves, than…their counterparts in other parts of the West" (Orloff 2001: 152). In short, motherhood and child rearing are seen as purely private matters that women themselves must find the time and resources to undertake.

Time is also in short supply. As Juliet Schor pointed out over a decade ago, Americans work longer hours than their counterparts in other rich countries (1991), they take fewer and shorter holidays, and have fewer public holidays. Women adopt familiar strategies to make time; notably, they are more likely to be employed part-time than men so that they can also shoulder their unpaid work of care. But this pattern of employment, the fact that women earn less than men, and the persistence of men's and women's jobs, have perpetuated the moral hazard of men avoiding their fair share of the work of care. Increasingly, mothers who can afford to do so employ women from poor countries to care for their children, who, in turn, often leave their own children with relatives – so adding to the global problem of care. On the other hand, because TANF includes funds for child care, former welfare mothers are able to avoid some of these problems.

The assumption in the United States today is that mothers (parents) need little public provision to care for children. The implications for social reproduction, especially when combined with universal employment, tend to be avoided. The two At-Home Infant Care programs that Christopher Beem (2005) discusses are one attempt to mitigate the problems being generated: Beem suggests that these programs might provide a model for a universal policy of paid parental leave for low-income families. Such a move away from the logic of the Poor Law to the logic of democracy is to be welcomed, but would leave untouched the wider problem of social reproduction. One difficulty is that only mothers who are in paid employment are eligible for the Infant Care programs, and Beem proposes to retain this feature if the programs were extended. But this is to cling to the logic of the Poor Law and to the principle that benefits should be given to the able-bodied only in exchange for employment. The figure of the undeserving (poor) citizen thus still looms large in the background.

Another difficulty is that social reproduction, the task of providing for the welfare and care of citizens, is much broader than the work of mothers or fathers, but in Beem's discussion, as in many feminist arguments about care, the wider public problem disappears. This disappearance makes it all the more easy to overlook that the preoccupation with employment is part of the problem of social reproduction in all its dimensions. Caring for citizens takes second place to employment and the logic of the Poor Law. The time and resources required for social reproduction are being sacrificed to the demands of global labor markets and capitalism.

The alternative is to move away completely from the logic of the Poor Law to the logic of democracy. A basic income for all citizens – which would open up time and resources to citizens and help put social reproduction at the forefront of debate – would be a crucial step in this direction.

A basic income and reciprocity

In *Citizenship and Social Class,* T.H. Marshall saw the British legislation of the 1940s as abolishing the Poor Law and the Poor Law mentality. Marshall wrote that the "significance of [the] final removal" of the disenfranchisement of those receiving relief "has, perhaps, not been fully appreciated" (1963, 83). His words are still apt. The provision of benefits without loss of rights is a major step forward in the process of democratization. Citizenship ceases to be conditional, a privilege, and the maintenance of a minimum standard of living through public provision becomes a universal right or entitlement. Marshall writes of a "universal right to real income which is not proportionate to the market value of the claimant" (100).[35] In other words, welfare becomes part of citizenship; the care of citizens is part of public policy.

But Marshall was too optimistic. The Poor Law mentality has persisted, and over the past quarter century has gained new influence at the expense of the universalist logic of democracy. The proponents of workfare argue that full citizenship is conditional on employment, and that respect depends on that particular contribution. In the United States universalism has received much less support than in some European countries and has generally been outweighed by the Poor Law mentality and a minimalist view of democracy. Nonetheless, it animated Social Security (though this is sometimes seen as a reward for life-time employment), and in the 1960s Charles Reich argued that public provision should be seen as a form of property right that represented "part of the individual's rightful share in the commonwealth, and provided a basis for individual well-being and dignity in a society where each man cannot be wholly the master of his own destiny" (1964: 785–86). Marshall also took for granted that husbands were breadwinners and wives were available to provide care in the household. Thus, to fulfill his hope of abolishing the Poor Law, a new approach to the care and welfare of citizens and to their self-government and standing is required. This must follow the logic of democracy: that citizenship is unconditional and that respect is owed because an individual is a citizen.

A basic income for all citizens, a policy that has been receiving attention in recent years, would be a significant step forward in keeping with the logic of democracy and would help recapture the time and resources needed for social reproduction. By a basic income I mean the regular payment of a sum of money by a government to each adult citizen with no conditions attached.[36] A basic income differs from the generous income replacement policies in some European countries precisely in being unconditional; marital and household status, and employment history are irrelevant.[37]

While there are few people who are now opposed to universal suffrage, there is widespread reluctance to see a decent living standard as an analogous democratic right. Nonetheless, a basic income can be compared to the suffrage. If the vote is essential for participation in collective self-government, then a decent standard of life is essential for individual self-government and participation in social life more generally. Universal suffrage is the emblem of equal citizenship, and underpins an orderly change of government through free and fair elections, so enhancing citizens' security. A basic income is the emblem of full citizenship, and provides the security required to maintain that political standing and individual self-government. Both the vote and a basic income can be seen as fundamental rights in Henry Shue's sense of rights that "specify the line beneath which no one is to be allowed to sink." Rights are fundamental "if enjoyment of them is essential to the enjoyment of all other rights" (1996: 18, 19). A basic income provides the life-long security that helps safeguard other rights, ensures that citizens are able – that is, have the opportunities and means – genuinely to enjoy their freedom and helps promote respect (compare Gaffaney 2000: ch. 5).

Hayek argued that the deleterious effect of employment on freedom could be combated if there were sufficient gentlemen of private means (1960: 125). One way of looking at a basic income is as a democratization of this argument at a lower standard of living. The idea of a basic income does not, in itself, specify an appropriate income level. This is a crucial question, and the subject of considerable debate. In part, the different levels advocated depend, of course, on evaluations of cost, but I shall leave these aside to highlight some of the implications of the logic of democracy. If cost proves a decisive obstacle, then we need to be clear about what is being given up and what that means for citizenship and democratization.[38] Arguments for specific levels of a basic income also depend on the reasons for an interest in the policy. If it is supported as a means to relieve poverty or a way to promote flexible labor markets, the suggested level is likely to be lower than if the concern is social reproduction and democratic citizenship.

The logic of democracy requires that a basic income be set at a level sufficient to ensure that citizens can enjoy what I call a modest but decent standard of life. That is, a standard sufficient to provide them with a meaningful degree of choice about how they live their lives and the ability to participate in social, cultural, economic, and political life to the extent they wish. A basic income would provide citizens with a wide range of opportunities, because ex hypothesi they could live on it, including the opportunity not to be employed. A basic income would therefore make it possible for mothers – and fathers – to care for their children full-time if they wished. The opportunity would be universal, available to all citizens, and so would begin to provide some remedy for the problem of social reproduction. But a basic income in itself could not solve the wider problem, which can only be addressed by other areas of public policy.

One of the most significant consequences of a basic income would be for women's self-government. For the very first time all women could be economically independent. Mary Wollstonecraft argued in 1792 that if women were to enjoy freedom and the rights of citizens they must have economic independence – whether married or single. In the interwar years in Britain, some feminists hoped that a child endowment could break the nexus between men's wages and mothers' standard of living and "once for all, cut away the question of the maintenance of children and the reproduction of the race from the question of wages" (Rathbone 1986 [1927]: 219).[39]

Not all contemporary feminists support a basic income; some have argued against the idea on the grounds that it would reinforce the status quo. Given the existing private and public sexual division of labor and occupational structure, women's lesser earnings, and lingering beliefs about the proper tasks of men and women, a basic income might merely give women an incentive to undertake more unpaid caring work and bolster free riding by men. Would men take advantage of the new opportunity? Whether the work of care would be shared more fairly, or feminist fears realized, is an empirical question. However, the outcome depends in part on how a basic income is argued for. Men would more likely begin to do their fair share if the debate about its introduction drew attention to their free riding; that is to say, if questions are asked about the relationship between marriage, income, and citizenship; about caring for citizens and time; about the relation between paid and unpaid work and thus the meaning of "work"; about the place of employment in a democracy; and about social reproduction. Only then would questions begin to be raised about the institutional restructuring necessary for a solution to the problem of democratic social reproduction.

These questions have received little attention so far in discussions of basic income because, as in the controversies over "welfare," employment has remained a major focus. Ironically, despite the fact that a basic income stands at the opposite pole from welfare, the continuing grip of the logic of the Poor Law is evident in the discussions. The unconditional character of a basic income has provoked a great deal of apprehension and anxiety, and, in particular, much criticism has centered on two related questions; first, idleness and, second, the question already raised earlier, the practice of reciprocity and citizens' contributions. So let me begin with some comments about a basic income, free riding, idleness, and employment.

I have seen little evidence to suggest that the outcome of the introduction of a basic income would be a large number of idle citizens. That most people do not want to be idle is indicated by the extent of unpaid voluntary contributions of time and work, particularly from women. Significantly, Hayek did not expect his gentlemen of independent means to be idle. They would be indispensable in using their resources "in the service of aims which bring no material return," and which "the mechanism of the market cannot adequately take care of" (1960: 125). In debates about basic income it is not work in general or motherhood (usually ignored) that is the concern, but male employment, illustrated by the figure of a male surfer as the symbol of the free rider.[40] Significant numbers of men, it is assumed, would turn away from employment if given a basic income. The major problem of male free riding in caring work is rarely acknowledged.

The effect on employment of a basic income is another empirical question, and there is little evidence to draw on. One source is the five negative income tax experiments conducted in the United States and Canada between 1968 and 1980. Karl Widerquist has recently reanalyzed the evidence from these, and concludes that limitations of the experiments mean that no definitive answer is available about the effect on employment. There was some disincentive effect (most noticeable among married women and teenagers living with their parents) but there was no wholesale withdrawal from the labor market. Despite the enormous amount written about the experiments there is no consensus about policy implications, and whether the disincentive effect is seen as acceptable or not largely depends on the political views of commentators.[41]

It is sometimes forgotten that the unconditional character of a basic income means that it would act as an incentive for employment as well as a disincentive. Individuals could choose to supplement their income through employment, even low-paid employment, and so it could act as a subsidy for low wages. Alternatively, individuals might refuse to accept very low pay and unsafe or unsanitary working conditions and take advantage instead of the other opportunities a basic income provides.

Other questions rarely asked in either debates over welfare or basic income are whether universal employment is feasible (especially with jobs that pay a living wage with good benefits and conditions),[42] or, even more important, why in the twenty-first century, with high productivity levels and rapid labor-saving advances, universal employment is required. There is some evidence to suggest that it is not. Robert Goodin, for example, has argued that The Netherlands can be regarded as post-productivist. Citizens there seem to "spend very substantially less time in paid labour and unpaid household labour combined than do people in any of the other nine OECD countries...they experience very low rates of poverty....Both their temporal autonomy and their economic autonomy are thus well-served" (2001a: 30–31).[43]

I now turn to the second major anxiety about an unconditional basic income, the issue of reciprocity, or the social web of interdependence, and making a contribution. Like "welfare," a basic income, it is argued, breaches the principle of reciprocity – the principle of doing "one's fair share [in] a cooperative scheme from which one expects to benefit" (Gutmann and Thompson 1996: 303) – because recipients get something for nothing.

Stuart White (2005) has considered the reasons for making public assistance conditional, and he concludes that doing so is neither unjust nor illiberal (see White 2003). In part, his argument rests on empirical outcomes (for example, individuals' human capital will be increased, teenaged parents' child-rearing capacities improved, or the claims of the poor will be legitimized) that cannot be definitively assessed at present. It also rests on the claim that, because societies such as Britain and the United States are unjust in many respects, both reciprocity and employment requirements must be fair in themselves so that existing disadvantages are not consolidated. Thus, in *The Civic Minimum,* White sets out four criteria for a fair work-test, one of which is income adequacy (2003: 134–35).[44] Gutmann and Thompson also propose fair workfare, including the requirement that employment must pay enough "to enable adults to lift their families out of poverty" (1996, 296).[45] Such criteria pose problems for reciprocity because in low-wage economies, such as the United States or Britain, employment often leaves families below the poverty line. For example, from 1995 to 2000 the proportion of poor children in the United States living in working poor families rose from 32 to 43 percent; in 2001 it fell to 40 percent (Child Trends 2004).[46] Increases in the Earned Income Tax Credit have helped to combat poverty but reciprocity would be better served by higher wages, or, better still, by a basic income.

White presents his argument in a Rawlsian framework emphasizing moral reasoning. Moral reasoning is important but is not synonymous with political argument. Self-government and full standing for citizens, and the relationship between employment, labor markets and social reproduction, are political issues. In the present political climate, as White (2005) notes, the danger is that disadvantage would be further entrenched and lesser citizenship would result from the imposition of unfair conditions. However, the danger runs deeper still: lesser citizenship cannot be avoided when conditions are imposed.

The debate about conditional benefits is not confined to "welfare." A variety of proposals that introduce conditions into receipt of a basic income have been made; Anthony Atkinson's participation income is the best known (1996: 67–70). These proposals often extend the contribution required to include, for example, looking after children as well as employment. However, the democratic problem is not only a matter of widening what counts as a contribution or the fairness of the conditions, but goes back to Marshall's difficulty in sorting out what counts as a task of citizenship. Which tasks are to count and how it is to be decided if the criteria for performing them have been met? Is there to be another large, intrusive bureaucracy to police the fulfilling of contributions and exacting penalties? More fundamentally, the problem is that there would undoubtedly be some individuals who did not, or refused to, make the designated contributions even if these were broadly defined. Imposing conditions on some citizens for provision of benefits already divides the population into the more or the less deserving, those who are free and those who must be coerced. Some citizens are thus already set apart from others. What, then, would be the standing of those who made no designated contribution? Conditional benefits inevitably reinstate lesser citizenship; the old undemocratic notion of citizenship as a privilege rather than a universal right is still alive in arguments about public provision, contributions, and reciprocity.

Another variant of the reciprocity argument is that to call for an unconditional basic income as a democratic right is to ignore duties. Citizens who benefit from the cooperative scheme that is social life have a duty to contribute their fair share in return. Workfare is a way of ensuring that there are no free riders, that all citizens do their duty (I leave aside the question of why the idle rich are not similarly coerced into their duty). Indeed, the claim has been made that "if there are duties, then there has to be some element of conditionality in citizenship."[47] However, it does not follow from my argument that a decent standard of life is a democratic right, that duties are unimportant or irrelevant. To argue against workfare or for an unconditional basic income implies nothing about rights or duties in a general sense. There only seems to be a connection because of the narrow understanding of reciprocity in the claims about benefits, reciprocity, and contributions.

A narrow, contractual or economistic sense of reciprocity is presupposed in discussions of both workfare and a conditional basic income.[48] The assumption is that a specific contribution is owed directly and immediately in return for a benefit, rather like a wage in employment. Or, to put this in terms of rights and duties, if there is a right (say, to TANF), then there is a correlative duty (employment or another form of contribution) attached directly to that right. It needs to be emphasized, first, that no such duty is demanded of other beneficiaries of public provision. Second, to see every right as having a correlative duty directly attached is only one conception of the relationship between rights and duties. Furthermore, in social life, outside of the market, few areas of reciprocity operate in such a narrow, contractual fashion.

I have already referred to the broader understanding of reciprocity; social life is a web of mutual aid and forbearance, a dense network of interdependence or reciprocity, which includes rights and duties which have no strict correlation with each other.[49] The narrow, contractual view of reciprocity echoes the idea of an original contract and the move from a state of nature to civil (that is, political) society. The claim is that the move takes place because humans benefit from political society. But there are two ambiguities here. The first is that if the state of nature is not a social state (so the benefits are those of social life itself) the problem arises that, as Hobbes and Rousseau show, the natural condition is not human either. If the state of nature is portrayed as social then reciprocity, the web of mutual aid and forbearance, is already in place (and what exactly are the benefits?).[50] Social life is the network of reciprocity, the cooperative scheme, but nothing follows from this conceptual point without much further argument.

Social life can be organized in many ways, and to posit a specific form of social order is go far beyond a conceptual point. A great deal more discussion and specification of principles, values, and institutional arrangements is then needed to decide what is a just or democratic society. And here the second ambiguity comes to the fore. To maintain social life, contributions have to be made. But in which direction do they flow? I earlier raised the question of vertical and horizontal contributions, but this is a problem only in civil society – that is to say, in a modern state – because only then are duties owed vertically to the state as well as horizontally among citizens. Workfare is mandated by the state in return for benefits and the benefit and the duty are directly linked. Yet arguments about schemes of cooperation, free riders, and duties seem instead to refer to failure to give what is owed (horizontally) to fellow citizens or to do what is necessary to maintain the general well-being – but then the problem of specifying what counts as duty of citizenship reappears. For example, if the tasks of motherhood are seen as a contribution in return for workfare or a conditional basic income does that imply that such tasks are those of a citizen rather than a private individual? If motherhood is brought into citizenship, then what are the implications for the familiar, minimalist view of democracy that separates public citizenship from private motherhood (and fatherhood)? There are other problems, too, in deciding what constitutes doing one's fair share; do the duties, for example, depend on the distribution of benefits? The latter question is not usually raised in debates about welfare, but perhaps poor citizens, rather than being open to coercion, owe less than the better off,

We all rely every day, to a large extent implicitly, on countless acts that look forward to other reciprocal acts that we expect in the future, or reflect actions that have assisted us in the past; we rely, that is, on the performance of duties. Reciprocity stretches over time and space. Neither mothers nor all those engaged in caring work or education demand an immediate reciprocal contribution from, for example, young children, the sick, infirm, elderly, or pupils in return for benefits; their work is not conditional upon a contribution. Indeed, love, not expectation of reciprocity, is seen as motivating the work of wives and mothers. Providing for the welfare of citizens and the work of, and time devoted to, the social reproduction of citizens who can actively participate in a democratic polity cannot depend on immediate reciprocal contributions.

One of the lessons from great political theorists such as Hobbes or Hegel is that narrow, contractual views of reciprocity always depend on the wider web of social interdependence, and, if extended too far, contractual practices undermine their own social grounding. The social reproduction of citizens includes careful attention to ethics, but moral education is all the harder when the welfare of citizens is subordinated to the labor market, and the logic of the Poor Law takes precedence over the logic of democracy. The rapid changes now taking place provide the opportunity not only to rethink current policies but also to consider how to put employment in its democratic place. Societies in which time for motherhood and fatherhood becomes a luxury, economic insecurity is widespread, inequality is growing, and public provision for the welfare of citizens is under continuous threat are unlikely to be stable in the longer term.

A basic income is, I have argued, a necessary step forward – but it is not sufficient. The social reproduction of citizens goes well beyond the private caring work of wives and mothers and equitable sharing of that work by husbands and fathers. Public provision is also needed to sustain and strengthen democratic citizenship. A basic income cannot in itself provide good quality education in well-equipped schools, affordable housing, access to health care, violence free neighborhoods, access to cultural amenities, or the cultivation of individual capacities within the democratized institutions of a robust democracy. Reforming welfare requires the elimination of the Poor Law; reforming the relationship between employment and the social reproduction of citizens is part of a much bigger process of democratization.

Notes

1 I am grateful to Larry Mead and Chris Beem for their careful reading of drafts of this chapter, for criticisms and helpful suggestions. I also thank Mary McThomas for her assistance and Gary Chartier for discussions. I dedicate this chapter to the memory of my old friend and former student (who wrote her honors thesis on motherhood): Teresa Brennan 1952–2003.

2 I shall use "welfare" to indicate the circumscribed usage of the term in the United States, in contrast to the much broader welfare provision in most other rich Western countries. Workfare means that assistance is conditional upon employment in either the public or private sector.

3 States now receive a fixed grant for the program from the federal government and are able to set most eligibility rules for beneficiaries.

4 In 1979 only 17 percent of British social expenditure went to means tested benefits but by 1995 it was 36 percent (Wilding 1997: 722). Sweden's active labor policy is often cited too, but, unlike the United States and Britain, Sweden has few means-tested programs and has very generous income replacement policies and support for parents, so the context is different.

5 Marshall equivocated about social rights, and his argument about citizenship was thus more complex than these quotations suggest; in places, especially in his later writings, his argument points towards recent claims that social rights are outdated (see Pateman 1996).

6 Though this is not exactly as Mead envisaged: by workfare he was referring to employment in the public sector.

7 Workfare is one element in the wider category of means-tested policies that create the paradox that a given group "must first be singled out as *different* from ordinary citizens. But if the group is that different, how can they ever by any social policy initiative become like 'ordinary citizens'" (Rothstein 1998: 159).

8 Universal suffrage has been much harder to achieve than is usually supposed. For example, women won the vote in Switzerland only in 1971, they still lack the franchise in Kuwait, and neither men nor women have the franchise in Saudi Arabia. In the United States voting was only democratized in practice after the Civil Rights Act of 1965 ensured that African Americans could freely cast a ballot, and in a few states felons are still disenfranchised for life.

9 Minimalist and economic theories of democracy owe a good deal to Joseph Schumpeter (1943).

10 Moreover, virtues such as frugality and thrift sit uneasily with an economy that depends on continuous consumption and high levels of individual indebtedness.

11 In fact, there were too many men and families to fit into the workhouses and outdoor relief survived in the form of a system of Labour Yards (where half the relief was paid in kind), and here is "the historical origins of a workfare principle…in exchange for receiving assistance recipients must undertake some work activity" (King 1999: 229; on the Labour Yards, see 229–32).

12 This view is associated in particular with the work of Charles Murray, but it is hardly new (on dependency, see Fraser and Gordon 1994).

13 These problems need to be tackled through the appropriate therapeutic channels, whether they derive from illiteracy or health problems (though the war on drugs is a singular failure) and lie outside my concerns here. If criminal behavior is involved there are numerous laws to deal with it.

14 A small-scale study from 1996 to 1998 in New Jersey of single mothers who were sanctioned for noncompliance found that they were confused about why they had been penalized, and no significant differences existed between those who then complied and those who did not. It is reported that in other research caseworkers were also found to be confused about the new laws (Smith and Gunn 2002).

15 Based on data from the 2000 census, the U.S. Census Bureau found that in 400 fields full-time, year-round women workers earn only 74 cents compared to the dollar earned by their male counterparts.

16 President G.W. Bush has also introduced a Healthy Marriage Initiative. Leaving aside religious objections to childbirth out of wedlock, it is hard to see why single motherhood, in itself, is a problem, even though it is a difficult task when women are mired in poverty. If mothers lack parenting skills then that is a problem to be tackled directly. In Sweden, over half of all births were to unwed mothers by 1990 but conditions for, and social perceptions of, unmarried mothers are very different from those in the United States. Reference in often made to empirical research to show that children fare poorly in the absence of an intact two-parent family. However; the methodology of much of this research can be questioned (see Lister 2001).

17 Nor does so-called nonwork count in a more literal sense. Nonmarket activities are not calculated in estimates of GDP. There are now efforts to remedy this, but the division between public work in the labor force (primarily male) and private activities in the household (primarily female) was built into the United Nations System of National Accounts (see Waring 1988).

18 Marshall goes on to say, "but the community is so large that the obligation appears remote and unreal."

19 He ignored the problems this raised about women citizens in 1949, when he first presented the lectures that became his essay. They were not subject to postwar conscription, and, if they were married, were regarded as under coverture (that is, as part of the legal person of their husband) for tax purposes and not allowed to make a tax return as individuals.

20 Gutmann and Thompson draw on Judith Shklar's argument about earning. I am not sure that acquiring respect is a capacity.

21 Structural adjustment and privatization are often seen as applying only to developing countries, but New Zealand provides perhaps the most complete example of the application of these economic dogmas. Other rich countries are beginning to follow this example, but at least in the countries of the Commonwealth, there is a considerable gap between the views of citizens about the responsibilities of governments and current government policy (see Knight, Chigudu, and Tandon 2002).

22 Brennan (2003) discusses the prime directive; that is "we shall not use up nature and humankind at a rate faster than they can replenish themselves and be replenished" (164).

23 Cott also notes that in 1996 a report "from the U.S. General Accounting Office found more than *one thousand* places in the corpus of federal law where legal marriage conferred a distinctive status, right or benefit" (2; see also Pateman 1988).

24 The common law doctrine under which (in Blackstone's words) "the husband and wife are one person in law; that is, the very being, or legal existence of the woman is suspended during the marriage, or at least is incorporated and consolidated into that of the husband" (Blackstone 1899 [1765]: 442).

25 In 1996, "65 percent of elderly female Social Security recipients received benefits based at least in part on their husbands' work histories" (Ackerman and Alstott 1999: 145; see also Pateman 1989).

26 In Australia, a child endowment scheme was introduced in New South Wales in 1927 and at federal level in 1941; family allowances were introduced in Britain in 1946, and continue as a universal child benefit; a child tax credit has also been introduced (either can be paid to the custodial parent).

27 It is the feminist, not the republican, view of motherhood that generates (my formulation of) Wollstonecraft's dilemma, on which Beem draws.

28 Under the Federal Emergency Relief Act (1934) "three times as many children and almost three and a half times as many single-mother families were receiving federal emergency relief as had received any mothers' aid."

29 These replaced a tort liability system, and the programs were based on standardized criteria and eligibility, and realized risk (Nelson 1990: 141).

30 In the late nineteenth and early twentieth centuries there was also a welfare system for Civil War veterans: "After 1890, what amounted to disability and old-age pensions were paid quarterly from the federal Treasury to all applicants who could claim to be Union veterans, as well as to others who could claim to be dependents of soldiers who had died during or after the war." Between 1880 and 1910 a quarter of federal expenditures were allocated to such pensions (Skocpol 1992: 65). Military service, along with employment, have been the contributions required of men, and are seen as primary political obligations. But political theorists have rarely paused to consider the political obligations of women, or, indeed, if they have any.

31 Support dropped especially between 1960 and 1973, and 1991 and 1993.

32 Religious fundamentalism also became increasingly influential. Campaigns were launched for family values and against single motherhood, but opposition to abortion (and also in some cases contraception) contradicts the goal of lowering the incidence of births out of wedlock. The administration of G.W. Bush has promoted partnership between religious organizations and government in delivering welfare services.

33 In 1974 Old-Age Assistance and aid to blind and disabled people were absorbed into SSI, but these were not seen in quite the same way as AFDC.

34 Gilens (1999) presents evidence about the role of the media in fostering these perceptions, so it is hardly surprising that figure of the African American welfare queen became so prominent.

35 I called this Marshall's strong or democratic view in *Democratization and Citizenship in the 1990s*.

36 The policy has attracted supporters from different parts of the political spectrum for a variety of reasons ranging from social justice to flexible labor markets, and has been supported by Nobel Prize winners James Meade, Herbert Simon, and James Tobin. Information can be found at http://www.basicincome.org/; for the United States at http://www.usbig.net/; and for Britain at http://www.citizensincome.org/. The policy is being widely discussed in Europe and South Africa and has adherents in the United States. In 2002, the Irish government published a Green Paper on Basic Income, and in early 2004 Brazil became the first country to enact legislation for a basic income, to be phased in gradually. The academic discussion was sparked off in earnest by Philippe Van Parijs (1995). There is now a large literature on basic income (for an introduction see Van Parijs 1992; *Boston Review* 2000; see also Pateman 2003; 2004).

37 The idea of a basic income has a competitor; stakeholding, or basic capital, in which a lump sum is paid to each individual on reaching adulthood (see Ackerman and Alstott 1999). In the political culture of the United States a stake is likely to be more immediately appealing than a basic income. In the United Kingdom the Blair government has already taken a step toward stakeholding by instituting a Child Trust Fund. For each child born on or after 1 September 2002 the government is providing £250 which is invested and will be available to the child at age eighteen. At age seven, the government will make a further contribution (the amount not yet determined) and parents and others can add up to £1200 per year to the child's Trust Fund account. Such measures are welcome, but, still, I believe that if democracy and citizenship is the concern a basic income is to be preferred (see Pateman 2003).

38 The net cost of a basic income is less than it may appear at first sight. It would replace means tested and some other programs, and the tax-transfer system would still operate. In the last analysis, cost is a political question. Since 2000 many hundreds of billions of dollars have been devoted to tax cuts, to subsidies to the agricultural and steel industries, sent up in space and spent on warfare. In the 1960s, the proportion of GDP comprising public spending, mostly welfare programs, in United States and the Scandinavian countries was roughly the same. By the 1990s, the latter were spending twice as much as the United States, and some other European countries fifty percent more (Rothstein 1998: 18). And Sweden in 2003 had a budget surplus and seemed to be in good economic shape.

39 Rathbone also hoped that child endowment would open the way for men and women workers to be paid the same for the same work. But the feminist case was overshadowed by pronatalist arguments and the more general argument that child endowment was important in the relief of poverty.

40 Rawls used the figure of the surfer to discuss this problem and he appears on the cover of Van Parijs's book.

41 "The experimental results seem to be a scientific Rorschach test in which an observer can see whatever she wants to see." The findings were complex but much of the commentary ignored the complexities. Nor did the experiments measure the possible long run shift in the labor supply or the demand (Widerquist 2005).

42 Unemployment rates in America are often compared favorably to those in Europe. However, this neglects the very high incarceration rate in the United States; in 1996 1.63 million individuals were in prison, a number that had increased threefold since 1980. In the short run the size of the prison population means tighter labor markets – male unemployment was understated by about 2 percent in the mid-1990s – and means that those imprisoned were more likely to be unemployed in the long run: "sustained low unemployment in the future will depend on continuing expansion of the penal system" (Western and Beckett 1999: 1031). (My thanks to Bob Goodin for alerting me to this article.) Expansion has continued and by mid-2002 there were 2 million inmates.

43 There will, no doubt, always be a few idle drones but a robust democracy can afford them. The use that citizens choose to make of their freedom is open to no guarantees. Self-government entails that they decide for themselves how and when they will contribute

or whether they will contribute at all. In the last analysis, if the cost of democratization and a basic income as a fundamental right is the existence of some drones, then it is worth paying.

44 For his five criteria for fair reciprocity and a formulation of the "contributive obligation," see White (2003: 90–91).

45 The other requirements are that governments make employment and child support available. Gutmann and Thompson also argue that if any parents refuse employment they must be coerced into supporting their children. They note that this "comes close to a policy of forced labor," but claim that the "alternatives are morally worse" (300) – not an argument that I find convincing, especially from democratic theorists.

46 A working poor family is one in which in a two-parent family one parent worked at least thirty-five hours per week, or a single parent worked twenty hours, and the family income (in 2001) was still below $18 (Child Trends 2004: 104).

47 An anonymous reviewer.

48 For a discussion of different models of reciprocity in the context of workfare in Australia, see Robert Goodin (2001b: 579–96). For further criticism of contractual conceptions of welfare see, for example, Robert Goodin (1998: 141–58), and King (1999).

49 For convenience, I am writing of duties here but I should be referring to acts that ought to be performed. For the reasons why I see acts that ought to be performed as distinct from both obligations (self-assumed by individuals) and duties (attached to stations and offices), see Pateman (1985: 27–30, 34).

50 I criticized some earlier versions of the benefits argument in *The Problem of Political Obligation* (1985: 121–25).

References

Ackerman, B. and A. Alstott. 1999. *The Stakeholder Society.* New Haven, CT.: Yale University Press.

Atkinson, A. 1996. 'The Case for a Participation Income'. *Political Quarterly* 67(1): 67–70.

Beem, C. 2005. 'Restoring the civic value of care in a post-welfare society'. *Welfare Reform and Political Theory.* New York: Russell Sage Foundation.

Beveridge, W. 1942. *Social Insurance and Allied Services.* New York: Macmillan.

Blackstone, Sir W. 1899 [1765]. *Commentaries on the Laws of England,* 4th edn., Book 1. Chicago: Callaghan and Co.

Boston Review. 2000. 'Symposium: Delivering a Basic Income'. October/November.

Brennan, T. 2003. *Globalization and Its Terrors: Daily Life in the West.* London and New York: Routledge.

Child Trends Databank. 2004. Available at: http://www.childtrendsdatabank.org/ (accessed January 2004).

Cott, N. 2000. *Public Vows: A History of Marriage and the Nation.* Cambridge, MA: Harvard University Press.

Dean, M. 1991. *The Constitution of Poverty: Toward a Genealogy of Liberal Governance.* London and New York: Routledge.

Fraser, N. and L. Gordon. 1994. 'A Genealogy of "Dependency": Tracing a Key Word of the U.S. Welfare State'. *Signs* 19(2): 309–36.

Gaffaney, T.J. 2000. *Freedom for the Poor: Welfare and the Foundations of Democratic Citizenship.* Boulder, CO: Westview Press.

Galston, W. 2005. 'Conditional citizenship'. *Welfare Reform and Political Theory.* New York: Russell Sage Foundation.

Gilens, M. 1999. *Why Americans Hate Welfare: Race, Media, and the Politics of Antipoverty Policy.* Chicago: University of Chicago Press.

Goodin, R.E. 1998. 'More than Anyone Bargained For: Beyond the Welfare Contract'. *Ethics and International Affairs* 12: 141–58.

—— 2001a. 'Work and Welfare: Towards a Post-Productivist Welfare Regime'. *British Journal of Political Science* 31(1): 13–39.

—— 2001b. "Structures of Mutual Obligation." *Journal of Social Policy* 31(4): 579–96.

Gordon, L. 1994. *Pitied but Not Entitled: Single Mothers and the History of Welfare, 1890–1935.* New York: The Free Press.

Gutmann, A. and D. Thompson. 1996. *Democracy and Disagreement.* Cambridge, MA: Harvard University Press.

Hayek, F. 1960. *The Constitution of Liberty.* Chicago: University of Chicago Press.

Hirschmann, N. 2003. *The Subject of Liberty: Towards a Feminist Theory of Freedom.* Princeton, NJ: Princeton University Press.

Kerber, L. 1998. *No Constitutional Right to be Ladies: Women and the Obligations of Citizenship.* New York: Hill and Wang.

King, D.S. 1999. *In the Name of Liberalism: Illiberal Social Policy in the United States and Britain.* Oxford: Oxford University Press.

Knight, B., H. Chigudu and R. Tandon. 2002. *Reviving Democracy: Citizens at the Heart of Governance.* London and Sterling, VA: Earthscan Publications.

Lister, A. 2001. 'Understanding the Burdens of Judgment: Moral Pluralism, Causal Ambiguity, and the Limits of Consequentialist Public Reason'. Ph.D. dissertation, University of California, Los Angeles.

Locke, J. 1997 [1697]. 'An Essay on the Poor Law'. In M. Goldie (ed.) *Political Essays.* Cambridge: Cambridge University Press.

Marshall, T.H. 1963. 'Citizenship and Social Class'. In *Sociology at the Crossroads and Other Essays.* London: Heinemann.

Mead, L.M. 1986. *Beyond Entitlement: The Social Obligations of Citizenship.* New York: Free Press.

—— 1992. *The New Politics of Poverty: The Nonworking Poor in America.* New York: Basic Books.

—— 2005. 'Welfare Reform and Citizenship'. In L. Mead and C. Beem (eds), *Welfare Reform and Political Theory.* New York: Russell Sage Foundation.

Michel, S. 1993. 'The Limits of Maternalism: Policies Toward American Wage-earning Mothers During the Progressive Era'. In S. Coven and S. Michel (eds) *Mothers of a New World: Maternalist Politics and the Origins of Welfare States.* New York and London: Routledge.

Mink, G. 1990. 'The Lady and the Tramp: Gender, Race, and the Origins of the American Welfare State'. In L. Gordon (ed.) *Women, The State, and Welfare.* Madison, WI: University of Wisconsin Press.

Moon, J.D. 1988. 'The Moral Basis of the Welfare State'. In A. Gutmann (ed.) *Democracy and the Welfare State.* Princeton, NJ: Princeton University Press.

Murray, C. 1994. 'What to do about Welfare'. *Commentary* 98(6): 29–34.

Nelson, Barbara. 1990. "The Origins of the Two-Channel Welfare State: Workmen's Compensation and Mother's Aid." In L. Gordon (ed.), *Women, The State, and Welfare.* Madison: University of Wisconsin Press.

Orloff, A. 2001. 'Ending the Entitlements of Poor Single Mothers: Changing Social Policies, Women's Employment, and Caregiving in the Contemporary United States'. In N. Hirschmann and U. Liebert (eds) *Women and Welfare: Theory and Practice in the United States and Europe.* New Brunswick, NJ: Rutgers University Press.

Pateman, C. 1970. *Participation and Democratic Theory.* Cambridge: Cambridge University Press.

— 1985. *The Problem of Political Obligation,* 2nd edn. Berkeley: University of California Press.

— 1988. *The Sexual Contract.* Stanford, CA: Stanford University Press.

— 1989. 'The Patriarchal Welfare State'. In *The Disorder of Women: Democracy, Feminism and Political Theory.* Stanford, CA: Stanford University Press. First published in 1988 in A. Gutmann (ed.) *Democracy and The Welfare State.* Princeton, NJ: Princeton University Press.

— 1996. *Democratization and Citizenship in the 1990s: The Legacy of T.H. Marshall.* The Vilhelm Aubert Memorial Lecture, University of Oslo.

— 2002. 'Self-Ownership and Property in the Person: Democratization and a Tale of Two Concepts'. *Journal of Political Philosophy* 10(1): 20–53.

— 2003. 'Freedom and Democratization: Why Basic Income is to be Preferred to Basic Capital'. In K. Dowding, J. De Wispelaere and S. White (eds) *The Ethics of Stakeholding.* London: Palgrave Macmillan.

— 2004. 'Democratizing Citizenship: Some Advantages of a Basic Income'. *Politics and Society* 32(1): 89–105.

Rathbone, E. 1986 [1927]. *The Disinherited Family,* 3rd edn. Bristol: Falling Wall Press.

Reich, C. 1964. 'The New Property'. *Yale Law Journal* 73(5): 733–87.

Rothstein, B. 1998. *Just Institutions Matter: The Moral and Political Logic of the Universal Welfare State.* Cambridge: Cambridge University Press.

Sandel, M.J. 1996. *Democracy's Discontent: America in Search of a Public Philosophy.* Cambridge, MA: Harvard University Press.

Schor, J. 1991. *The Overworked American: The Unexpected Decline of Leisure.* New York: Basic Books.

Schumpeter, J. 1943. *Capitalism, Socialism and Democracy.* London: Allen & Unwin.

Shklar, J.N. 1991. *American Citizenship: The Quest for Inclusion.* Cambridge, MA: Harvard University Press.

Shue, H. 1996. *Basic Rights: Subsistence, Affluence, and U.S. Foreign Policy,* 2nd edn. Princeton, NJ: Princeton University Press.

Skocpol, T. 1992. *Protecting Soldiers and Mothers: The Political Origins of Social Policy in the United States.* Cambridge, MA: Harvard University Press.

Smith, J. and J. Brooks-Gunn. 2002. 'How Mothers Cope When their Welfare Grant is Cut'. *Social Policy Journal* 1(4): 63–83.

Teles, S. 1996. *Whose Welfare? AFDC and Elite Politics.* Lawrence, KA: University Press of Kansas.

Van Parijs, P. (ed.) 1992. *Arguing for Basic Income.* London: Verso.

Van Parijs, P. 1995. *Real Freedom for All: What (if Anything) can Justify Capitalism?* New York: Oxford University Press.

Waring, M. 1988. *If Women Counted: A New Feminist Economics.* New York: Harper & Row.

Western, B. and K. Beckett. 1999. 'How Unregulated is the U.S. Labor Market? The Penal System as a Labor Market Institution'. *American Journal of Sociology* 104(4): 1030–60.

White, S. 2003. *The Civic Minimum: An Essay on the Rights and Obligations of Economic Citizenship.* Oxford: Oxford University Press.

— 2005. 'Is Conditionality Liberal?' In L. Mead and C. Beem (eds) *Welfare Reform and Political Theory.* New York: Russell Sage Foundation.

Widerquist, Karl. 2005. 'A Failure to Communicate: What (if Anything) Can We Learn from the Negative Income Tax Experiments?' *Journal of Socio-Economics* 34(1): 49–81.

Wilding, P. 1997. 'The Welfare State and the Conservatives'. *Political Studies* 45(4): 716–22.

13

AN INTERVIEW WITH CAROLE PATEMAN (2009)

Interview questions by Terrell Carver and Samuel A. Chambers

An oral interview was conducted and recorded in 2009 by Terrell Carver at Cardiff University, Wales, where Pateman has held full-time and visiting appointments. What follows is a version lightly edited with Pateman's help.

This book collects your writings from four different decades in order to make the case for you as an 'innovator' in the field of political theory. But is this how you think of yourself? How do you conceive of your relation to the field of political theory, and how have you seen that relationship change over the years?

Forty years is a long time and, not surprisingly, my view of myself has changed over that period. When I started out in academic work, given my background, it was in a state of total academic innocence. Even when I was working for my degrees, including the DPhil, and writing *Participation and Democratic Theory* (which was published before I got my DPhil), I did not appreciate that some of the more recent books which I read and commented on had been written by such big figures in political science. But of course in Britain in the 1960s the study of 'politics' had not yet become professionalized 'political science' and the writers were American, so perhaps it is understandable. And if I had known perhaps I couldn't have written the book, since I had very little confidence. And while I was writing *The Problem of Political Obligation* and *The Sexual Contract* I just worked on the problems; I wasn't consciously thinking of how I was doing something innovative, although in the case of the latter book I knew that no one else had looked at theories of original contracts in this way. Now that I have had many years of reactions to my arguments and have seen how my work is received and referred to (or not, as the case may be) I can see that at least some of it is innovative.

So which piece would you pick out?

Well, for example, in the *Problem of Political Obligation* - which is less well known than the other two books I have mentioned - the major question I asked was why political obligation was a problem. I think that is an innovative question. I'm not sure that I am completely up to date with the political obligation literature but usually when I come across a piece the tacit assumption is that there is no general problem about political obligation. So the typical procedure is to discuss which justification is the most plausible. My question was not new; it was central to classic theories of original contracts, generated from the premise of individual freedom and equality, but it is a question that has been repressed in the last half century of political theory because political theorists take the legitimacy of the modern state for granted.

But I did not answer your question about my relationship to political theory. That is not altogether straightforward because, on the one hand, almost all my work deals with very central questions in political science and political theory: democracy, political obligation, contract theory, welfare and so on. So in that way it is fairly conventional. But, on the other hand, right from the beginning I have taken a critical approach. In that respect I do not think my relationship has changed that much over the years; it is still critical. I have continued as I began. The difference is that 40 years on I now appreciate how critical my approach has been and how much at variance my arguments are from the standard arguments in political theory and the areas of political science I have touched on. Of course political theory has changed a lot since I started.

Can you comment on that?

When I began ... when I think back to my student days and immediately afterwards, there was not nearly so much academic political theory. There were fewer people in it and very much less was published. I began my work before the journal *Political Theory* started and now journals proliferate. And there were not so many books either. I was taught political theory before Rawls's major book was published. This is pre-history, as it were, back in the mists of time. Now there is a proliferation of everything. The field has really changed in that respect; it is another academic world. What have I lived through in political theory? Its death was being discussed in the 1960s, but since then there is the development of the Rawls industry, the development of academic feminism, the decline of Marxism and left theory in general and the rise of analytical egalitarian political philosophy, the rise of postmodernism, the development of rational choice, deliberative democratic theory, critical race theory, all the reinterpretations of the classic texts and challenges to the conventional 'canon' of the texts and so on. There is a niche for all approaches now. All this has happened since I started. And my relationship to it is that I have not aligned myself with any one authority or any one school of political theory - although many critics of *The Sexual*

Contract try to put my book in one of the conventionally labelled boxes. I work on the problems that I am interested in, and my approach is fairly eclectic. I work on something, using the material that seems appropriate, until it looks satisfactory to me and then I stop.

Could you pick out a couple more areas besides obligation where you think you have been an innovator or have asked innovative questions?

In my first book, I would single out two things. First, my criticism of the idea that there was one 'classical theory of democracy'. Second, the fact that, rather than insisting that a normative ideal of active citizenship was still relevant, I looked at the empirical evidence. The argument at the time was that (the then new) empirical surveys showed that a theory of democracy that emphasized active citizenship and participation was unrealistic. I looked at the evidence that was being presented and thought, 'well, you can interpret this in a different way', and I also introduced additional evidence to support my argument that participation was something that was learned.

In my second book on theories of original contracts I think the most innovative idea was that of 'the sexual contract' itself. No one had made the argument that there was another dimension to the original contract, that it was more than the social contract, or had read the classic texts to look at the implications of what they had to say about the sexes for their idea of an original pact. Nor had anyone linked the arguments of the classic theorists to actual contracts that help constitute major social institutions. For example, Locke, Hobbes, etc., all discuss marriage but their arguments had not been put in the context of coverture and the subordination of wives.

Perhaps I should also add that in my most recent book, with Charles Mills, *Contract and Domination*, in my chapter on 'The Settler Contract', I present another reading of the story of the original contract.

Given that the political theory canon has now been reworked by at least four decades of feminist criticism, what recommendations would you give to a colleague in political theory for teaching that canon today?

Not all my colleagues have yet caught up with feminist scholarship. Let us get that point out of the way first! Yet in light of the fact that there has been so much feminist scholarship on the texts, anyone who is thinking of teaching or studying the history of political thought needs to be acquainted with the feminist rereadings, reinterpretations and commentaries. But talking to and teaching students I find that not all of them are introduced to this body of scholarship – even though it got under way in the 1970s. 1979 is a particularly important year, for instance, since that was when Susan Okin's pioneering book on the texts came out, along with a number of articles. One difficulty is that feminist writers are critical of basic assumptions and arguments in political theory, and not everyone wants to scrutinize these assumptions to integrate this work into the teaching of the history of political thought.

But there is also another question besides teaching the canon. It is not only that the texts included in the conventional understanding of 'the history of political thought' can be read very narrowly, but the writers who have been included in the canon have been very limited. Women theorists and, especially, feminist thinkers were excluded. This began to change in the 1990s so that now some anthologies and books in the history of political thought include neglected figures. For example, increasing attention is now being paid to Mary Wollstonecraft, and Mary Astell is gradually creeping in. If one wanted to be cynical, it might be pointed out that the inexorable publication, tenure and promotion mills always require new grist. Incidentally, I did not – could not – initially learn about Wollstonecraft or Astell from political theorists. I first heard about them in the early days not from academics but from feminists who were writing for a broader audience (feminism was not academic to begin with; it gained a foothold in universities later), and literary theorists were a long way ahead of political theorists, including feminists, in studying them.

So one approach is to enlarge the canon, and another is to single out a history of feminist political thought. I occasionally teach a graduate course on this and have been doing so for some years, but when I began I believe there were very few courses of this type, perhaps one or two others. One thing that is very striking is that many of the earlier feminist theorists were extremely well known in their own day and they engaged with famous theorists – the ones who are conventionally taught – and they wrote about the major questions, problems and topics that political theorists are concerned with. Yet, despite the explosion in political theory, they were ignored for so long.

So would your recommendation be to go for a history of feminist thought or for a reworking of the canon that picks up major figures as you go along?

It is not necessary to choose, there is plenty of room for both, and no doubt other approaches too. I find it hard to see how the classic texts can be read in the old way any more; my reading of the texts has been completely transformed, well, transformed twice over actually. More recently I have been doing some reading from a critical race theory perspective. This is a newer development and the parallels with the development of feminist scholarship are fascinating. Here are more aspects of the texts that have been ignored or glossed over (including by myself until recently), such as embarrassing passages about Africans in Kant, or the fact that he lectured on the idea of 'race' for decades. Now we have scholars showing us not only how the arguments in the texts helped shape structures of sexual power but also their contribution to racial power and colonialism.

Where would you place yourself within the current spectrum of feminisms?

That is not very easy to answer, but in so far as it emphasizes the connections between race and sex I have made a contribution to that area in *Contract and Domination*. I have had a problem for a very long time with the common classification of feminism into liberal feminism, radical feminism, etc. This suggests that there is nothing distinctive about feminism and that it should be understood as an outgrowth of well-known political theories. Yet feminist thinkers raised fundamental questions about central assumptions of those same theories and cannot be merely added on. This is why I think the classification is very misleading about the history of feminist thought. I rather unwisely - well, unwisely looking back at it - used the term 'radical feminism' in the Preface to *The Sexual Contract*. I was attempting to indicate how I became alerted to various problems not identifying myself with a particular school of thought (as conventionally classified), but some critics immediately leapt on this and claimed that my book was an example of the genre.

More recent developments, such as the emphasis on the differences between women, have resulted in much illuminating work and have reminded us of a great deal that it is all too easy to forget or ignore. But at the same time, preoccupation with difference can lead to an infinite regress or to marked reluctance to make any generalizations, and to the neglect of sexual power structures and of some of the basic problems that were at the forefront when I first started getting involved in feminist work. Many of these problems are still with us, even though the form that they take has not remained static over the years. Problems such as women's poverty, men's monopoly of the better-paying jobs and upper levels of the occupational structure, violence against women, the sex trade, exclusion of women from positions of authority ... none of these very basic problems have gone away, and looking round the world they are as urgent as ever. So, as you might suppose, I have a problem with the term 'post-feminism' or the notion that feminism today has little in common with feminism 40 years ago - or 140 years ago, come to that.

One of the most popular terms over the past few years is 'intersectionality', which is used to refer to the fact that one is not, say, only a woman but is also poor, non-white, afflicted by debilitating illness and so on. That no one can be characterized by merely one attribute is true and important. However, as Rousseau once remarked, it is not possible to talk about everything at once. And I discovered how hard it is to try and say anything of substance, even in broad terms, when dealing with more than one of these categories while writing my part of *Contract and Domination*. One of the tasks we set ourselves was to discuss the intersection of the sexual and racial contracts, but it was not at all easy to decide what exactly I was going to write about in Chapter 5, 'Race, Sex and Indifference'.

What do you see as the long-term impact of well-known feminist thinkers, e.g. yourself, MacKinnon, Butler, etc. (your choice)?

I do not think this is a question that it is possible to answer. If you look at what happened to feminist thinkers in the past, as I have said already, many of them were extremely well known in their own day but were forgotten or ignored very quickly. Take Mary Wollstonecraft; in the 1790s she knew the leading radicals of the day, she joined with them in attacking the power of aristocracy and property, and hierarchy more generally, only she went much further and extended her criticisms to the power of men over women and conceptions of masculinity and femininity. Like them she defended the French Revolution, and even went so far as to go and see it in person. She wrote the first reply to Burke's *Reflections on the Revolution in France*, drew on and transformed the arguments of the Scottish Enlightenment, and, although Rousseau was her favourite author, she roundly criticized him. In short, she was in the thick of the intellectual activities of her time and her books were widely read. But, like Mary Astell before her, who was also well known and whose books went through several editions, she disappeared from view very rapidly and her writings were then forgotten. So who knows what might happen, even if people like MacKinnon are known outside of universities, who knows whether they will be read or remembered in another three or four decades? That is not to say that their ideas will not be remembered. Many feminist ideas are now in general circulation, usually in watered-down form, but whether particular figures will be known, I don't think you can say.

What political strategies are there for undoing patriarchy? I think it has been a central focus of your work, and that it is about power, the sexual binary, gender, etc. So I think it is a good question.

It is a good question - and one of the perennial questions - but I am afraid that I do not have a good answer. It is a very difficult question without any easy answers, and a huge task in practice. In general, I think we need to go on doing what we have been doing for a very long time and doing it in a much bigger and better way. That is, we need to attack on all fronts at once, whether it's trying to undo patriarchal modes of thought in universities, trying to make societies and economies 'woman friendly', trying to change laws and institutions, to change sexual relations and views about masculinity and femininity, to reduce inequality and eliminate poverty, to eliminate violence against women, to bring about a much more peaceful world and get rid of the arms industry, to foster democratization and so on, and so on. There have obviously been many changes over the last 40 years, but there is still a very long way to go. Another question is which changes have been in the right direction or at least have the potential for moving in the right direction. For example, in the last quarter century, especially in Britain and the United States, society has become markedly more commercialized, and, as part of that, much more sexualized, and commodification has increased; there is virtually nothing now that cannot be sold as a commodity. The sex industry has expanded enormously since I wrote my pages about prostitution in *The Sexual Contract*. It has become global and is a multi-billion dollar business. I do not have much sympathy for recent arguments by some feminists who proclaim that prostitution is 'transgressive' or empowering for women. Women in the trade may, if they are not at the bottom end of the business, make money, but to see this as transgressive rather than as part of sexual power structures seems to me to mistake commercialization and commodification for freedom. It also assumes that treating women's bodies as commodities to be sold in the market has no implications for conceptions of sexuality and women's position in the wider society.

I am intrigued by the 'we' in your answer. Have you had much experience with men coming on side for this, or do you find that they are not interested, ignoring it, don't get it and can just be pushed out of the way? ... I am interested about coalition politics across the sex binary.

I certainly wouldn't want to rule out men! There are men who are sympathetic and willing to be the men's auxiliary, as it were, and who understand what the problems are. Quite apart from anything else, men still largely hold the reins of power so their support, or at least acquiescence, is required much of the time to achieve change. But there are many more men who make no effort to understand the problems or who do not welcome sexual equality and women's rights and many men remain actively hostile. The women's movement and feminism have had an impact; indeed, this can be seen both from the resistance they have provoked and the way in which people who have never displayed any opposition to women's subordination now frequently and quite cynically invoke the poor treatment of women by this or that group, or in this or that country, to further their (non-feminist) political agendas. Resistance to sexual equality and women's freedom can be seen in many different areas from, for instance, attempts to reinforce the powers of husbands, the harassment of women workers and women in legislatures, to the erosion of women's access to reproductive health care in the United States. General indifference, or worse, to women's position is revealed in the global statistics on women's poverty, maternal death rates, illiteracy rates and malnourishment, and continuing legal discrimination in a number of countries.

How do you see yourself and your work in relation to liberalism today? Is liberalism a project to be renewed or abandoned?

The term 'liberalism' is extraordinarily ubiquitous and the answer to this question depends on what you mean by it. I have thought for some while now that 'liberalism' has been so over-used, and stretched to cover such a wide range of arguments and theories, that it had become more of a hindrance than a help. I try not to use it, unless the meaning is clear. I do not see the work that I have been doing on theories of an original contract and the sexual and racial contracts as an analysis of liberalism. My view is that contract theory, though obviously related to liberalism, is a distinct tradition of argument.

As to your question about renewal or abandonment, if you mean by 'liberalism' basic rights and liberties, individual freedom, consent to government, equality under the law and so forth ... well, why would you want to reject it? But my question would be whether 'liberalism' has a monopoly on constitutional and political rights. Surely, these are part of democracy and democratic theory. I do not think liberalism in this sense should be abandoned; rather renewal is called for. The point is to build on it, transform it, democratize it. One difficulty with such a project is the so-called war on terror. That is being used to inflict considerable damage to the rule of law, civil liberties have been curtailed, there is detention without trial and 'renditions', and there has been a huge increase in executive power. We are now in a position of having to defend basic liberties and rights, including habeas corpus, while, in this strange world we now inhabit, at the official level all the rhetoric is about democracy and freedom.

But a right that is missing from most liberalism is the right to a decent standard of living - in my work on basic income I have been calling this a democratic right. We now have an extraordinarily wealthy world but there are billions of people who live in dire poverty or destitution. And there is one branch of 'liberalism' that stands resolutely against any such right, exemplified by neo-liberalism, the branch embodied in the economic and political doctrine that has been so influential over the past quarter century. Privatization, reduction of public provision and deregulation have been rigorously enforced around the world. And what I like to call the official view of democracy, a very minimalist form, has become identified not only with 'free and fair' elections but also with a particular, neo-liberal form of a market economy. But privatization cuts off avenues of democratic accountability and participation that may have existed. Maybe the avenues were more in principle than in practice, but at least they were there in principle. Once everything is privatized they are gone. And neo-liberal economic dogmas have been responsible for the rapid increase in inequality and economic insecurity since the late 1970s, both domestically and globally. But their power has already peaked in Latin America, and the current economic crisis over which the apostles of neo-liberalism have presided may see the end of it. We have to wait and see.

It sounded from what you said about contract initially that contract as a concept and a way of addressing problems was something over and above liberalism and over and above free market theory, you might say. Is that the case? Or is it a broader approach?

Contract theory and liberalism come out of the same intellectual complex but that they are not coextensive, as can be seen quite simply from the fact that not all liberals are contract theorists. For instance, John Stuart Mill is usually taken to be a liberal *par excellence* but is not a contract theorist. The reason that contract and liberalism are so often taken to be indistinguishable today is because of the Rawls industry and his 'liberal' theory, which contains a rather bloodless and attenuated version of contract theory. In fact, in contemporary contract theory 'contract' does no real work; it is merely a metaphor. Following Rawls, what is called contract theory is a mode of moral reasoning. Classic theories of an original contract were very different, and I like to think that my own work follows in that tradition – although I want to see the end of contract theory. Early modern theories were political theories about the justification of the modern state and its power structures, including sexual and racial hierarchies. They are a long way from contemporary theories about moral reasoning and 'our intuitions' about justice. My co-author Charles Mills has done sterling work in modifying a Rawlsian approach to take account of racial supremacy, but we disagree about the usefulness of contract theory.

Of course, contract is also a commercial device, a valuable commercial device, but that is another matter from the neo-liberal approach that, ideally, sees contract as constitutive of social and political life; it clings to the fantasy of contract all the way down. It involves an abstractly individualist perspective that shares some assumptions with Hobbes. As I argued in *The Problem of Political Obligation*, Hobbes's individualist logic shows that contract depends on the non-contractual basis of contract – an argument made much later by theorists such as Durkheim and Parsons – a basis that is undercut by contract itself when not kept firmly in its place but seen as a practice that creates social life. Without non-contractual relationships, as Hobbes sets out so clearly, the only solution is Leviathan, now an even more terrifying figure than in Hobbes's time.

Could you assess the progress (or otherwise) on 'organizational democracy' and 'feminism and democracy' since you began to address these questions?

I think there has been more progress on feminism and democracy, in some areas at least, than there has been in organizational democracy. Management may have been flattened somewhat in some areas, but you do not hear much about workplace democracy in Britain or the United States. There is the occasional publication, co-operatives, especially in the Basque country, still have a fair number of supporters, and Employee Stock Ownership Plans are often mentioned in this context in the United States, but it is not a topic that excites much popular attention. Even standard union activities are now at a very low ebb. There has been a precipitous decline in the United States and Britain in union membership.

We are in a very different political and economic context now than when I wrote my first book and discussed participation in the workplace. Three decades of neo-liberalism have hardly been hospitable to workplace democracy. It raises even more complex questions than when I was looking at it 40 years ago, given the huge economic changes since then. The old industries, where workers were organized, were paid decent wages and had long-term jobs, are in decline or have vanished. These were breadwinner jobs, which in those days were jobs for white, male workers. Now the service sector has vastly expanded, the majority of women are in the paid workforce, a workforce which is now multiracial, and many jobs are temporary, part-time, low-paid, with few or no benefits. The workforce is now supposed to be 'flexible', but what are the implications of 'flexibility' for democratizing workplaces? Moreover, corporations have become absolutely gigantic entities that operate globally. Democratic theorists have had very little to say about how to reduce the power of corporations and democratize them. This is a really big problem.

But there are other interesting developments, particularly in Brazil with participatory budgets – although, now that participatory budgeting has been taken up by the World Bank and in development circles, it may be that what I long ago called pseudo-participation will be all that is left. Most political scientists, if asked about having more citizen participation, would say that budgets must be left to experts; citizens cannot meddle in that area. Yet very large numbers of people, including very many poor people, have participated in the Brazilian budget process. Electoral democracy is rather tattered these days and citizens' level of trust and their confidence in government and established institutions has been in decline for some time. To introduce a genuine, robust form of participatory budgeting would be a very good way to begin a process of democratization, as would be an extension of the use of citizens' juries and deliberative polling, which rarely involve decision-making.[1] Something that I have been suggesting, and John Bernheim wrote about some years ago, would be to experiment with an alternative to elections. Starting at the local level, a random sample of citizens could be chosen to investigate and decide on a solution to a specific problem. People enjoy taking part in the deliberative polls and citizens' juries, and take their task seriously, so why not give them a modicum of decision-making power?

Feminism and democracy have fared rather better, at least in the sense of electoral democracy. Women have made some inroads into electoral politics – a large number of countries now have quotas of various kinds for women in legislative bodies – and in 2008 the Spanish cabinet was full of women and even the Spanish Defence Minister was a young pregnant woman ... that is a big change! But that is still exceptional. In addition, views about masculinity and femininity have changed, and many feminist ideas that were seen as extreme 40 years ago are now in wide circulation. Women's rights are now firmly on the international agenda, and there are a multitude of grass roots movements and organizations working to improve women's position. And in universities, particularly in the US, there is hardly one that does not have a women's studies or gender studies programme, and these areas are big publishing business. But the process has been very slow; it was not until the 1970s that legal discrimination began to be finally eliminated in Britain and the United States, and formal civil and political equality was won. Overall, men still monopolize most of the authoritative positions. Women are still not seen as citizens and political actors in quite the same sense as men. And as I said earlier, the old problems are still with us, including an appalling level of violence against women. Women are still seen as one of the spoils and one of the weapons of war. In no country is women's human right to physical protection fully secured. So it does rather depend on what you are looking at how optimistic or pessimistic you will be on the question of feminism and democracy.

Do you have any views or comments on the National Assembly for Wales, which at least briefly had majority female representation? Comments or views in relation to either democracy or feminism?

Hurrah for the National Assembly for Wales! It is often conveniently forgotten that women are half of humankind - we are not 'a group' or 'a minority'. As a matter of equity, justice and democracy there should be around 50:50 women and men in parliaments and other decision-making bodies in major institutions. But even today that is something which people often find rather extraordinary; the belief is that too many women pose a problem. Yet having such a large majority of men is not seen as a problem, despite the dire state of the world that has resulted from their decision-making. However, even if women were equitably represented it does not mean that they are all going to be feminists, because women's political views differ widely, just as men's political views do, and they, like men, have careers in political parties. So it is a mistake to think that this would be an easy solution that is bound to lead to big changes that help women. But there is evidence to suggest that even with a much smaller percentage of women there might be some change in the right direction. A lot depends too on vigorous women's movements outside of legislatures.

How would you describe the current condition of the 'welfare state' in the US and/or UK or elsewhere?

The first thing to be said is that, although there have been many attacks on the welfare state in the recent past and various parts have been eroded, in Western countries it is still with us. Despite the power of neo-liberal doctrines and governmental support for targeted and means-tested programmes, it has not been dismantled, although social provision in poor countries has suffered greatly under structural adjustment policies imposed by the IMF. And a major reaction to the current crisis, exemplified in California, is to ravage social programmes while preserving the prerogatives of the rich. However, increasingly individuals have become seen as consumers or customers for services available for payment and not citizens with *rights* to public services. A democratic view of the welfare state is becoming overshadowed by an economic view. It has become widely believed that rich people (particularly those in banks) require large monetary incentives, tax cuts and special treatment to get them to do their bit. Poor people, in contrast, are assumed to react to coercion and thus we have seen welfare turned into workfare, even though the jobs may not pay enough to live on. In short, we have a new version of the nineteenth-century Poor

Law. Employment has been central to the development of Western welfare states and for a long time the focus was on the male breadwinner. Today the idea is that all able-bodied adults must be in the flexible workforce. This was demonstrated in the 1996 welfare reform in the United States that ended a particular programme providing assistance to single mothers to stay at home to look after their young children. So we have the very odd situation that the wealthier we become, and the more productivity increases, the more insistence there is from policymakers and governments on employment. A twenty-first century policy would be to uncouple subsistence from employment and increase disposable time.

Nonetheless, universal services remain very popular, as the attachment to the National Health Service in Britain demonstrates, and Social Security – retirement pensions – in the United States. People in general support and want welfare states, though they want them to be run both efficiently and for their benefit, not for the benefit of bureaucrats and managers. One of George W. Bush's policies was to privatize Social Security, but he did not get anywhere with it (I should add that in US terminology Social Security is not 'welfare', which refers to targeted, residual programmes). Indeed, Social Security is more important than ever, because companies have been shedding traditional pensions and about two-thirds of Americans now rely on schemes funded from pre-tax income that are run by private investment management companies, which of course make a nice profit from this, but which have been decimated since the financial collapse . There is also widespread desire for change in provision of health insurance, now provided largely through employers, and some 47 million people are uninsured. But we have to wait and see what will be the outcome of the legislation by the Obama administration to tackle the problem.

One of the central questions is what should 'a welfare state' look like? By that I mean does 'welfare' in the phrase 'the welfare state' refer only to public provision for the poor and provision to rescue people from accidents of fortune (such as health care) or from the vagaries of the market (such as unemployment benefits), or does it refer to the well-being – the welfare – of the population as a whole? The latter I see as a democratic way of looking at 'welfare'. And it would mean, if taken seriously, that public spending should be directed first and foremost to that end. It would require, for example, drastic cuts in the sums spent on subsidies to businesses, on corporate welfare, and especially eliminating colossal spending on weapons and warfare. A decent standard of living for everyone is central to a democratic welfare state, the major reason why I support a basic income for all citizens.

And, as I have emphasized in my work in this area, for a long time women in the United States and Britain were lesser citizens of the welfare state. And, despite the reforms of recent years, women still tend to gain less from the welfare state over their lifetime than men do, and women are more likely than men to be poor; in poor countries neo-liberalism and structural adjustment have vastly increased the burdens on women. Welfare states have always depended upon the unpaid work of women in the household, but in poor countries, where women do much of the farming, they now are working harder than ever, often in extremely adverse circumstances, to keep their families going.

Is there much hope for realising the 'basic income'?

One imponderable at present is what will be the outcome of the economic crisis generated by neo-liberalism and deregulated finance capitalism. Will it lead to a major rethinking? If so, then that may well open a space for serious consideration of basic income. But in general I think that there is some hope, although a basic income may not be introduced for reasons that I would like.

One hopeful sign is that basic income has proponents across the political spectrum - although I admit that this can be a two-edged sword. For example, Charles Murray recently published a book arguing for a basic income, but he sees it as replacing the welfare state. That is not, of course, how I envisage it. While basic income could replace some programmes, my argument is that a flourishing democracy requires ample public provision, including a basic income at a level that I call sufficient for a modest but decent standard of life. The fact that proponents come from both right and left means that 'basic income' has a variety of meanings for its various advocates, and so the politics of implementation are likely to be complex. Not everyone agrees that a basic income should be set at subsistence level or that it should be unconditional. So, for some it can be seen as little more than another form of poor relief, and others stress its compatibility with a flexible labour market or that it could act as a supplement to low wages. In the academic literature, many arguments are in terms of social justice.

Another reason for hope is that the idea of a basic income has support around the world. For instance, Brazil has legislated for a basic income, and the Irish government published a Green Paper on it a few years ago; there is a good deal of discussion in Germany (where a prominent businessman supports it); there are popular movements in Canada, in Spain, in some Latin American countries, and a big grassroots movement in South Africa. Another encouraging development is that some aid and development people are rethinking their long resistance to cash grants for people in poor countries; there is evidence now that such grants work very well and can help local markets to get going again. There has also been a fascinating experiment with basic income in Namibia. There is a lot of room for such endeavours, and basic income is well suited to poor countries. One of its great virtues is that it is simple to administer and relatively cheap, and there are no poverty or unemployment traps. What is required is for everyone to be registered, an up-to-date means to provide the payment and some measures to prevent fraud. There is no need for a large expensive army of bureaucrats and snoopers.

But I do not want to minimize the resistance to basic income. Recognition of a universal right to a decent standard of life is a long way off. Inequality has been growing for a quarter century. In the US real wages have been, at best, stagnant for most of that time, and globally some 2.5 billion people live on less than $2 a day, and inequality will intensify as a consequence of the global economic crisis. The two objections to basic income that get raised over and over again are cost and idleness or free riding. But cost is not really an economic question but a political one. It is a question of how public resources are allocated and what kind of society we want to live in. At present, Western and many other governments always find the funds for armaments while declaring that it is hard to finance the welfare of citizens or to assist the global poor.

The objection about idleness actually mirrors the discussion of welfare and workfare. In both cases the question is whether recipients of the benefit are getting 'something for nothing'. Would a basic income result in massive idleness and a nation of wastrels? I have seen no convincing evidence to suggest that this would be the case. The question that is rarely asked is how realistic it is to suppose that everybody - globally? - could be employed, and at a living wage. That seems to me more pie in the sky than the policy of basic income. Technology is displacing labour, people are getting 'downsized' all the time, very low-wage jobs proliferate, and the push is towards industrialized corporatized agriculture rather than enabling people to feed themselves in sustainable ways. Perhaps the current crisis might cause more questioning of the economic path we are on. But, in any event, for some time now the evidence has seemed conclusive that we are on an ecologically unsustainable trajectory. A global basic income has a vital place if saner policies are ever introduced - in time.

Could you comment on the 'warfare state'?

This is such an enormous topic ... but let me make a few remarks. The post-war welfare state has also been a warfare state - well, how many states are not warfare states? But there does seem to have been a disturbing change from the turn of the century. The resort to military force has now seemingly become a first rather than a last resort. This has a great deal to do with the proclamation of the so-called war on terror. Raise the cry of 'terrorism' and now any government, whether elected or headed by the military, a tinpot despot or authoritarian ruler, has virtual *carte blanche* to start obtaining yet more weapons and waging war against sections of their own population or against other countries. And in the case of the onslaught on and destruction of Iraq (which even today, 2009, does not have a properly functioning electricity and water supply or sewerage system) we have witnessed the appalling spectacle of the governments of the United States and Britain, two countries that like to present themselves as models of democracy, 'justifying' aggressive warfare through deceptions and lies. No attention was paid to the historically unprecedented numbers of citizens around the world, some 13 million, or perhaps many more, who took to the streets to register that they did not consent.

To return to the 1960s for a moment, one of the things that I was doing was taking part in the anti-nuclear movement. 'Ban the bomb', as we called it. We were asking for unilateral disarmament by Britain, in the hope that everyone else would follow suit. But that didn't happen. British governments today still cling to the idea that having nuclear weapons somehow gives them the grandeur of a great power. However, there was some progress, and I am sure the anti-nuclear movement played a part ... for a while it looked fairly hopeful. It is very depressing that we are now in a position where nuclear weapons are proliferating again. To state the obvious, outrage about proliferation is extremely selective. Iran must not have nuclear weapons, yet in the United States the Israeli nuclear arsenal is virtually a taboo subject; India's nuclear pursuits are assisted and a blind eye was turned to Pakistan.

I earlier referred to one consequence of the warfare state, that is, the allocation of resources to guns rather than butter. According to the Stockholm International Peace Research Institute (SIPRI), in 2008 global military spending was $1,464 billion, an increase of 4 per cent in real terms over 2007 and of 45 per cent since 1999; imagine what could be done with such money to provide a basic income and proper living conditions in poor countries. Chalmers Johnson has recently highlighted the economic distortion in the United States, where the infrastructure is in a dire state thanks to the diversion of resources into the warfare state. Even without counting the wars in Iraq and Afghanistan, 'defence' spending has doubled since the mid-1990s. In recent fiscal years it exceeded $1 trillion. The Department of Defense's planned expenditure was larger than all other nations' military budgets put together. Johnson also stresses how difficult it is to obtain a proper estimate of the resources that go into the US warfare state because a great deal of it is hidden away in, for example, other departmental budgets, and some projects are classified. There is also one area of US 'aid' relevant here. In 2008 Israel was given $2.4 billion 'aid', almost all of which was used to buy weapons (mostly from the US) which are used in its continued aggression against its neighbours, particularly against the Palestinian people, infrastructure, economy and society. Moreover, the production of the means of destruction is all too often accompanied by bribery and corruption – war business is extremely profitable. Britain has provided an excellent example of this in the case of BAE Systems and the Saudis - and the enquiry that Prime Minister Blair wanted quashed.

Casualties in present-day wars are overwhelmingly civilian. Sophisticated high-tech weapons kill and maim large numbers of civilians, but they are not required. There are some 640 million small arms circulating and a brisk business in torture equipment. Bombs, in particular, inflict horrendous civilian casualties. 'War' in many cases now seems to consist largely of bombing, ranging from the 'shock and awe' variety, depleted uranium, cluster and phosphorus bombs, unmanned drones and the newest DIME bombs, to the 'ordinary' bombs dropped on civilians in poor countries. And one should not forget the large areas of the world scattered with landmines and the continuing toll of casualties. The civilians being slaughtered are overwhelmingly in poor countries and non-white.

One recent change is the notion that wars fought by rich white countries must leave their armed forces virtually intact, while the huge casualties of the other side are not even officially counted. Alternatively, proxies can be enlisted to fight the 'war on terror', as in Somalia, where the Americans gave the green light for the Ethiopians to invade (and did a bit of bombing and rendition themselves). The result is one of the worst humanitarian situations in the world, although little attention is paid to it – but then, there are numerous armed conflicts to which little attention is paid, including the Congo where the dead now number around 5 million and horrendous atrocities have been committed against civilians, not least women. I have already noted the connection between the warfare state and the erosion of the rule of law and civil liberties, but another disturbing development is the privatization of warfare. 'Private contractors', who less euphemistically used to be called mercenaries, are becoming more and more prominent, and the companies that supply them are expanding rapidly and making huge profits. In the first Gulf war in 1991 there was one private contractor for every 100 US soldiers, but by the time of the fourth year of the occupation of Iraq there was one for every 1.4 soldiers; among the British contingent private contractors outnumbered soldiers by three to one. In one case of a battle in 2004, US marines were reported to be under the command of mercenaries. These developments raise fundamental questions for democracy and the democratic principle of civilian control over the military and the conduct of warfare. We ignore them at our peril.

A few last remarks: the question of the warfare state is closely related to your previous question about feminism and democracy. Both are undermined by the growth of militarization. I have already touched on erosion of the rule of law and civil liberties, and the increasing use of 'private contractors' in warfare eliminates democratic accountability. Hyper-masculinity is also encouraged. 'Shock and awe' bombing brings to mind Burke's distinction between the masculine sublime, which inspires awe, and the beautiful, represented by weak and lisping femininity. Again, restraints against violence towards women, albeit hardly effective, are frequently swept away completely in warfare. The destruction and diversion of resources particularly affects women and their children, who fill camps for refugees and displaced persons. Without a change in the foreign policies of Western countries and in conceptions of development it is hard to be optimistic about a more peaceful world in the near future.

Note

1   Pateman's updated and somewhat altered views on this subject can be found in the published version of her 2011 Presidential Address to the American Political Science Association, *Perspectives on Politics* (forthcoming).

INDEX